CW00589128

155 |

SOCIAL QUESTIONS OF TO-DAY

EDITED BY H. DE B. GIBBINS, D.LITT. M.A.

WORKHOUSES AND PAUPERISM

SOCIAL QUESTIONS OF TO-DAY

Edited by H. de B. GIBBINS, D. Litt. M.A.

Crown 8vo., 2s. 6d.

A series of volumes upon those topics of social, economic, and industrial interest that are at the present moment foremost in the public mind. Each volume is written by an author who is an acknowledged authority upon the subject with which he or she deals, and who treats his question in a thoroughly sympathetic but impartial manner, with special reference to the historic aspect of the subject.

The following Volumes of the Series are now ready.

TRADE UNIONISM—NEW AND OLD. G. HOWELL, M.P., Author of *The Conflicts of Capital and Labour*. Second Edition.

PROBLEMS OF POVERTY: An Inquiry into the Industrial Condition of the Poor. J. A. HOBSON, M.A. Third Edition.

THE CO-OPERATIVE MOVEMENT OF TO-DAY. G. J. HOLYOAKE, Author of *The History of Co-operation*. Second Edition.

MUTUAL THRIFT. Rev. J. FROME WILKINSON, M.A., Author of *The Friendly Society Movement*.

THE COMMERCE OF NATIONS. C. F. BASTABLE, LL.D., Professor of Political Economy in the University of Dublin.

THE ALIEN INVASION. W. H. WILKINS, B.A., Secretary to the Association for Preventing the Immigration of Destitute Aliens.

THE RURAL EXODUS: Problems of Village Life. P. ANDERSON GRAHAM.

LAND NATIONALISATION. HAROLD COX, B.A.

A SHORTER WORKING-DAY. H. DE B. GIBBINS, D.LITT. M.A.

BACK TO THE LAND. HAROLD E. MOORE, F.S.I.

TRUSTS, POOLS, AND CORNERS. J. STEPHEN JEANS.

THE FACTORY SYSTEM. R. W. COOKE-TAYLOR, Author of *The Modern Factory System*, etc.

WOMEN'S WORK. LADY DILKE, AMY BULLEY, and MARGARET WHITLEY.

THE STATE AND ITS CHILDREN. GERTRUDE TUCKWELL.

MUNICIPALITIES AT WORK. FREDERICK DOLMAN.

SOCIALISM AND MODERN THOUGHT. M. KAUFMANN, M.A.

MODERN CIVILISATION IN SOME OF ITS ECONOMIC ASPECTS. W. CUNNINGHAM, D.D.

THE HOUSING OF THE WORKING CLASSES. F. BOWMAKER.

THE PROBLEM OF THE UNEMPLOYED. J. A. HOBSON, M.A.

LIFE IN WEST LONDON. ARTHUR SHERWELL, M.A. Second Edition.

WORKHOUSES AND PAUPERISM. LOUISA TWINING.

Other Volumes are in preparation.

METHUEN & CO., 36 ESSEX STREET, W.C.

WORKHOUSES AND PAUPERISM

AND

WOMEN'S WORK IN THE ADMINISTRATION
OF THE POOR LAW

BY

LOUISA TWINING

METHUEN & CO.
36, ESSEX STREET, W.C.
LONDON
1898

" Workhouses, under a prudent and good arrangement, will answer all the ends of charity to the poor, in regard to their souls and bodies; they may be made, properly speaking, nurseries for religion, virtue and industry, by having daily prayers, and the Scriptures constantly read, and poor children Christianly instructed."

· Speech of WILLIAM III, in Parliament, 1698. . ·

PREFACE

WHEN it was first suggested that this narrative of events connected with the administration of the Poor Law should be written by me, including the period from 1853 to 1897, I felt the same reluctance as in 1880, when I thought of publishing a small volume on "Workhouse Visiting and Management during 25 years",—a reluctance arising from the personal character which this narrative must take; but this feeling is overruled by another consideration which may be held to overbalance that reluctance, which is, that, being of this personal character, the history of the progress of events could not be correctly given by any one who did not take part in it from the beginning, and of these few, hardly one is now left. I can only trust, therefore, that whatever appearance of egotism there may be in this narrative, will be considered to be unavoidable, and that it will be believed my only desire is to give a clear and chronological view of events and efforts which have been made during the long series of years in which I have been permitted to work in the cause of reform.

I can only hope that in doing so I shall not be found to give offence to any persons, or class of persons, with whom I have been brought in contact. In describing the evils and abuses which I have witnessed, it may be unavoidable that I have done so, though most unwillingly, but I have been compelled to tell the truth as it appeared to me, and I always felt that the blame was chiefly due to the system, rather than to those who carried it out. With regard to the narratives of my public work, as the proceedings of Boards of Guardians are, rightly, made public through the press, I shall not, I trust, be supposed to have betrayed any confidences in relating them, nor have incurred ill-will by doing so. On looking back over the more than 40 years since I was first led to visit one of our great State institutions, I can only feel wonder and surprise at the small amount of opposition and obstruction that I met with from all who were in authority, and could not therefore be expected to see the evils which they had become accustomed to. More particularly is this the case with regard to the central authority, the then Poor Law Board, which I, a woman, had the audacity to invade, as an utterly unknown individual, whose aims and objects could not possibly be known to the officials who presided there, but yet who listened to my statements with the utmost attention and courtesy. And here let me say, that this has ever since been my experience, and that from several of the succeeding Presidents, I and those working with me, have received the same kind and courteous reception and hearing. I cannot help adding that on the most recent occasion on which we approached the Local Government Board, in December, 1896, at an interview kindly granted us as members of the "Workhouse Nursing Association", by Dr. A. Downes, and Mr. Knollys, it was with real gratification and thankfulness that I heard an expression of satisfaction and recognition of what I had been able to do in the course of so many years. To know that my efforts had been received in this friendly spirit, as helpful and not antagonistic, was sufficient reward for all the labour and anxiety that had been encountered, knowing that it had not been wholly in vain, but crowned, we may hope, with a large amount of success.

Perhaps I may name one other motive which has influenced me in making this narrative of past work public, and that is, the regret I feel at the growing tendency of the present day and generation to ignore the results of the past and of former experience. I can hardly be mistaken in believing this to be a serious drawback and hindrance in the work of social reform, yet it cannot be denied that it is prevalent. In carrying out my own plans, some of which were afterwards adopted by others, it has struck me as a remarkable fact, that the experience gained during many years by myself and my fellow workers, was not consulted or desired, at least as a starting point for guidance, but in many cases, deliberately ignored, with the result that much precious time was lost in working out problems which had already been solved, and difficulties were encountered which might have been avoided. I am quite sure that this spirit did not prevail to the same extent formerly, and I venture to raise this note of warning to some of the eager workers of the present day. I may add here that my object in giving the names of my numerous correspondents has been to shew the widely spread interest in the subject so many years ago.

One of my objects in this review of the past and present has been, it will be seen, to press and enforce still more strongly, my conviction of the part which women are called upon to take in carrying out the Poor Law.

I see no reason why some should not be employed as relieving officers, at least in conjunction, with men, for it can hardly be denied that women have done, and are doing, good work as visitors to the poor, by investigating the condition and needs of their families. But at least, there might be co-operation in this part of the work, and even unofficially, they might be of great use and assistance in carrying out the objects of the too often overworked officers. The German system, known as that of Elberfeld, of a thorough visitation of the poor, has frequently been quoted in connection with this question, and might be, at least partially, adopted with advantage. *

I think I shall have shewn in the following pages the advance that has been made within the last few years in both these directions of women's work and co-operation with charity—an advance which enables us to look forward with confidence and hope to still further progress in the future.

* Suggestions have long since been made for women to act as Relieving Officers, or assistants, and a leaflet was written some time ago advocating the adoption of the plan, but I am not aware that it has been sanctioned, though the advantages of such co-operation are obvious, and it is now being again brought forward and urged upon the authorities. At the beginning of 1893 a Woman Relieving Officer, the first of her kind, was appointed temporarily to a Warwickshire district. The Oswestry Guardians have again chosen a woman, who did the duty for several months during her husband's illness, and it is because she was so perfectly efficient as his substitute that they elected her to succeed him.

September, 1897. *Rochester.*   L. T.

CONTENTS

WORKHOUSES AND PAUPERISM

CHAPTER I

RETROSPECT

THE first publication that called my attention to the subject of Workhouses, was a Pamphlet of eight pages (published by F. & J. Rivington), in 1850. Its title was, "A plan for rendering the Union Poor-Houses National Houses of Mercy." [1] I hardly know why it should have attracted my attention, for at that time I had not seen a Workhouse, nor known anybody who had entered one, but it expressed exactly the thoughts that I entertain to this day, contained in the following words. "This class of the Poor has hitherto been generally neglected in our schemes of charity, though it must be evident to those who have examined the subject, that the righteous principle of relieving the destitute, which is the foundation of our Poor Law system, cannot be carried out to its due extent—especially in a moral and religious sense—by means of legal enactments, without the co-operation of private charity." This is surely a remarkable statement, made nearly thirty

[1] The "Diary of a Workhouse Chaplain" had been published in 1847, and in 1855 a Lecture on "Workhouse Visiting," by the Rev. J. S. Brewer, was given in a volume of "Lectures to Ladies on Practical Subjects."

years before "charity organisation" was thought of or advocated. The "Plan" is then sketched out, and these recommendations made; 1. there must be "a licensed Chaplain"; 2. a "well-educated matron", 3. "Union Visitors, for the following objects", and amongst these objects we cannot fail to observe the germs of many of the good works of later days, or years; "to contribute and collect money to form a fund for assisting orphans, friendless, and other destitute, persons, upon their leaving the House; for purchasing religious books to distribute among them; for providing a suitable Library for the use of the inmates; for increasing the comforts of the sick and aged, as far as the authorities would permit; and for all other purposes necessary for carrying out the scheme to which the provisions of the Poor Law would not extend." One object to be kept in view by the Visitors was to "watch the development of the characters of the younger inmates, with a view of obtaining places in service for those who should prove themselves worthy of patronage".

4. Visitors were to meet occasionally in order to carry out these objects. Hints are also given of other plans which might grow out of the central one, such as, for the men, employment in agricultural labour (Farm-Colonies, as recently suggested and in many countries carried out), and even a "House for training Nurses to attend the Poor in sickness, similar to St. John's House in London", (then just coming into existence). We can hardly fail to see in this sketch of nearly fifty years ago, the singular forecast of much that has since grown up and is in full exercise at the present day, such as the organisations for befriending Workhouse Girls, both in London and the Country, the Workhouse Girls Aid Committees, Nursing Associations,

and lastly, the now generally advocated co-operation of private charity with the Poor Law. I cannot remember that there was any outcome of this anonymous Pamphlet till the year 1857 saw the embodiment of most, if not all, its suggestions, in the scheme for establishing a "Workhouse Visiting Society," a paper "on the condition of Workhouses," having been contributed by me to the first Social Science Congress held at Birmingham in that year; and in 1858, an influential Committee was formed, including all persons, men as well as women, who in that day, were foremost in promoting good works, our Society being affiliated to the Social Economy department of the larger and comprehensive "Association for the promotion of Social Science"; I acting as the Honorary Secretary and carrying on the general work during all the years of its existence.[1] During this period a Journal was started as the organ of

[1] The objects of the Society as described in the first Circular issued in 1858, are as follows: "This Society was established to promote the moral and spiritual improvement of workhouse inmates, of whom there are upwards of 117,000 in England and Wales; and will provide a centre of communication for all persons interested in that object. Acknowledging the importance of moral influence over all classes of inmates, the chief object at which the Society aims is the introduction of a voluntary system of visiting, especially by ladies, under the sanction of the Guardians and Chaplains, for the following purposes:—

1. For befriending the destitute and orphan children while in the schools, and after they are placed in situations.

2. For the instruction and comfort of the sick and afflicted.

3. For the benefit of girls of good character, as well as of the ignorant and depraved."

It was added, that "the sanction of the Poor Law Board has been obtained to this mode of action."

the Society and published till 1865, at first monthly, and then quarterly, and a perusal of its 32 numbers would, I think, be a surprising revelation to many workers of the present day, shewing, as it would do, the fact that all the questions, at present so eagerly discussed by some who, no doubt, believe themselves to be the first to discover abuses, or to suggest remedies for them, were known to, and considered by, those thinkers and workers of forty years ago.[1] I have before me a goodly volume consisting of numerous Pamphlets of various sizes, treating of all the questions that are now engaging public attention and interest, from 1850 to 1870. To give even a list of these would take up too much space, but I must name some of them; the " Experiences of a Workhouse Visitor ", by Mrs. Sheppard, of Frome, though without her name, was published in 1857, and also " Sunshine in the Workhouse ". " Begin at the beginning, a Plea for Industrial Schools ", was reprinted from the Irish Quarterly Review, of 1859,

---

[1] I may be permitted to give an extract from the " Letter to the Members of the Workhouse Visiting Society," as given in the last No. of its Journal (32) January, 1865, these being the closing words, after 7 years of publication.

" If this Journal has done anything to lessen the ignorance and dispel the darkness that has hung over the subject of which it treats, we are thankful; and if the battle with indifference, ignorance and obstinacy,—in a word, with *red tape* of various shades and degrees of strength,—has occasionally been wearisome and depressing, not to say despairing, we have been sustained and cheered in our work, from time to time, by having been permitted to see the blessing of God in some results of our labours, and to feel the reassuring conviction that we have at least

" Sown some generous seed,
Fruitful of further thought and deed."

this being a review, amongst other papers, of an article by me, on "Workhouses and Women's Work", in the Church of England Monthly Review of 1858. In 1861 a paper was read by Mary Carpenter at the Social Science Congress at Dublin, on "What shall we do with our Pauper children?" At the same meeting a Paper was read by Frances Power Cobbe on "Friendless girls and how to help them", being an account of the "Preventive Mission", at Bristol, started by the writer and Miss Elliot, for befriending Pauper girls, the pioneer of all subsequent efforts on their behalf. In Macmillan's Magazine of that year an article appeared by the same writer, called "Workhouse Sketches", gathered from her experience at Bristol, giving an admirable picture of the then state of things, and well calculated to arouse attention to the subject. In the same year the "Ecclesiastic" gave a Paper on "Our Workhouse Poor", in a review of the "Journal of the Workhouse Visiting Society". Then there was a "Friendly Letter to Under Nurses of the Sick, especially in Unions", by a Lady, foreshadowing the efforts to be made in this direction in future years. Ireland was not left out in this movement of sympathy, and in 1861, the Medical officer of the Cork Union Workhouse wrote of his "seventeen years experience of Workhouse Life, with suggestions for reforming the Poor Law and its administration", as a result, he says, of the recently established "Ladies Workhouse Visiting Society" there, in a most instructive and exhaustive Lecture.

Suggestions "How to save Infant Life, with hints on the establishment of Homes for Pauper Children", was published by a member of the "Ladies' Sanitary Association" in the same year. In 1862 "Workhouse Education", was written with the same object.

The "Statistical and Social Enquiry Society" of Ireland published several Papers on the "Workhouse System", "The difference between the English and Irish Poor Law", etc. In 1859, when a Commission on the Education question was appointed, I was asked to contribute evidence in Section 4, Question 9, relating to Pauper Schools, especially regarding girls; and the following is an abstract of my replies. "*Industrial* education is advancing in a right direction, being made a prominent feature in Pauper District Schools, yet in none of the *Workhouse* Schools that I have visited, is this sufficiently attended to, nor can it be, as long as they are under the same roof as adults, and practical work can only be taught by communication with them. Yet for these children, boys as well as girls, intellectual education alone is nearly useless. Inquire into the history of the women and girls to be found in the adult wards of workhouses, and they will be found to have been, generally speaking, brought up in Pauper Schools, the effects of which, also generally speaking, I believe to be fatal to girls, the larger proportion of whom are orphans. From herding together masses, or even any number, of these children, without family affections or any attempt at their cultivation, I should expect only the worst and most unnatural results."—I then suggested some remedies, such as the appointment, 1, of a superior class of persons over Schools, both District and workhouse, 2, abolishing the custom of employing Pauper Nurses from the Workhouse, 3, the practice of mixing up casual with permanent children; then, "I am convinced that *women* should have a greater share in this work; no Boards of Guardians, and no officials, can be expected to manage Girls' Schools, neither can *male* Inspectors alone inspect them. There should be no School without Lady Inspectors (and, strange as it may seem, none are even appointed for the needle-work or the domestic arrangements), and constant Lady Visitors, who would cultivate the affections of the children, and help to counteract the fatal effects of life in an Institution, and in a mass, for girls. Education in the Schools, however conducted, will be in a great measure thrown away, unless a certain amount of protection is extended to the girls after they leave them; and without some such plan, the previous care will be in a great degree thrown away, as any one acquainted with the condition and temptations of friendless girls will own. It is my firm belief that nothing but an infusion of *voluntary* labour and interest into this portion of educational work will ever make it completely successful.—The Lady Visitors and Inspectors should act under the Guardians or Poor Law Inspectors, and on all points connected with the Girls' Schools, send in their reports to them; there would thus be that communion of labour which alone can procure successful results." It will be observed that some of these suggestions have already been carried out, but that Women Inspectors, so long and anxiously desired, are still in the future, with the exception of one for the Boarded-out children, and one for Industrial Schools, inadequate in number even for these limited spheres of work.—In the year 1862 an elaborate Report of 86 pages, including two tables of statistics, was presented by the Poor Law Inspector, Mr. Andrew Doyle, to the President of the Poor Law Board, apparently issued as a result of the Education Commission already named, of which Mr. Senior was named one of the Commissioners, giving not

merely a history of Pauper education before 1847, but
also the effects of the system since then, and the evidence
of various witnesses.—The contents of this Report would
be most valuable for present consideration, but it is
hardly likely to be referred to in these days.

That the care of Pauper children was anxiously considered at that time is shewn by all the literature
that discussed the subject; "Suggestions respecting the
orphan children now in Workhouse Schools and in Workhouses", was addressed by the Chaplain of the Central
London District School, the Rev. S. Valentine Edwards,
to the President of the Poor Law Board, in 1863, its
"text" being taken from No. 2 of the "Workhouse
Visiting Society's Journal".—In the same year a Pamphlet
of 55 pages on "The Maintenance of the Aged and
necessitous Poor a National Tax, and not a local Poor-
rate", was written by Mr. Henry Pownall, a magistrate
of Middlesex and Westminster, giving in an Appendix the
amount raised for Rates for the relief of the Poor in each
of the Parishes of the Metropolis in 1856, as well as of
the Unions.

We have lately heard a good deal of the new plans for
the children of the Chorlton Union, but in 1865 we find
a pamphlet on the same subject, "the education of Orphan
Pauper Children", by Mr. Charles Herford of Manchester,
who desired "the appointment of a special Committee to
consider whether any improvements can be made in the
present arrangements" for them. It is remarkable to read
amongst other wise suggestions, the following words, urging
that "the number of persons really interested in their
welfare shall be multiplied as much as possible, so that no
child shall be left without some kind friend to whom he

or she can look with a certainty of finding encouragement
and help, if need be, in time of difficulty. And in order
to do this we must reverse the system adopted in England
in the disposal of orphan children of massing them together
in large schools, we must break the mass into fragments
as small as is found practicable, and approach as nearly
as possible to nature's plan of division into families."

Then in 1865 begins the discussion on the care of the
Sick, a Pamphlet on " Workhouse Hospitals " being written
by Dr. Stallard, of London, based on the deaths of the
two men in the workhouses of Holborn and St. Giles',
which may be said to have brought the matter to a climax,
after years of consideration and representation, which could
now be no longer overlooked or ignored. All his suggestions are valuable, but I will only quote one; " It would
seem essential that at least one member of the Poor Law
Board should be acquainted with Hospital duties and
requirements!" This being then, as now, quite the most
important and special of all their duties. Admirable are
also the suggestions concerning Hospitals for towns, as well
as for smaller, or Cottage, Hospitals, for Country Districts.
It is strange to reflect that more than thirty years after,
so much still remains to be carried out in the treatment
of the Sick Poor. In 1866 the subject was followed up in
Fraser's Magazine, by Mr. Edwin Chadwick, who wrote
on " the Administration of Medical relief to the destitute
Sick of the Metropolis ", as a late Commissioner of the
Poor Law Enquiry, of which he was the sole surviving
member; classification, consolidation, and separation of the
various classes of Paupers being amongst his chief recommendations, quoting Miss Nightingale in support of his
views. I wish I could give more than this brief mention

of this admirable article, which fills twelve pages of double columns of small print, for no one, even at the present day, can deny the claims of so eminent a man to be listened to on these matters. .

Another important step towards action was made in 1866 by the holding of a Public meeting of the " Association for the improvement of London Workhouse Infirmaries", held at Willis's Rooms, the Honorary Secretaries of which were Mr. Ernest Hart, Dr. Francis Anstie, and Dr. Joseph Rogers, the Earl of Carnavon being in the Chair. A Report of this is in the volume I am quoting from, but in the large and comprehensive Committee it is remarkable to find no names of any women, though to the action and discoveries of such, the movement was largely indebted. Amongst the numerous speakers who followed the long and able speech of the Chairman, I shall be excused if I quote a few words spoken by Mr. Ernest Hart, who, though inaugurating the present public movement, could not deny or ignore the fact, that the way for it had been opened and made plain by those who had began it at least thirteen years before, by making known in the Public Press and in other ways, the secrets of these hitherto hidden receptacles of sickness and misery. " He might say that he was in a position to adduce independent testimony as to the general moderation of the descriptions given of some of the Infirmaries, and this too, from some of those ladies who long before the inspections were made, had been working in the wards through the benevolent interest they took in the patients. He thought he might fairly mention the name of one of these ladies, and he was satisfied that the name of Miss Louisa Twining would be known to them all.

Miss Twining wrote, 'I can fully bear my testimony to the need of reform in Workhouse Infirmaries, and having read your descriptions of places I know, I must say they have not been so strong as I expected'." At that time I was constantly visiting the Strand Union, in Cleveland St., St. Giles' and St. George's, Blooms-bury, and the Holborn Union Workhouse, then in Gray's Inn Lane. The remedy suggested at the meeting for the state of things which had been described, was set forth in the following resolution; "That with a view to the humane and efficient treatment of the sick Paupers, it is desirable to consolidate the Infirmaries of the Metropolitan Workhouses, to support them by a general metropolitan rate, and to place them under uniform man-agement in connexion with the Poor Law Board." "That a deputation be appointed to wait on the President to ascertain whether he will be willing to bring in a Bill for the purpose", was next proposed by Mr. Davenport Bromley, M.P., and supported by Sir J. H. Shuttleworth, who had been one of the Metropolitan Commissioners of Poor Laws, thirty years before. At this meeting one of the Guardians of the Strand Union, and one from St. Giles's, were present, as well as the Rev. F. D. Maurice.

In the same year this association reprinted "an account of the condition of the Infirmaries of London Workhouses", from the "Fortnightly Review," by Mr. Ernest Hart, which had preceded the meeting by one month.

In 1868, the subject was again brought before the notice of the "National Association for the promotion of Social Science", in a Paper by Dr. Stallard, on "Poor Law Administrative Reform", and in the discussion which followed, Mr. Charles Buxton, M.P., being in the chair,

Sir Harry Verney, M.P., took part, and read a letter from Miss Nightingale.

Amongst the measures undertaken for the help of Pauper children, I must name one begun in 1802, called the "Marylebone Preventive Mission for Workhouse Girls", the first of the kind in London, though following closely upon that begun in Bristol in 1801, to which I have already alluded; "occasional Papers" were printed for private circulation, by Miss Tucker, of Upper Portland Place, who was the chief originator and supporter of the movement. In 1868 an important Paper was contributed to the Social Science Congress held at Birmingham, by Joanna Margaret Hill, (well-known for her constant efforts in this cause) on "How can we eradicate the Pauper taint from our Workhouse children?" In this Paper allusion is made to the recent work, published the same year, on "Children of the State", by Florence Davenport Hill; and the reply to the question in the title is the description and advocacy of the "Boarding-out system", as carried out in Scotland, as well as to a certain extent, in Ireland, France, Russia, Germany and the United States, probably then brought forward for the first time as adapted to the orphan and deserted Pauper children of England. In 1869 a sermon was preached in Trentham Church, by the Rev. G. L. Edwards on "Love to the brethren, more especially in relation to the orphan and deserted child of the Workhouse", with the text, "God setteth the solitary in families", dedicated to the Confirmation candidates.

In 1870 we come to the Memorial of eleven ladies to the President of the L. G. B. recommending the system, all well-known workers in the case, and including the name of Miss Preusser, the first to carry out the plan at

such meetings as these will call public attention to some of the wants of our poor orphans and destitute children; and whether by Committees of Visitors in the Workhouse, or District Visitors for our villages as well as towns, kind Christian friends will be forthcoming, who will co-operate with the Poor Law guardians and others in improving the condition, and brightening the future, of our Pauper children." I cannot refrain from quoting Mr. Portal's last sentence and resolution, which is as applicable to the present day as when it was spoken; "That, though great difficulties exist in establishing District Schools in agricultural districts, yet, where practicable, they deserve encouragement; and that *idiotic* and *weak-minded children* should be removed from all schools to central Asylums". Finally, 27 years ago, the rule was laid down that "One trained Nurse, adequately paid, should have general charge of the Hospital and Infirmary." Allusion is also made to the sad want of a suitable place of worship in workhouses, Chapels in those days being almost unknown. [1] Stress is laid on the necessity of Lady Visitors to Workhouses, by which "mercy drops on workhouse sorrows." The extension of such conferences was decided upon.

This brief review of the principal papers and publications of twenty years up to 1870, will, I trust, prove that the subject has not been neglected up to the present time, and that it is not for want of effort and representation that so much still remains unaccomplished; but without

---

[1] The first Workhouse Chapel was built at Cuckfield in Sussex in 1860, by the exertions of the chaplain, the Rev. H. Hawkins. Since that time these separate buildings have gradually increased in number, but are not yet by any means as general as they should be, the Dining-halls being still frequently used for services.

these early efforts, probably no results would have been attained.

I cannot omit from this retrospect of 47 years, a reference to perhaps the most important of all the utterances on the subject of Pauper children, the Report presented to the Local Government Board in 1874 by Mrs. Nassau Senior, who had been appointed in the previous year, Inspector of Schools under the management of the Board. It is probably known to few at the present day, and I cannot but regret that its admirable recommendations had not been considered by those who were called to give evidence on the recent commission on Pauper Schools. The Report consists of 80 pages, and its object is described in these words: " I have given my attention almost exclusively to questions affecting the physical, moral and domestic training at the Schools. I have not attempted to judge of the scholastic work, as I required all the time allowed me, for looking into the matters on which I knew that you more especially desired the judgment of a woman. I divided the inquiry into two parts,— first, as to the present working of the system in the Schools,—secondly, as to the after career of the girls who had been placed out in the world." To carry out these objects, the 17 Metropolitan Schools were visited, and later, some country districts in England and Scotland, in order to compare the physical condition of the children in the Metropolitan Schools with those placed in private families. Orphanages and other Schools were also visited, besides others in Paris, as well as boarded-out children. For the second object, no fewer than 650 girls were inquired for, who had been placed out in service during two years, and in addition to this, the careers of girls who had left the schools five years before, having been not less than five years at School. A few valuable statements of these results can only be given here, but "two points have especially to be borne in mind—1. That these schools have to deal with bad material.—2. That great improvement has taken place in the management of workhouse children since the Workhouse Schools have been abolished in London, and distinct and separate schools have taken their place." The observations resulting from the whole inquiry are comprised under two heads, 1. in School, 2. in the World, the first including the classification of children, sanitary conditions, moral and industrial training; the second, choice of situations, Supervision, Guardianship, Protection when out of place. Under the head of "classification", Mrs. Senior laments the failure to make provision for the "physically afflicted," either as regards sight or imbecility, an omission which we still have to deplore, and we shall cordially agree in her remark, that "as long as there is no legal power to detain them in a place of safety, no plan seems to offer a fair prospect of success." The entire separation of the Infants from the mass of the school, under the care of nurses assisted by the older girls, is strongly recommended, even so far as to the use of entirely separate buildings, the training being excellent as a preparation for service. Not only would this be a gain for domestic training, but a great moral gain for the girls; "one of the greatest objections to the plan of bringing up girls in large schools is, that they are unable to get the cherishing care and individual attention that is of far more importance in the formation of character than anything else in the world. It is the fault of no one in particular that at a large

school a girl's affections are not called out. The officers
have so much routine work to go through, that it is
absolutely impossible for them to give sufficient time to
individualising and influencing the girls under their care.
The inquiries I have made on all sides have convinced
me that what is wanted in the education of girls is more
mothering." The division of children into separate groups
or families, is also advocated, and "if a successful beginning
were made of a return to something like a family arrangement in the Infant Schools, the same principles might be
afterwards carried out with regard to the whole system of
Union Schools." Under the head of "Sanitary conditions"
there are admirable remarks on school-room arrangements,
dormitory arrangements, food, exercise and play, such as
I venture to think, could only be made by an experienced
and competent *woman*, more especially as regards the
clothing of the girls, frequently the same by night as by
day. With regard to the staff of these schools, we are
told, "the higher the culture of the superintendents and
matrons, the more power will they have at command.—
Where the object in view is to raise successfully a low
class of minds, a very high class of officer is wanted, and
the position must be made one that they would accept.
The Boards of Management might be more willing than
they now are, to extend the powers of the head officers of
their schools, if people of high education and culture were
found to fill these posts."

With regard to the children of vagrants, a class to which
attention is now being largely directed, the Report recommends
that such should be dealt with in the same way as is
pointed out in The Industrial Schools Act (Clause 14), but
a clause would have to be added, authorising the magis-

2

trates to order the detention of a child in school, on the parents taking their discharge; or that those also should be detained who have entered and discharged themselves three times in one year; this would serve as a check upon the desire of parents thus to rid themselves of their children. Other suggestions concerning the age of protection for children, have already been carried out, saving them not only from the ill-treatment of employers, but of their own relations also. From all these suggestions arose the movement which resulted in the " Metropolitan Association for Befriending Young Servants " and other beneficent work, such as Homes for Girls leaving their places, who must otherwise return to the School or the Workhouse. [1] Some few extracts from the " Conclusion " of this admirable Report, shall close this retrospect of past years and work, conclusions which have now, in great measure, permeated the tone of public opinion on these questions in England. " I was unfavourably impressed with the effect of thus massing children together in large numbers, ... I considered the physical condition of girls in the schools, and their moral condition on coming out of them, disappointing and unsatisfactory". Boarded-out children were then visited and inspected with this result. " I received the same impression everywhere, in favour of the free and natural mode of life afforded by cottage homes." The arguments for and against this system are then most ably and fully stated. " Thus, I am forced to believe that the system of

[1] The first of such Homes was opened in 1861 in New Ormond St., and was certified by the Local Government Board the following year, under the Act obtained by the efforts of the Hon. Mrs. Way, who had already started a Home, or rather a School, for Workhouse girls at Brockham, in Surrey.

large schools is not a good one for girls, and that where
it is not possible to place a girl in a family, she should
be brought up in a small school, where individual influence
can be brought to bear on her. The plan for the education
of Pauper children that I should like to see adopted, would
be that the orphan children should be boarded-out in
cottage homes. In the next place I should wish to break
up the present schools, and to educate the deserted children
apart from the casual children. For both classes of children
I would adopt schools of a more home-like character,
arranged on the Mettray system, each house containing
not more than from 20 to 30 children of all ages. Should
this be pronounced impossible for the present, I would
recur to the plan of using some of the existing schools as
Infant establishments, in which girls after 12 years of age
should receive special training; and I would re-class the
remaining Schools, using some as Hospitals, and the others
as Schools for boys and girls. These I should like to
divide into two classes. In one set of schools, permanent
inmates only should be received, in the other, casuals only;
so that the special system of training which I wish to see
adopted for them, might be carried on in establishments
exclusively devoted to this purpose."

I am of course not aware how far this valuable Report
may have been considered and studied by those who have
recently given so much attention to the subject, nor do I
know if it is still accessible to them, [1] but it seems to me
that no more useful and practical document exists, and it
is well worthy of study by those who have the welfare of
these children at heart. The testimony it offers, besides,

[1] A copy of this Report is in the Library of the Women Guardian's Society, 4, Sanctuary, Westminster, S.W.

to the urgent need of Women Inspectors, can also hardly be overlooked, one only still being found on the staff of the Local Government Board, notwithstanding that the first experiment was so eminently successful. [1] We cannot help noting the result of all these efforts in the various reforms which have taken place since that time, and this may encourage workers in the cause to persevere in their efforts for what still remains to be done.

[1] One Lady Inspector of Schools has been added since this was written.

CHAPTER II

RETROSPECT (*Continued*)

A RETROSPECT of 30 or 40 years cannot be complete without some statements concerning the actual state of things, and the condition of Workhouses, at the time when I first began to visit them. These I will give (in addition to my own Diary) from the experience of eye-witnesses, and those who were concerned in the management of these our State Institutions, under, as was supposed, the "New," or reformed, "Poor Law." One of the chief of these witnesses was Dr. Rogers, who was appointed medical officer to the Strand Union in 1855 (two years after I began to visit there, in Cleveland St.), at the munificent salary of £50, a year, out of which he had to provide drugs. I cannot give a better picture of the then state of things (to which public attention had never been drawn) than by quoting some extracts from his book, as given in the "Queen's Commemoration number of the British Medical Journal," June 19, 1897.

"THE STRAND WORKHOUSE AS IT WAS.

"Dr. Rogers, so well known for his efforts in regard to the establishment of mortuaries and the abolition of intramural interment, was in one sense the hero of workhouse reform. In 1855 he was appointed medical officer to the Strand Workhouse at the munificent salary of £50 per annum, out of which he was to provide all drugs. The master of the workhouse was a man who might have been the original of "Bumble" in *Oliver Twist*. He had been a policeman in Clare Market, and had somehow ingratiated himself with the chairman of the guardians, who kept an *à la mode* beef shop in that locality, and whose niece he subsequently married. The "nurses" were pauper inmates, usually infirm and more often drunk than sober, who were remunerated for their services by an amended dietary and a pint of beer, to which was added a glass of gin when their duties were peculiarly repulsive. Underneath the dining hall was the laundry, with the fumes of which it was filled four days out of the week, while the lying-in ward was immediately above the female insane ward, the presence of a noisy lunatic or two in which no doubt greatly conduced to the wellbeing of the parturient women. The ward for fevers and foul cases contained but two beds, and was separated from a tinker's shop by a lath and plaster partition only 8 feet high. As to this ward, we cannot do better than quote Dr. Rogers's own account:

"It was altogether unsuitable for the reception of any human being, however degraded he might be; but it had to be used. I remember a poor wretch being admitted with frost-bitten feet, which speedily mortified, rendering the atmosphere of the ward and shop frightfully offensive. At first I was at a loss to know whom to get to go through the offensive duty of waiting on him. At last a little fellow called Wiseman undertook the task, the bribe being two pints of beer and some gin daily, with steaks or chops for dinner. Presently the patient was seized with tetanus, and after the most fearful sufferings, died. He was followed almost immediately afterwards by poor Wiseman, who had contracted from his patient one of the most malignant forms of blood-poisoning I ever saw.

"These two successive deaths took place whilst the tinker was plying his business on the other side of the partition which separated this ward from his smithy. This place was an utter disgrace to the Board, but they never attempted to alter it whilst I was there. I have referred also to the nursery ward. This place was situated on the third floor, opposite to the lying-in ward. It was a wretchedly damp and miserable room, nearly always overcrowded with young mothers and their infant children. That death relieved these young women of their illegitimate offspring was only what was to be expected, and that frequently the mothers followed in the same direction was only too true. I used to dread to go into this ward, it was so depressing. Scores and scores of distinctly preventable deaths of both mothers and children took place during my continuance in office through their being located in this horrible den.

"The male insane ward was used also for epileptics and imbeciles, and is described by Dr. Rogers as 'ludicrously unsuitable.' Immediately outside the male ward there was a continuous beating of carpets by the able-bodied inmates, from which the guardians reaped at least £400 a year; the noise was so great as to preclude any possibility of sleep, and the dust so thick as to prevent the windows of the ward from being opened till the day's work was done. Such was the condition of a workhouse infirmary in London but little more than thirty years ago; mediæval as the horrors narrated no doubt appear, we must insist most emphatically that similar conditions may be and have been found at this present moment in Workhouse Infirmaries in the provinces and in Ireland. Surely no act of mercy in this year of charity is more needed than the sweeping away of these abominations.

" As has already been indicated, two resolute persons had for years devoted their energies to the attempt to remedy the abuses we have sketched. One was Miss Twining, who after years of appeal to the Guardians of the Poor and the Poor Law Board, succeeded in abolishing the system of entrusting the care of the sick poor to the Sairey Gamps and Betsy Prigs. The other was Dr. Rogers, who maintained a sturdy but unequal fight against the prejudice of the Board of Guardians, the treachery of their clerk, and the brutality of the Workhouse Master. In 1862 the Poor Laws were considered by a Select Committee of the House of Commons, and Dr. Rogers volunteered to give evidence; he was courteously encouraged by Mr. H. B. Farnall, the one permanent official who showed any consideration for the welfare of the sick poor, of whom he was the metropolitan inspector.[1] Dr. Richard Griffin, of Weymouth, and Dr. Fowler, of Bishopsgate Street, drew up documents illustrating the abuses referred to, but the Committee took

[1] I should like to endorse all that is said of this excellent man, who permitted me to accompany him in his inspection of several London Workhouses, at this time. One cannot help asking the question, was this state of things reported by him to the Central Board, and if so, were they powerless against the apathy and ignorance of the Guardians?

these as read, and practically shelved their evidence. Dr. Rogers's evidence, given impromptu, received rather more consideration, and his recommendations as to the provision of drugs being undertaken by the guardians instead of the medical officers, were partially adopted, though the prejudice of the permanent officials prevented them from being carried into effect till many months and, in some instances, years, had elapsed. In 1865 he succeeded in inducing his own Board of Guardians to appoint a superintendent nurse, and he also increased the cubic space of some of the sick wards by raising the ceilings; even then the floor space was so limited that there was no room for the patients to get out of bed at the side, and they could consequently only do so by the foot! This is the sum of what was accomplished during ten years' strenuous agitation, and will well indicate how hopeless was the outlook at the time of the institution of the *Lancet* Commission, the efforts of which, and the subsequent steps taken by its members, are mainly responsible for the reforms which followed.

"The Commission of 1865 was suggested in April, by Mr. Ernest Hart, then on the staff of the *Lancet*, who drew up the scheme of inquiry, and with whom Dr. Francis Anstie and Dr. Carr were associated in the necessary investigations. These comprised inspection of all the Metropolitan Workhouses into which admission could be procured, with a particular reference to eight main points. First of all there had to be considered the general characters of the infirmary buildings, their suitability to the purposes for which they were intended, the accommodation which they provided, and the proportionate number of inmates. The great point made by the Commission

was the patchwork character of the workhouses, which had
originally been intended for the reception of able-bodied
inmates, and had been more or less inefficiently adapted
to the infirm.   In many of them the proportion of healthy
to sick was not more than 1 to 8, and of the whole number
of inmates—some 33,000—it was computed that nearly
27,000 were on the sick list.   The disadvantage of having
the sick and healthy under one roof is obvious, but this
was not the full extent of the evil, for patients with con-
tagious fevers were often kept perforce in the common
wards, wards in which there was less than 500 cubic feet
of space per patient.   With regard to the buildings the
Commission trenchantly divided them into three classes—
those which were utterly unfit, those which with some
alteration might be adapted to the reception of chronic
cases, and those which fairly fulfilled the purposes for
which they were constructed.   Many and grave were the
defects reported in the ventilation, cleanliness, and furniture
of the wards, whilst the sanitary arrangements and provisions for personal cleanliness were often abominable.   The
system of nursing was carefully investigated, and found to
vary between a small but fairly efficient staff of paid nurses
with pauper help, and the consignment of the care of the
sick to those who had been brought to the workhouse,
not by disease, but by intemperance.   The quality of the
provisions and their management were on the whole satisfactory, but the dietaries, in spite of Dr. Rogers's efforts,
varied considerably at the various institutions, in many
of which no sufficient provision was made for meeting
the natural fastidiousness of invalids.   The medical officers
were found to be practically all overworked, and the
Commission strongly recommended that they should be

relieved of the expense of providing and the labour of dispensing the drugs. There can be no doubt that some medical officers were tempted to eke out their miserable pittances by providing as little medicine as possible. An extreme case is that of a gentleman who was medical officer of the Westminster Union till Dr. Rogers's appointment in 1872. This philanthropist "did not believe in medicine," and treated all his patients with water coloured in various ways, and flavoured with peppermint and other essences. The Commission next investigated the histories of epidemics in various workhouses, and urgently advised the construction of isolation wards. Finally the question of mortality was taken up, both from the general point of view and that of the special causes affecting its rate. The Commissioners found a great excess in the mortality from zymotic diseases, as, indeed, could only have been expected, and also a terrible death-rate among the infants born in the Institutions.

"The findings of the Commission produced a profound impression; a national evil had been laid bare, and a national remedy was called for. Hence the labours of the Commissioners were terminated by the appointment of Dr. Edward Smith and Mr. Farnall by the President of the Poor Law Board, to conduct an official investigation into the matter. Meanwhile, as the result of a meeting at Dr. Rogers's house, the Workhouse Infirmaries Association was formed, with Mr. Ernest Hart, Dr. Anstie, and Dr. Rogers as Honorary Secretaries. Mr. John Storr generously put down £100 to float the Society, which speedily prospered and did much good work in further enlightening the public mind. This was in January, 1866. In the following June, Mr. Ernest Hart, acting on the

statements of the superintendent nurse, got Lord Carnar-
von, a member of the Society, to obtain from Mr. C. P.
Villiers, then President of the Board, an inquiry into the
management and condition of the Strand Workhouse.
This was held by Mr. R. B. Caine, one of the official
inspectors, whose report was bitterly biassed against Dr.
Rogers, whom it blamed as the cause of the state of
affairs through not having made proper representations to
the guardians. Soon after the Poor Law Board sent a
circular letter of inquiry to all the Metropolitan workhouse medical officers. Dr. Rogers called them together
to discuss a general form of reply, and from this meeting
arose the Poor Law Medical Officers' Association, of which
he was so long chairman.

"Mr. Ernest Hart's article in the *Fortnightly Review* for
April, 1866, of which 50,000 copies were reprinted, com-
pleted the stirring up of the public mind, and the title
'Hospitals of the State' has passed into common speech.
Then followed a mass meeting in St. James's Hall, and an
enormous and influential deputation to the President of
the Poor Law Board. Mr. Gathorne Hardy (now Lord
Cranbrook) then succeeded to that position, and in 1867
brought in and carried his famous Metropolitan Poor Bill,
which was largely drafted on the lines laid down by Mr.
Ernest Hart, and incorporated many suggestions from
Dr. Rogers. Out of this have grown the Metropolitan
Asylums system and the institution of the present suitable Workhouse Infirmaries.

"Although the reforms already mentioned have long
prevailed in the Metropolis, the condition of provincial
Workhouse Infirmaries, particularly in the smaller towns, is
far less satisfactory. For the last three years the British

Medical Journal, as the result of Commissions of Inquiry into the workhouses of the provinces and Ireland, has demanded the same treatment for their sick poor as obtains in the metropolis. In many provincial infirmaries the 'straw sack' was found to be still in use, the 'assistant nurse' was still receiving her £12 per annum, and night nurses were few and far between. The unpaid pauper had charge of the nursing in many an infirmary, and for the infirm, the sick, and the helpless imbeciles to be mixed up together was the rule rather than the exception. Small wonder could therefore be felt at tragedies such as those in the workhouses of Oldham and of Newton Abbot. Of individual houses we may mention Bath, where the Commissioner found a building of 230 beds for the accommodation of the sick with no hot water laid on. Here the day nursing was done by one nurse with three untrained assistants. Night nursing there was none, nor even a bell by which assistance could be summoned. At Bristol there were two paid nurses to 132 patients; at Bedminster, two to 128; at Truro, one to 78, and at Falmouth, none at all. At Sedgefield, among other scandals, confinements took place in a corner of the general ward."

Let us also hear what Francis Power Cobbe says in her "Workhouse Sketches", contributed to Macmillan's Magazine in 1861, her experience having resulted in the scheme which was set forth at the Social Science Congress, held at Dublin the same year, of "Help for destitute Incurables." She asks, "how do we accomplish the third end of the Poor Law, and afford support and comfort, *void of all penal element*, towards the sick and helpless who have no other Asylum?... the fundamental principle of workhouse management is incompatible with the proper care of the sick. The Infirmary is an accident of the House, not its main object, and proper Hospital arrangements are consequently almost impracticable. The wards are hardly ever constructed for such a purpose as those of a regular Hospital would be, with proper attention to warmth, light and ventilation. In some cases their position entails all sorts of miseries on the patients—as for example, the terrible sounds from the Wards of the insane. In another court a blacksmith's shed has been erected close under the windows of the Infirmary, and the smoke enters when they are opened, while the noise is so violent as to be quite bewildering to a visitor. Can we conceive what it must be to many an aching head in these wretched rooms? The furniture of the Workhouse Infirmaries is commonly also unsuited to its destination. The same rough beds (generally made with one thin mattress laid on iron bars) which are allotted to the rude able-bodied Paupers, are equally given to the poor, emaciated, bedridden patient, whose frame is probably sore all over, and whose aching head must remain, for want of pillows, in nearly a horizontal position for months together. Hardly in any Workhouse is there a chair on which the sufferers in asthma or dropsy, or those fading away slowly in decline, could relieve themselves by sitting for a few hours, instead of on the edge of their beds, gasping and fainting from weariness. Arrangements for washing the sick and for cleanliness generally, are most imperfect. We cannot venture to describe the disgusting facts of this kind known to us as existing even in Metropolitan Workhouses, where neither washing utensils are found, nor the rags permitted to be retained which the wretched patients used for towels.[1] Again, in other Workhouses, cleanliness is attempted · to an extent causing endless exasperation of disease to the rheumatic sufferers and those with pulmonary affections, to whom the perpetual washing of the floor is simply fatal. In new Country Workhouses the walls are commonly of stone—not plastered, but constantly whitewashed—and the floor not seldom of stone or brick also, and without carpets. Conceive a winter spent in such a prison; no shutters or curtains, of course, to the windows, or shelter to the beds, where some dozen sufferers lie writhing in rheumatism, and 10 or 15 more coughing away the last chances of life and recovery. But even the unfitness of the wards and their furniture is second to the question of medical aid and nursing ... Low as the salaries usually given to Workhouse surgeons are, they are, with very rare exceptions, made to include the cost of all the drugs ordered to the patients. It would seem as if the mere mention of such a system were enough to condemn it. In many cases we believe it would swallow up the whole miserable salary of the surgeon, and go far beyond it, were he to give to the pauper sufferers the anodynes they so piteously require, and to the weak, half-starved, scrofulous and consumptive patients, the tonics, cod liver oil, etc., on which their chances of life must depend .... Besides the anomalous arrangements of wards and medical attendance in Workhouses, which are actually Hospitals without Hospital supervision, there remains a third source of misery to the inmates—the *Nurses*. It is easy to understand

[1] These facts were told by me to the Inspector Mr. Farnall, who was quite unaware of these and some other practices, and was glad to be informed of them.

that the difficulty of obtaining good nurses in ordinary Hospitals is doubled here. Indeed it is rarely grappled with at all, for women hired by the Board are so invariably brought into collision with the Master and Matron, that even the kindest of such officials say (and probably say truly), that it is best to be content with the pauper nurses, over whom at least they can exercise some control. [1] The result is, that, in an immensely large proportion of houses, the sick are attended by male or female paupers, who are placed in such office without having had the smallest preparatory instruction or experience, and who often have the reverse of kindly feelings towards their helpless patients. As *payments*, they usually receive allowances of beer or gin, which aid their too common propensity to intoxication." This admirable article ends with a detailed account of the proposed plan for "Destitute Incurables", by which it was suggested that voluntary help should supply additional comforts, and even pay for trained nurses for such patients who might be placed in separate wards; but though the scheme was accepted by many Unions and even adopted, by some, it was ultimately decided that such co-operation of voluntary charity with the Poor Law, could not be legally carried out; nevertheless, it was one more step towards the humane consideration and treatment of this helpless class. A circular on the subject was sent out by the Workhouse Visiting Society to every Board of Guardians, besides being published in the *Times* and many other papers, and numerous replies were received. In 1861 a Home for

[1] It is strange to find this statement made so long as 36 years ago concerning the chief difficulty at the present time in procuring the best nurses for Workhouses.

Incurable Women was opened in New Ormond St., adjoining the Home for Workhouse Girls, with the object of saving some of the most respectable of such persons from the hardships of the Workhouse, a portion of the payment being received from the rates, and several of such sufferers were received during the first few years, four being at once admitted. Two of these were from Marylebone Workhouse, and the West London Workhouse, then situated at Smithfield. The first Report of this Home was written by Miss Cobbe. It can hardly be necessary to give further proofs of the need of reform that existed 30 and 40 years ago; but nothing could have been done without the aid of the Press, and this was happily given; in this review of the past, I cannot therefore refrain from noticing some more efforts that were made in this direction, to which I have already alluded. In 1857 I wrote the first letter to *The Guardian*, on the subject of " Homes for the Aged Poor ", viewed in the light of Workhouse deficiencies; this was followed by many others, and a leading article, all of which were reprinted in a small volume on " Metropolitan Workhouses and their Inmates ", published by Longmans, in the same year, though this had been preceded by another pamphlet in 1855, " A few words about the Inmates of our Union Workhouses ", urging the visitation by Ladies, and the training of Nurses for the Sick. A letter from me to the *Times* on " Workhouse Nurses ", was admitted in 1858, and from that time may be dated a continued flow of correspondence to various periodicals and magazines.

In connection with this subject I will add the following " Suggestions, from the Members of the Workhouse Visiting Society on the condition of the Sick in Workhouses, 1864, containing as they do, the germ of all that has since been urged and effected in the cause.

"As the results of the Committee on the Poor Laws will be brought before Parliament during the present Session, we desire to submit to members the following points, which appear to us the most important concerning the treatment of the poor in Workhouses. These points arise out of the fact that Workhouses are now, in a far greater degree than formerly, institutions for the reception of the sick poor, Hospital accommodation not having increased in proportion to the needs of the population. We, therefore, beg to suggest the following inquiry, viz., if Workhouses, as at present constituted, are fit places for the treatment of the Sick, by reason of the following facts?

" 1. The appointment of a Medical man, who is expected to supply medicines for his patients out of his salary. [1]

" 2. The custom of employing Pauper Nurses, with (in many cases), not even one paid, or responsible, superintendent for the Sick.

" 3. The general construction of Workhouse Wards, want of ventilation, suitable furniture, and comforts, such as are supplied to Hospitals; extras not being permitted to be given by friends, by order of the Poor Law Board.

"We beg, therefore, to remind members that at the Committee of Inquiry the following suggestions for improving the condition of the sick were made, and we earnestly desire now to see them carried out:

" 1. The appointment of additional Medical Officers, either as Inspectors (as in the case of the Lunacy Commissioners in Workhouses), or, as constant attendants, with pupils (as in Hospitals).

[1] Still a far too prevalent custom. 1897.

" 2. The employment of trained and competent nurses.

" 3. The admission of voluntary benevolence to the Sick wards, so that the Rates should not entirely bear the cost of these improvements." A visitation and inspection of Workhouses by competent medical men is then suggested, and these words follow. " The projected removal of some Workhouses from London seems to offer an opportunity for making improvements, and suggests the question whether it would not be desirable to separate the wards for the sick and incurable from the *Workhouse*, in order that they might be arranged on different principles without encouragement to Pauperism." A Deputation waited upon the President to convey these views. [1]

Other means of publicity, and explanation of the existing state of things, were given by the Parliamentary Commissions which were held in 1861 [2] (House of Commons) and 1888 (House of Lords) at both of which I gave evidence, and amongst other measures of reform, urged the desirability of electing women on Boards of Guardians, though this, the greatest of all the changes carried out, was not an accomplished fact till the year 1875, when a lady was placed on the Kensington Board, to be followed 21 years

[1] The following Deputations to the Central Board have taken place. In 1858 four gentlemen went before Mr. Bouverie, then President; in 1860 a deputation of Physicians addressed Mr. Villiers, and in 1884, our Association expressed its views to Sir C. Dilke, then President, I and several ladies being present, introduced by Sir E. Colebrooke. The last deputation was in 1896, when a large number of the members of our Association, both men and women, represented our hopes and desires to Mr. H. Chaplin, President. A report of this can be obtained at 4 Sanctuary, Westminster.

[2] And not concluded till 1864.

after by 900 women, although there are still 300 Unions and four Counties at the present time without any.

In later years, two more commissions were appointed, that upon Hospitals in 1891 (House of Lords), though not connected especially with Poor Law Institutions, and on Poor Law Schools in 1896, on both of which I had the opportunity of expressing my opinions on the subject of the education of children, and of the condition of the sick in Workhouses and Workhouse Infirmaries. The necessity of trained, as a substitute for Pauper, Nurses having been fully demonstrated, it became necessary to consider how the supply was to be obtained, and this led to the beginning of the "Workhouse Infirmary Nursing Association" in 1879, the result of a Conference between myself, Lady Henry Scott (now Lady Montagu) and Constance, Marchioness of Lothian, who from personal visitation of the sick and incurable in St. Pancras Workhouse, had become impressed with the great need there was of more efficient nursing, superintendence, etc. On visiting the President of the Local Government Board (Mr. Sclater-Booth, afterwards Lord Basing) we found him sympathetically inclined towards our views, and the plan was started at a meeting at Lady Lothian's house in 1879. Since that time the work has grown, and though merely a voluntary Association, and one commanding but little sympathy from the Public (who consider that the Rates ought to do all that is required), we have trained and supplied over 800 Nurses, and spent more than £3000 in the work. But even that is found to be inadequate to the needs of all England, which we are quite unable to supply, even though another Association has started work on our lines for the Northern

Counties, since 1891. [1] But considerations for the future must not come into this chapter, and are reserved for a further and final one.

I can hardly attempt to enter into all the details of work carried on during this preliminary period, in addition to the constant meeting of the Workhouse Visiting Society. One influential gathering was held at Mrs. Gladstone's house in 1860, with the endeavour to obtain the co-operation of London Physicians, in a petition concerning the sick inmates of workhouses, which was largely signed by them, and was presented by a Deputation to the President, the Rt. Hon. C. P. Villiers.

But as early as 1857 the subject was brought before the House of Commons by Lord Raynham (as I have mentioned), when a petition, for which I worked hard to get signatures, was presented. This endeavour to obtain an inquiry was based upon the revelations as to the condition of St. Pancras Workhouse, made after an inspection by Dr. Bence Jones, which much resembled those reports made of other Workhouses, in 1861. In 1858 I wrote an article in the " Church of England Monthly Review ", afterwards reprinted as a pamphlet, and in 1880 it was incorporated in a little volume of "Recollections of Workhouse Visiting and Management during 25 years" (now out of print).

In 1855 Dr. Edward Sieveking brought forward the subject of training nurses from the able-bodied inmates of Workhouses, and the plan was recommended by the Poor Law Board, but it was found to be impracticable

[1] We acknowledge with satisfaction as another outcome of our work, the Workhouse Association for Ireland and Irish Workhouses, begun in 1896.

owing to the lack of suitable and respectable women to be found amongst them. In 1866 I addressed a " Letter to the President of the Poor Law Board," to which was added the Letter to the *Times* on " Workhouse Nurses", and the evidence given by me at the Commission of 1861, and this was followed by another " Letter" in 1887, on " some matters of Poor Law Administration", both being published as pamphlets.

The most important result of all these efforts was the official Report, ordered by the Poor Law Board, and carried out by Mr. H. B. Farnall, Metropolitan Inspector, and Dr. Edward Smith, which issued finally in the Bill of 1867, introduced by the President, the Rt. Hon. Gathorne Hardy,[1] for the entire separation of the sick from the other classes of inmates in the Workhouse, and to be placed under the control of other officers, at least as far as the Metropolitan District is concerned, a reform which it is earnestly desired may ere long be extended to other regions also, as the only hope for the satisfactory treatment of the Sick Poor.

In order to carry out still further the object of this Chapter of " Retrospect", I may perhaps be allowed to add the names and expressions of some of my early correspondents on these subjects, to prove, as I have already stated, that there existed, even in those days, a real and important feeling and interest concerning them.

In my volumes of many valued autographs, the first correspondence is with the Strand Union Board of Guardians, in 1853, and was continued in the following years till 1858, the chief subject being the admission of Lady Visitors, the Poor Law Board being also com-

[1] Now Lord Cranbrook.

municated with, when Mr. Matthew Talbot Baines and Lord Courtenay were President and Secretary; two chairmen of the Strand Union also wrote personally on the matter. Correspondence was also held with many other Boards on the same subject in 1857, the West London Union (then at Smithfield), being one, Mr. Butterworth, of Fleet St., kindly interesting himself in the matter, the result being that a Committee was formed with the Lady Mayoress (Mrs. Finnis) as President, which carried on its work till the Workhouse was removed to Holloway. Mrs. de Morgan was at that time a valuable ally as Visitor to St. Pancras Workhouse, where a Committee of Visitors had worked before the "Workhouse Visiting Society" began its labours; her experiences were afterwards published in a Pamphlet called "A London Workhouse forty years ago." Communications were held in 1863—4 with Dr. King, of Brighton, whose acquaintance I made there, who warmly took up the cause and was the means of interesting Colonel Moorsom in it, who later became Chairman of the Board of Guardians. Other correspondents were Mr. J. W. Cropper, long a Guardian at Liverpool, where he did a great work in supporting the nursing reforms carried out by Agnes Jones, and was the means of establishing the first separate Home for the treatment of Pauper Epileptics. In 1865 Dr. Anstie (one of the Commission appointed by the Lancet) Mr. G. Lyall, M.P., Rev. W. Denton, Mr. Ewart, M.P., Mr. Oldfield, of Emsworth, Mr. Charles Herford, of Manchester, Dr. George Burrows, Mr. Wyndham Portal, of Malshanger, and Mrs. Gladstone, were correspondents; at her house two important meetings were held in this year, 21 persons being present, many of whom were London Physicians, giving their names to a petition on the subject of "Destitute Incurables".

In 1866 Miss Berwick, of Dublin, took up the cause of visiting in the large Workhouses there, and carried on her interest in it till her sad and untimely death, with her brother, in the memorable railway accident from fire in Wales; amongst other early correspondents must be named Miss Tucker of Portland Place, in connection with the Preventive Work for the Girls of the Marylebone Schools at Southhall, and her brother, Mr. H. Carr Tucker; Elizabeth Bell, who began the Girls' Industrial Home in Gloucester Place, Miss Fraser, a devoted visitor at Camberwell Workhouse, Lady Hatherley, Lady Salisbury, the Hon. Mrs. Maclagan, Miss Florence Davenport Hill, Miss Ellis, of Leicester, Miss Luard, in Essex; in 1870, Miss Preusser, of Windermere, the early promoter of Boarding-out, Dr. Elizabeth Blackwell, and Lady Meath. Letters were also received from the Colonies of Adelaide and Western Australia, and from Philadelphia; from Mr. Samuel Benton (long a valued and prominent member of our "Workhouse Nursing Association"), Dr. Arthur Tawke, Dr. Tom Robinson, Mr. W. Vallance (Whitechapel), Dr. T. Dolan, (Halifax) and up to 1879, I had as correspondents the following members of the Poor Law Board, Dr. Bridges, Medical Inspector, Mr. H. B. Farnall, Mr. H. Longley, Mr. R. Hedley, Mr. Murray Browne, Mr. H. Lockwood, Inspectors, and up to the present time, Dr. Arthur Downes, Rev. R. Phelps, Oxford, and Sir J. T. Hibbert, under whose Presidency of the North-Western Poor Law Conference, held at Preston in 1879, delegates were present from various Poor Law Unions, and for *the first time ladies were admitted*, a circumstance worthy to be recorded, and

in connection with which I will give the following extract
from the President's opening address.

" We have also the unusual presence of the lady inspect-
or of the Local Government Board, Miss Mason, who has
since her appointment, which has now, I think, existed for
about three years, shown how well a lady is capable of
doing the work which has been entrusted to her hands.
We have also another compensation to-day. It is that
on the platform and in other parts of the hall our meeting
is graced with the presence of ladies.

" I believe it is the first time that ladies have given us
the benefit of their presence, but I am sure that I am
right in saying that Poor Law administration is a work
which ought to be, and I believe is, attractive to many
ladies. We have now in many parts of the country lady
Guardians, and we have ladies taking a great interest in
everything connected with Poor Law administration.

" Therefore, I think it is especially right and proper that
we should see amongst us to-day the ladies who have so
kindly given us their presence."

Dean Gott (then of Worcester), Lady Montagu, and the
Rev. J. P. Wright, of Oldbury, Bridgnorth, may also be
named as amongst the correspondents of later years.

The first letter received from the Press was from the Editor
of *The Guardian* to which, through the long course of forty
years, we are deeply indebted, as being the first Periodical
to give publicity to facts concerning the Poor Law, to the
then existing evils, and the suggested remedies and reforms.
The letter is dated February 20, 1857, four years after
my first visit to the Strand Union, the two little pamphlets on the subject of the " Inmates of Workhouses "
having been published (as already stated) in 1855 and

1857, and I had sent one letter to *The Guardian* previously.
It may be of some interest to give it here: " The Editor
of the Guardian presents his compliments to Miss
Twining, and encloses a notice by which she will
see that Lord Raynham proposes to move on March
3rd for a Select Committee on the management
of Workhouses. If there are any suggestions which Miss
Twining's knowledge of the subject suggest to her as
desirable to be made before the debate comes on, the
Editor will be very happy to receive anything which she
may wish to say upon it."—The next letter is dated July
21, 1857, after I had sent another letter, hoping it might
be inserted in *The Guardian*.

" The letter addressed by you to *The Guardian* on the
management of Workhouses, has, as you will see, been
printed as a leading article. It is not usual to do this
without the permission of the writer, but your remarks
appeared to me to be of so much value, that I was desirous of securing for them greater attention than they
would probably have received in the form of a letter, and
thus of promoting the object you had in view in writing
them. I have published them as a whole, though they
are long, because they form a whole in themselves. Permit
me to add that if you should hereafter have any further
practical suggestions to make on this subject, on which it
is very desirable to gain the ear of the public, I should
be glad to receive and consider them."

I need hardly say that this kind and welcome invitation
was gladly accepted and acted upon during the whole
period up to the present time.

The next letter is from Lord Brougham, dated October 4,
1857, to whom the Pamphlet had been sent, and as it

led to the first Paper on the subject being read at a Public Meeting, the " Social. Science Congress ", held at Birmingham in that year, of which Lord Brougham was President, it may be of interest to give its contents. " Lord Brougham presents his compliments to Miss Twining and begs her to accept his best thanks for the valuable present of her tract, to which he has called the attention of the Council of the Birmingham Congress. But he would suggest the expediency of her sending a paper on the subject in order to raise a discussion on questions so important. Although the time fixed by the rules for receiving Papers has expired, if Miss Twining sends, or causes any friend agreeing in opinion with her, to send, a short paper to Lord B. it will be received and presented." Thus it is seen how kindly these first efforts, made by a hitherto unknown person, were received and encouraged.

The next letters are from Sir Benjamin Brodie, in 1857, 1858 and 1859; one of which is in response to a request that he would join the Committee of the " Workhouse Visiting Society," then being formed. Mr. R. Monckton Milnes writes, Sept. 1857, to thank for the pamphlet, and says, " it seems almost an insolvable problem to make Workhouses generally more comfortable without increasing the rates, but there are clearly practical abuses of management, which the Poor Law Board can, and ought to, remedy." The then President of the Poor Law Board, Mr. E. P. Bouverie, succeeding Mr. M. Talbot Baines (to whom my first efforts were addressed in 1853), wrote fully on the subject of the admission of Lady Visitors, and rightly described the extreme difficulties of Workhouse management, owing to the heterogeneous collection of various classes under one roof and control, an amalgamation which, as has been often said, is attempted in no other country in Europe; six classes are enumerated, this remark being added, "they are not very easily made compatible." Lord Goderich writes from Newby Hall, Ripon, Sept. 1857, that "the subject is a very important one, and deserves much more attention than it has hitherto received."

Lord Shaftesbury wrote cordially in Sept. 1857, in favour of the visitation of Workhouses by Ladies, "who must have both zeal and patience", adding that "Lady Shaftesbury visits constantly at St. James's Workhouse, which is one of the best of all, and yet there is much to be done in it. I heartily approve of your Workhouse Visiting Society."

In 1857 and 1858 I received long and interesting letters from Lord Lyttelton, with valuable remarks on the Poor Law; "that it is quite essential that a legal system of relief, of whatever kind, should be such as to repel, rather than attract, the poor;—pauperism is essentially and ineradically, an evil state to be in, and one morally injurious to the character;" an opinion given after 20 years' experience of the working of the Poor Law, the tendency to relax filial ties and a sense of duty towards parents, being one of its greatest evils.[1] In 1857 and 1858 Charles Kingsley gave his warm adherence to the Society, asking to be directed what to do "with our own Workhouse and Guardians," and adding, "I shall be most happy to put myself under your orders." The next President of the Poor Law Board was Mr. Sotheron Estcourt, who wrote seven letters in 1858, kindly appointing

[1] In 1862 Lord Lyttelton presided at the Annual Meeting of the Workhouse Visiting Society, held at Burlington House.

a day for an interview at Whitehall; and also arranging for my giving evidence at the approaching commission on the Poor Laws. There is a remarkable sentence in one of his letters, of similar import to that of Mr. Bouverie just quoted, referring to the difficulties to be contended with; "which arise chiefly from the miscellaneous character of the inmates. Young, old and middle-aged, strong and weak, good and bad, idle and willing, are those congregated under one management. The Master who is fitted for one class will be unsuitable for another. I fear that unless we could effect a separation, palliatives are all we can hope for. But I shall much wish to learn your opinions."

The following extract from a letter from Lord Raynham, who first introduced the subject in the House of Commons in 1857, may be of interest. "Under all the circumstances I consider we had reason to be much pleased with the debate on Thursday, 25th (July). It was evident that the feeling of the House was in favour of inquiry, much more so indeed than I expected it to be, and I have great hopes that next session I shall be successful. The discussion alone may at once lead to some improvements, and I am sure you will not fail to make the most of the temporary advantage that may have been gained to the cause, by continuing with renewed energy your benevolent exertions in aid of the poor people whose condition we may hope to see, before very long, as much as possible, such as it ought to be." Sir George Nicholls, whose book on the English Poor Law is so well known and valued, wrote in 1858 to express "a deep interest in the subject." The Bishop of Oxford (Wilberforce) wrote thus; "I thank you for drawing my attention to this important matter. Many circumstances *have* brought before me the pressing importance of such a move, and I do rejoice that you have undertaken it. May Almighty God give you His blessing in conducting it;" and in 1861 the Bishop wrote again; "it is of great interest to me to learn of such good works being carried on on the part of our Church, and I rejoice that God has given you the charity and the energy to labour as you have done for these poor outcasts, and I pray Him to accept and bless your efforts for them." In 1859, Miss Yonge wrote to express her interest in some Nos. of the Journal of the "Workhouse Visiting Society," which had been sent to her, and giving a personal experience of her own, and other Unions.

In 1858, Mr. Charles Buxton wrote to thank for a paper on Workhouses, "as it is a subject I am studying with a view to an article in one of the leading Reviews, and I am anxious to have some conversation with you upon it." The letter ends with an invitation to dinner, to meet Sir Charles Nicholson, of Sydney, "who wants to form a channel for introducing Workhouse boys and girls from England." In the following year Mr. Buxton wrote that he warmly approved the scheme named in the Pamphlet concerning the opening of the Industrial Home for girls, and "will gladly move the requisite clause when any Poor Law Bill is brought forward."

Amongst my valued correspondents at this time Mrs. Jameson must be named, and her important contributions towards the formation of public opinion on all social questions cannot be overlooked. Her two lectures delivered in London in 1855 and 56, on the "Social Employments of Women", were published the same year, the first being on "Sisters of Charity at Home and Abroad", the second on "The Communion of Labour."

Her extensive knowledge of charitable work and Institutions on the Continent gives great value to her suggestions, and it is to be regretted that these interesting little books have long since been out of print. Numerous letters of encouragement and advice were received from her, up to the time of her death in 1860. I may be allowed, as the books may not now be readily accessible, to quote the closing sentences of the last lecture, which sums up the "conclusion" she had arrived at: "I would place before you this, once more, ere I turn to other duties, that most indispensable, yet hardly acknowledged, truth, that at the core of all social reformation, as a necessary condition of health and permanency in all human institutions, lies the working of the man and the woman together, in mutual trust, love and reverence. I would impress it now for the last time on the hearts and the consciences of those who hear me, that there is an essential, eternal law of life, affirmed and developed by the teaching of Christ, which if you do not take into account, your fine social machinery, however ingeniously and plausibly contrived, will at last fall into corruption and ruin. Wherever men and women do not work together helpfully and harmoniously, and in accordance with the domestic relations—wherever there is not the Communion of love and the Communion of labour—there must necessarily enter the elements of discord and decay. Despair we cannot, dare not."

Mr. Sydney Turner, officially connected with the Industrial Schools and other educational movements, wrote with cordial sympathy in 1860—61. In 1859 I received a long letter from the Bishop of Perth, Western Australia, who was then in England, and deeply interested in the questions concerning the convict system, and the emigration of women, on which he had been in communication with the President of the Poor Law Board; as the colony was resolved not to admit Convict Women "whether reformed or unreformed", they desired to know if it would be possible to obtain from the Workhouses any number of women who would be available for emigration. In a subsequent letter from Perth, the plan as carried out in one attempt is described as a failure, though the women were all well reported of by the Chaplains and other officers by whom they were sent; the result is attributed entirely to the fact that "all the good that had been done to them in England was more than undone during the voyage to this colony, owing to the contamination of intercourse." The conclusion arrived at is one long since acknowledged and acted upon, that "you cannot hope to send out your women as emigrants, with any reasonable prospect of favourable result, until proper measures are taken for supplying them with the necessary amount of care and religious training during the voyage." The necessity of there being good matrons in the Emigrant ships, is earnestly enforced.

In 1859 began the correspondence with the Poor Law Board (of which Mr. Villiers was then President) concerning the proposed "Industrial Home for Young Women" from Workhouses, communications having been made by myself and Miss Coutts as to the possibility of obtaining payments from Guardians for the inmates, the inquiry having also been made by the Strand Union Board. The Home was opened in 1861, but not certified till the following year.

That we had the cordial sympathy of Mary Carpenter during all her life of work, need hardly be said, closely connected as it was with her own aims and objects in social reform. In 1860 a correspondence began and was continued for many years, with Sir Walter Crofton, from the Castle, Dublin. As the Social Science Congress was to be held there the following year he suggests that the subject of Workhouses should be brought prominently forward, and "the ablest men that can be found will be required to preside at the different Sections"; "Social Economy" should be well presided over, Mr. Sotheron Estcourt being suggested for the post.

Early in 1880 communications were made to Miss Nightingale, whose sympathy was earnestly desired for our work. Being unable to reply personally, owing to her state of health, letters were received from Mr. J. H. Bonham Carter, saying that she felt the "greatest interest in the subject," and adding, "in Miss Nightingale's own path, it has always been her feeling that the best and most satisfactory results have been obtained by steady working, beginning in a very limited field;—should her long continued endeavours to raise the standard of Nursing generally, be attended with any result, I trust that the good may be felt by degrees to aid in improving the Nurses of Workhouses, as well as of Hospitals", a hope which is surely now being fulfilled.

But I must not further multiply these extracts, I will only give a few more names of the many who were interested in, and helped forward, our cause. Charles Dickens wrote in 1860, a note of cordial approval, saying he was then writing an account of a Workhouse he had just visited. Mr. William Cowper, the President of our "Workhouse Visiting Society," had constant communication with me, and was present at the Social Science Meeting at Bradford in 1859. Mrs. Nassau Senior, Dr. E. Sieveking (who had proposed a scheme of Nursing to the Epidemiological Society), Dr. Bence Jones (who carried out the investigation at St. Pancras Workhouse), Mrs. Ranyard, Miss Sturch, Mr. H. G. Bowyer (Poor Law Inspector), Mr. Tufnell, Inspector of Schools, the Rev. W. C. Lake, then on the Education Commission, Dr. Howson, of Liverpool, were all correspondents of 1860. And from 1859 I had the great advantage and privilege of receiving numerous letters from Mr. H. B. Farnall, Metropolitan Inspector of Workhouses, whom I have already named.

In 1863 Elihu Burritt, the American, was present at the Social Science Congress at Edinburgh, and wrote to express his sympathy and interest in the paper I read there. In 1861 Mr. Charles Hood wrote to convey his great satisfaction at the proposed Home for Incurable Women to be added to the Home for Workhouse Girls, and for which he kindly forwarded £100. The Rev. C. H. Eyre, Rector of Marylebone, and the Rev. J. H. Gurney, were both interested in the Marylebone Workhouse and Schools, and wrote about them. The Rev. F. D. Maurice, the Rev. T. R. Redwar, Chaplain of the Strand Workhouse, the Rev. Emilius Bayley (Rector of the Parish in which I then lived), Mrs. Tait and the Bishop of London (from 1860 to 1866), the Rev. Francis Paget, Mr. Arthur Helps, Mr. J. L. Motley, Sir James Paget, Lord John Russell, Mr. Gathorne Hardy, the Rev. J. E. Kempe, the Rev. Ernest Hawkins, the Bishop of Salisbury, the Bishop of Durham, Dr. George Buchanan, Dr. W. Farr, Rev. J. Erskine Clarke, Frances Power Cobbe, Miss Williams Wynn, Sir W. Bowman, Dr. Russell Reynolds, Miss Neave, Miss Marsh, Lady Eastlake, Lady Herbert, Mr.

George Lyall, Mrs. Monsell and Rev. T. T. Carter (of Clewer), Sir W. J. Hylton Joliffe, Rev. T. Dale (St. Pancras), and Lady Ebury, all wrote at this time. Mr. John de Liefde, visited the Homes in New Ormond St., and wrote warmly of them, besides contributing an article in "Good Words", containing praise and satisfaction with all he saw there. In 1866 the Editor of "John Bull", was "so struck with Miss T.'s Letter to the President of the Poor Law Board, that he ventures to ask her, whether, as a great favour, she would undertake to write a series of six Papers, with or without her name (the former would be the greater boon). The Editor desires to make the subject a special feature of his Paper during the recess, and he knows none so competent as Miss T. and hopes therefore that she will excuse the liberty he has taken in desiring her co-operation for so good an object." A few more names of sympathising correspondents may be added; Mrs. William Cowper writes from Broadland's, Mrs. Arnold from Fox How, Mr. Thomas Snow from Halifax, to urge that reforms should not be limited to the Metropolitan Workhouses, and to the sick wards alone, as he feared was suggested by Mr. Ernest Hart's Committee, for the needs of those in Country Districts were as great. The Chairman of the Strand Union cordially adopted our suggestions in 1866, thirteen years after the first exposures of the then state of things in that Workhouse had been made. Mr. Edwin Chadwick, whose sanction and approval was most valuable, the Bishop of Bath and Wells (Dr. Eden), Miss Pauline Irby, from Kaiserswerth, the Director of the Deaconess Establishment in Paris, M. Vermeil, and the Director of that at St. Loup, Canton de Vaud, M. Germond, were also correspondents. Dr. Henry Acland, one of the members of our Committee of Workhouse Visiting, wrote in 1866 to ask, "Am I to look on a Workhouse Infirmary as a Hospital?" Mr. Arthur Kinglake (Weston-super-mare) asks what he could do " as a Magistrate for Somersetshire, for the introduction of reforms and for the improvement of our suffering Poor, especially by means of further inspection?" Dr. Edward Smith of the Poor Law Board, who was able to carry out so many of our suggested reforms, wrote, and sent his Report on Metropolitan Workhouses; Mrs. Sarah Austin also expressed her interest in the cause. In 1865 a long letter was received from " a Workhouse Visitor at Birmingham ", Miss Joanna Hill, though her name was not then given, and I need hardly add that it was a valuable contribution to our experience; I also heard from Dr. Vaughan, Dr. Goulburn (who in 1866 opened my Home for Incurables in Queen Square), Frances de Bunsen, and the Rev. J. P. Norris. Mr. J. G. Goschen, when President of the Poor Law Board in 1869, gave his opinion as to different classes of Pauper Schools, in terms which might have been written yesterday, and expresses what we hear being said now on all sides. Dr. Edwin Lankester gave suggestions as to the possible help Coroners might give in cases of suspected cruelty in Workhouses (1870); the Bishops of Lichfield, and London (Jackson), Mr. John Macgregor, Mr. C. H. Bracebridge, Miss Jane Sinnett, and Bessie Rayner Parkes, Editor of the Englishwoman's Journal, which already in 1857 had brought forward the subject of Workhouses, may all be added, not forgetting Dr. Aschrott, the able and painstaking author of the book on the English Poor Law which should be read by all who study these subjects. The last name in this long list shall be that of Mr. Stansfeld, President of the Local Government Board in 1871, who wrote to ask for an interview, in words which I may be excused for inserting here; "it would be no less useful than interesting to me just now to hear something from your own lips of your experience and views on the great subject matter of Poor Law and Charity organisation arrangement." A subsequent visit was made to discuss the all-important and welcome proposal for the appointment of a *Woman* as Inspector of Poor Law Schools, in the person of Mrs. Nassau Senior, which may surely be reckoned as one of the greatest onward steps ever taken in Poor Law reform.

Out of this long list of over one hundred correspondents, but few are now left to receive the thanks and gratitude which I feel I owe them for their abundant kindness, sympathy and encouragement in the work I had then in hand.

PARAGRAPH
INTRODUCTORY TO, AND CONNECTING,
CHAPS. 1 AND 2 WITH CHAP. 3

HAVING now given a sketch of the Literature and extent of public opinion and knowledge on the subject of the Administration of the Poor Law and Management of Workhouses from 1850 to 1897; the next Chapter will offer a description of the actual condition of Workhouses as witnessed by myself, during many years of visiting in London. The pictures thus presented will, I believe, be considered to prove the need that was felt for action, and an appeal, not only to the authorities responsible for the management, but to the wider sphere of public opinion by means of the Press, which, up to that time, had been in complete ignorance of the condition of these our State Institutions, although supported by the public Rates, and ostensibly managed by Guardians, the representatives of the contributors.

CHAPTER III

EXTRACTS FROM MY DIARY
1853

MY first visit to a workhouse was on February 1, 1853, when I went to the Strand Union, in Cleveland Street, to see old Mrs. S——, who was obliged to give up her home and go in. I had obtained an order from the Chairman of the Board of Guardians, and the master and matron readily admitted us, and agreed to show us over the house. They were kind-hearted, old-fashioned people, and had charge of the St. Clement Danes Workhouse for many years, when it was on the present site of King's College Hospital. In visiting poor people in a district, I had often heard of some who were going in. One poor old lonely woman, in whom I felt much interest, was obliged at last to break up her home and depart. I often reproached myself with not going to see her, when I heard, in about six weeks after, that she had gone quite out of her mind and died. But in those days I fancied the workhouse was an inaccessible fortress, which could only be entered through great difficulties and dangers. At last this most respectable and good old woman, Mrs. S. who had supported herself by doing the best kind of flannel-work for the best shops, after struggling on month after month, was forced to give up, and her only comfort in going seemed to be the hope of seeing an old friend. I promised to visit her. Though she was near eighty when she went in, she yet lived some years, and was the chief object of my visits to the workhouse during that time. Her sufferings were great, and they were greatly aggravated by the treatment of the nurses. At the first visit I found a courteous reception. The kind master and matron asked me to go again to read to a poor sick woman to whom I had spoken. This was an opening which I gladly availed myself of, and as we were well known in the parish to which the workhouse belonged, and to the Chairman of the Board, no difficulty was in the way of my going into any ward as often as I could find time. At the very first visit, I was forcibly struck by what has been my conviction ever since: the *great* want which is *the* evil of workhouses—efficient supervision. The sight of numbers of young women, many of them with babies in their arms, left wholly alone, and with no other control than that of pauper women, appeared to me a most hopeless and unfortunate state of things.

Shortly before this visit I had read a pamphlet upon workhouses, published by Rivington, which confirmed many ideas I had previously had about them. From all I had heard from the poor, I felt sure they were not managed as they might be and ought to be.

I talked to one or two of the women in the sick ward. One spoke of having been a great sinner, but appeared to be very repentant. I offered to go again to read to her, and my proposal was willingly agreed to by the matron, who said "she would be glad if I would visit her." I determined to act upon this permission, and I continued to do so till her death; and afterwards I went on visiting Mrs. S——, and made other acquaintances. In the course of that spring I paid thirteen visits to the Strand Union. I thought the benefit might be extended by having other ladies allowed to visit; and as I knew the chairman, I applied to him on the subject, personally and by letter. I paid him several visits in Clare Court, and he seemed favourable to the plan, though he could do nothing of himself.

He appeared to be chiefly impressed with the conviction of the hopeless character of the younger women. An application to the guardians brought an answer that unpaid and voluntary efforts were not sanctioned by the Poor Law Board, and the offer was declined. So the matter ended for the time. The master and matron would have aided me, and thought that much might be done. The chaplain seemed a very inefficient person, and I never saw him.

1854.—As the difficulty seemed to rest with the Poor Law Board, and I could get no satisfactory answer from them, I determined to ask for an interview. The Rt. Hon. Matthew Talbot Baines was then President, and I was told he was a very good and benevolent man. April 8th was the day fixed for the interview. I went to Whitehall, expecting to find the "Board" to consist of a large number of gentlemen seated round a long table, and I had great fears and tremblings about it; I was quite haunted by the thoughts of it for many days beforehand, and I longed to get it over. I suppose I looked as if I was going to something formidable, for the porter or attendant who showed me in said, as we went up the stairs, "You need not be afraid, ma'am; you will find them

very nice gentlemen indeed;" and I was much relieved
by hearing that there were only Mr. Baines and Lord
Courtenay (the Secretary) present. They were seated at
a long table in a large room. The President had a very
agreeable appearance and manner, and quite encouraged
conversation. Lord C. said less, and had very much
of the official and discouraging air about him, as if he
thought me—as, no doubt, he did—a troublesome person
to meddle with their affairs. I believe, however, I fully
explained my cause. I even ventured to ask if they
could not give at least a recommendation to Boards of
Guardians that ladies should be allowed to visit; but that
was declined. Lord C. said, however, that if I could
get the sanction of *one* Board of Guardians they would not
refuse permission, and that would be a great step gained.
I think Mr. Baines quite admitted that good might be
done by what I proposed. When I mentioned something about the chaplain, they said a new one had just
received their sanction, and Mr. R—— was appointed.
I suppose such a result as this is as much as is ever
gained by an "official" interview, and I was obliged to
be satisfied. It was clear that this was not the real cause
of the guardians' refusal, for on representing to them what
I had done, and renewing my application, the offer was
still declined. I saw the new chaplain at the union and
at his own house, and he said he would gladly assist me,
owning he could do little or nothing with many of the
inmates, but feared to say anything to the guardians, as
he was so lately appointed. I felt greatly cast down and
discouraged. The porter was frequently changed, and
a new one was so rude and insolent that I quite dreaded
to go. Altogether I paid fewer visits this year—only

nine—though I hardly ever went without feeling it was a comfort to some, and meeting with old acquaintances who knew something about me, and must have been cheered by seeing a visitor.

1855.—Paid four visits to the workhouse, and I again saw the chairman about more regular visiting, but without effect. The good master and matron died, and I felt more discouraged still. The new ones did not seem as if they would do anything. The master had been formerly porter at the gate, and was a most unfit person; the matron was passionate, and much disliked, and the complaints were universal; yet the guardians were well satisfied, and said they kept order, and were economical— the best they could have.

During this autumn at Surbiton I went to visit the Kingston Union, with the chaplain. It contained 150 inmates, and appeared to be kept in very good order, as such a small number was quite under the control of two people, who were kind and fitted for their work. Even here the visits of ladies who would read to the old people would have been a comfort. The infirmary is a separate building, and is superintended by a separate matron. During this time I decided on writing something on the subject, and prepared a pamphlet, which was published at the end of the year by Longmans, "A Few Words about the Inmates of our Union Workhouses." I saw Mrs. Jameson one day, and asked her about it, and she quite advised my doing so; she had brought the subject forward in her lecture on "Sisters of Charity," and she said to me, "Strike whilst the iron is hot." I sent the manuscript also to Mr. Maurice and Miss Williams Wynn, and both approved of it. The subject of visiting workhouses was mentioned by the former in a circular he had printed about forming classes for women at the Working Men's College, and in the summer a lecture was given there by Mr. Brewer on "Workhouse Visiting."

1856.—My visit to a third workhouse was to see J. T——, in St. Giles's. He was in a ward partly underground, with a stone floor; the beds, sheets, and shirts were quite dirty and grey. He said he had not seen the matron more than once during four months, only the chaplain and the guardians occasionally; the nurse was an old Roman Catholic, with a bloated face, above seventy. To get in I had to wait with a crowd at the office door to obtain a ticket. Visits to the sick are only allowed once a week, for one hour.

March 8th.—I took Mrs. Jameson to see the Strand Union, as she was preparing her second lecture, "The Communion of Labour," and workhouses were especially to be brought forward. We agreed it was a most depressing sight, more so than any prison, for there seemed no effort working for good, or to combat the evil. There was then a civil porter, to whom I spoke, and said I hoped kindness would be shown to the poor, who often complained of their treatment.

March 17th.—I went with Mrs. Jameson to see the Roman Catholic establishment of the "Little Sisters of the Poor," at Hammersmith, where about sixty old and sick women are taken care of, exactly of the same class as in our workhouses; but the law or spirit of "love" reigned there. One sister said, "So disagreeable and arduous are our duties, that we have to think every morning of the motive of doing them—for the love of God." They get up constantly in the night to attend to the patients, and sit and live with them, eating of the scraps that they daily beg and collect in the neighbourhood; yet they said their health was excellent. In the garden was a separate house for miserable, sick, and idiotic children. Why cannot Protestants do the same works with the same motives? Many were in bed, but some were sitting up. They make up old clothes, and seldom buy anything new. One of the two sisters, founders of this order, came over from France to institute this house, but is now dead, at the age of thirty-six. Many of the inmates were Irish Roman Catholics, whom the sisters said they wished to save from the workhouse.

June 26th.—I went with Mrs. Jameson to see the St. Pancras Workhouse with Mrs. Tomlinson, who had been mentioned to me as being one of the committee forming for visiting the workhouse. We heard much of the new arrangements, and of the miserable old state of things. One poor woman said their sheets had not been changed formerly for months. The matron of the infirmary seemed a good woman, and paid nurses were just being tried; the schools were not then moved.

This year I paid seven visits to the Strand Union, besides others to St. Giles's.

Once I was kept waiting with a crowd for some time after the hour appointed, and of this I complained. It was snowing, and miserably wet. I saw the master, and was taken by him to the medical man, who seemed to be the authority. Of course, at first he denied that it could be otherwise; but when I convinced him how long we had been kept, and the injustice of depriving the poor people of half the short time allowed for visiting their friends, he said it should be looked to and remedied.

After I had left, he ran after me to say that he had ascertained it was all correct, and was much obliged to me for mentioning it.

December 15*th.*—I went to the Islington Workhouse to visit old F——, a blind man, who wished to see me. He had often told me accounts of his life there, and of his misery from the bad language, from which he had no refuge but by going to bed at six o'clock; but then he was woke up when the others came to bed, and was often disturbed all night. He was a very respectable man, and had seen better days. One of his expressions in speaking of the language was, " It makes my blood creep." The boys were taught to be as bad as the older men, by all being together. I could not hear much from him, as the nurse always took care to be close by on these occasions. One poor man in the ward was evidently quite half-witted, and they said he was a dreadful trouble, wanting to undress and go to bed in the daytime, etc. The nurse with all her talking and threatening, could not manage him, and a man was called in to assist. I talked to him, and begged him to read and be quiet. The poor creature said, " Well, I really will try," and he seemed softened and more reasonable. How little are the arts of persuasion known or tried by those who have this difficult work! Signs were not wanting that the subject was gaining ground as to interest and importance. There was even another pamphet published upon it, " The Duty of Workhouse Visitation, and how to do it," with a reference to Captain Trotter. I wrote to him about it, and sent him mine. I had an anonymous note from a workhouse visitor, rejoicing in my pamphlet, and sending me a little tract called " A Wide Field of Usefulness," urging the same thing.

I also heard from Miss B——, in Lincolnshire, who visited in the Lincoln Workhouse, and every account of success was an encouragement when at first I had seemed alone in my work.

I forgot to mention that one of my first encouragements was finding from Mrs. Plumptre that Mrs. Hare had attempted the plan of ladies' visiting in Sussex, and that the behaviour of the inmates was found to be greatly improved by their influence. It was this that first emboldened me to apply to the guardians for leave to introduce lady visitors.

1857.—The subject made great strides during this year, and our efforts were evidently blessed. In January I saw a letter in the *Guardian*, on the subject of " Homes for the Disabled Poor." I felt a strong desire to answer this with a few words about workhouses, which it seemed to me ought to and might be what we wanted for our poor. I wrote it without much expectation of seeing it in print, but it was inserted, and I felt very thankful, that the matter was at last brought before the public. At the end of last year, Mrs. Tomlinson had asked me to write something for their Ladies' Committee at St. Pancras, which she thought would encourage them; I did not know exactly what I had to say, but I began it, and found I had material enough for a long paper. After they had read it, it was proposed to publish it, and one or two newspapers were suggested. I took it with me when I went to Brighton, and finding that I had been successful with my first attempt in the *Guardian*, I determined to try for this also, and wrote it out directly, and sent it up on Monday evening. I was agreeably surprised to find it inserted as a leading article in the Wednesday's number, and a note from the editor explained that he thought it important enough to place it thus, which he did without waiting to ask permission.

In the course of February I saw a notice in the *Times* that a motion was to be brought forward in Parliament, for an inquiry into the management of metropolitan workhouses, by Lord Raynham. I had never heard of him, and was anxious to know his motives in taking up the subject. I ventured to write to him, and had a polite answer, saying he should be glad of any further communication. Just then the ministers went out, and the whole subject was postponed.

At this time I had a letter from Mrs. Sheppard, sent through Longmans, in answer to my pamphlet, speaking of her interest in the work at Frome, and telling me of what she had done. This grew into a correspondence, which continued at intervals with much interest for some years. Mrs. S. shortly after published a pamphlet called " Experiences of a Workhouse Visitor," and she sent me several extracts of answers she had received, all showing an awakening interest in the subject.

In March I went to Paris for a month, and during that time I visited several charitable institutions, with a view to comparing them with our workhouses. The result of these visits I published in a letter to the *Guardian* on my return. I had one answer, sent through the editor, from Dr. Chambers, wishing to see a " Maison de Santé " for men here, and saying that my account quite agreed with his own experiences when a medical student in Paris.[1]

---

[1] These suggestions are now being carried out by the Home Hospitals Association, etc., twenty-two years after.

In the course of the spring Mrs. S. suggested that I should publish together the several letters I had sent to the *Guardian*, which was the first idea I had of doing so. I began to arrange another pamphlet, therefore, and wrote a preface. Finding that Lord Raynham was again proposing to bring forward the subject, I wrote to beg an interview. One morning he called, and we had some conversation upon it; but it was difficult to understand his views or plan, for he talked in a very confused manner, and had evidently no personal knowledge of what he spoke about. I feared his youth and inexperience would not favour his cause, but he was willing to receive any suggestions.

Before this I had written to Mr. Bouverie (President of the Poor Law Board), on the subject of ladies' visiting, etc. I received from him a very official answer, not at all to the point, but renewing the old objections of "interference," a "divided management," etc.

Routine and order (so called) evidently haunted the minds of these good people, who have never had anything to do with the poor personally. One day Lord Raynham called to say he thought it would assist him if he could have a petition signed by several persons, which he might present in the House. He asked me to get it done. I said I would willingly get signatures, but how to set about a petition I had no idea. He said it was very easy, and left me to manage it. I felt utterly perplexed, but got a written-out form, which I copied, and expressed it as I thought suitably.

June 17*th*.—I set out with the petition first to Dr. Bence Jones, who, having had the inspection of the St. Pancras Workhouse, was, I knew, interested in the subject. I had an encouraging interview with him, and found him very kind and cordial; we had much conversation about workhouses. He was most desirous that a better system of nursing should be carried out, and wished Miss Nightingale had turned her attention to this point. He very readily signed it, and said he should always be glad to see me.

I then proceeded to Dr. Routh, in Montague Square, whom I had heard speak of the evils of workhouses at a meeting for the Cripples' Home, some weeks before. I found him also very friendly and interested in the cause, but he spoke hopelessly of the impracticability of the guardians. He advised me to go to Dr. Stewart, in Grosvenor Street; but as I was near St. Mary's, I thought I would try to find Mr. Hampden Gurney there. I waited in the vestry for him, and did not get much encouragement when he came, though he signed his name. Then to Dr. Stewart, who read the petition, and to my dismay told me that it would not do, being incorrect in one or two points! He wrote out a form, and told me I must copy it, and he would gladly sign it again. So my morning's work on a hot day seemed wasted, and I returned home. The next day I sent round a new copy to the three doctors, who all kindly signed it again. There was scarcely a week in which to get it all done. Every day I got some fresh signatures, and wrote to ask some to call here to sign it. Mr. Pownall, the magistrate, called for that purpose, and I was encouraged by a long conversation with him, his experience being very valuable; he quite agreed with all I said as to the influence of women. It was singular at the time how well everything fitted in. Captain Trotter called here; his chief idea seemed to be to get "converted characters" to manage workhouses, and did not think women could take any part in the management.

June 19th.—I took the petition to Miss Neave, at Westminster, by appointment; Mrs. Sheppard sent me up several names who would sign it, and a list to add to what I had already.

June 22nd.—I went to Mrs. Shaw, in Camhridge Square, a lady much interested in the work; and then I went to Mrs. Sidney Herbert, whom I had the good fortune to find at home, and who was very kind about it, and spoke about what she had done in Wiltshire. Besides, these, I sent to many; Mrs. Tait, etc. I found the latter had much interest in the cause, from having personally visited the workhouse at Carlisle, which was all hopeful and encouraging.

June 23rd.—I sent the petition to Lord Raynham, thinking the subject was to come forward this evening, but it was returned to me, as it was postponed till Friday, and I might be able to get more names. I was sorry to see it again, for it had been no little trouble and anxiety to me, and a great fatigue. All this, after all, was useless, which may make the trouble seem the more vexatious; but I do not regret it, for I believe it spread an interest in the cause in many quarters, and was the means of my personally reaching many.

June 24th.— I took the petition to the closing meeting at Queen's College, and got more signatures, Dr. Trench's among the number.

June 25th.—I went after breakfast to Kensington Workhouse, as being admirably managed, and they seemed to have no experience of bad ones. I made a long round on a scorching morning, and found many persons out; so I did but little. In the afternoon, just as I was going out again, Lord Raynham called to ask for the petition, as he was then going to the House. I asked if we could be admitted to hear the debate, and he told us to be there at six o'clock. There was a difficulty about our admission without tickets, but after some delay we got into the ladies' gallery, and there, by a singular chance, found the Misses Waldegrave, who had been here to sign the petition; they did not know the subject was to be brought forward. It was late before its time came, and the House was very empty. Lord R. came up to see if we were there. I asked him not to mention any names, but he wished to bring forward some of the instances I had told him off. He seemed nervous, and certainly did not make an effective speech, or enforce the important points. It was a pity to lose such an opportunity, and I quite regretted it; but there was some response and sympathy shown in the following replies. The inquiry was, however, not granted, but there was some mention of renewing the attempt next session. Many persons, however, believed that private efforts would do more than Parliamentary inquiry could effect.

June 27th.—I went with Mrs. Goodfellow to see the Holborn Workhouse; she and one other lady take a ward there. The matron, as usual, looked ordinary, and was dressed in a tawdry cap with flowers. The house looked old and dirty; the school was kept under the same roof, and a workhouse training was therefore inevitable. The matron owned she had great difficulty in finding proper persons among the paupers to be nurses.

July.—I heard, through Mr. Butterworth, that the Lady

Mayoress was proposing a Ladies' Committee for the West London Union. The first I had heard of this was in a note from Mr. Adam Clarke Smith, Curate of St. Andrew's, Holborn, forwarded to me by the editor of the *Guardian*, saying he should be glad to communicate with me on the subject of workhouse visiting, having read the letters. I wrote to him, thinking he proposed to visit the Holborn Union. I found, however, it was the same plan as the Lady Mayoress had formed. I wrote to her about it, and she called. It was getting late in the season to begin anything, but it seemed a pity to delay till autumn. After my return from Ramsgate we agreed to have a meeting at the Mansion House, if we could only collect half a dozen ladies.

In July my pamphlet was ready, and I sent out a great number. I had many encouraging answers, and much kind sympathy. Those who have never published anything can hardly imagine the endless delays and small difficulties that arise before even a pamphlet can meet the eye of the public. I was anxious to send it out before everybody had left town, but I only got it done the day before I left home for Ramsgate.

I heard again from Mr. Butterworth, hoping I would join the committee.

July 22nd.—I went to the anniversary of the Highgate Penitentiary, and met Mrs. Tait. She spoke of what they had done at Carlisle, where no chaplain was appointed, and told me that, before leaving town, the bishop was to have a meeting of gaol chaplains, and another of workhouse chaplains. when the subject of ladies' visiting would be especially brought forward. I sent a packet of pamphlets for distribution at this meeting. This seemed another very hopeful sign.

August 21st.— A meeting at the Mansion House for the proposed committee. About twelve ladies were present, and three or four clergymen from the parishes forming the union. Mr. Butterworth spoke for the guardians, who seemed favourable to the plan now, after great opposition. About twenty ladies' names were put down as willing to join in the work. I saw Miss Fraser, and had some talk with her, finding her much interested in the cause. Another meeting was proposed at the union, in a fortnight, when plans were to be arranged.

This took place August 31st. Wards were appointed to the different ladies, and we all went over the women's side of the union. The master and matron seemed friendly, and the prospect was promising; the numbers were not overwhelming, and all seemed comparatively in good order to begin with.

September 7th.—I went for the first time, and had a long conversation with the master and matron, and visited the workroom which was appointed me. They seemed decent old women, and pleased to be read to.

October 12th.—I was unable to attend again till this day, when there was a committee. I found difficulties had arisen with the guardians which seemed threatening. It showed how very careful we must be not to interfere with such jealous officials, or move out of our own line of work.

In August I heard about the approaching meeting for the promotion of Social Science (a society inaugurated in the spring), to be held at Birmingham in September. I thought it possible that the subject of workhouses might come into the department of Social Economy, so I wrote to the secretary, Mr. Hastings, and heard that it would be included, and he was anxious for information upon it. Here was another opportunity and opening. He asked if I could write a paper upon it, which I agreed to do, and I had then every hope of being able to attend the meeting. I wrote a paper, which took about half an hour to read. It was with great difficulty I accomplished it, at a time of anxiety and trial at home; but I felt it to be a duty to do it, and that it would be quite wrong to lose an opportunity of spreading an interest in the cause.

At this time I saw the account of what Dr. Sieveking had proposed as to training nurses from workhouses many years ago; it was now brought forward again in the *Waverley Journal.* I wrote a letter to the September number in answer to the plan, not thinking it practicable as workhouses are at present constituted. Dr. Sieveking called, and I had some conversation with him; he brought me all the papers printed by the society which had proposed the plan, and seemed to think it feasible. Mrs. de Morgan sent me a paper to forward to Birmingham with mine, as I was unable to attend. I wrote to every member of the society, and especially in this department, likely to be interested in it, to secure their attention to the subject, and from many I had very encouraging and pleasant answers—some writing to me to send a paper upon it, not knowing I had already done so; but all expressed an interest in the cause.

This summer I had a visit from Miss Tucker (mentioned to me by Mrs. Sheppard), whom I found to be the lady who had sent me an anonymous letter long ago, expressing interest in my first pamphlet, and enclosing a little tract, "A Wide Field," etc. She visits at Marylebone,

and spoke with deep interest of the work, earnestly
desiring to see the doors of workhouses opened for the
purpose chiefly of spiritual instruction for the inmates.
She proposed that an association should be formed for
the purpose of combining persons interested in the cause,
but I could not see my way to it then. In a visit from
Mr. Hastings afterwards, he proposed what seemed to
me to be an opening to it—viz., that a sub-committee
should be formed in the Social Economy Department
for this subject especially; much better than forming a
fresh association, of which there are so many already.

At the end of this year I determined to renew my
application to the Strand Union Board of Guardians,
feeling that the success of the West London Committee
was an additional motive for attempting another. This
time I applied through Mr. Hutton, the clergyman of one
of the parishes of the union (St. Paul's, Covent Garden).
From him I found that the objection was believed to be
with the Poor Law Board. I determined then once more
to address them, and mentioned that the majority of the
guardians were (as I had been told) in favour of the
proposal. The answer from the Poor Law Board was,
of course, cautious, as usual, but gave a sanction to the
plan, subject to their prohibition should inconvenience
arise. This seemed a great step gained, but it was of
no avail. I found that Roman Catholic and Dissenting
guardians objected to the proposal and said they had an
equal right to the privilege, etc.; so the plan was once
more stopped.

In the spring of this year, just as I was going to Paris,
I received a note from Miss E. S——, asking if I could
take her to a workhouse, as she wished to visit one. I

could not arrange it then, but on my return I took her with me to the infirm wards at the Strand Union, and she continued to visit them regularly, which has been a great pleasure to the poor people. They speak of her visits as "quite reviving and cheering."

During the year I paid twenty visits to the workhouse. I went chiefly to the infirm wards, where I had many acquaintances; but occasionally I visited the sick, and once or twice I went to the "Shed," where I found Mrs. W——, of seventy, had been placed on her entering, and remained a fortnight. It was a miserable place with a brick floor, and oakum and hair picking is carried on there. I read to them, and found them very attentive, and some of the elderly ones spoke properly.

One day, when I was visiting Mrs. W——, the porter came to tell me the master said I was not allowed to visit there; it was against the rules. I spoke to him as I came out, and expressed my surprise, but I knew him to be a very low and insolent man, and that it was of little use to talk to him. He was formerly the porter at the gate. At the end of this year, I heard, to my great joy, that the master and matron were leaving. There was universal satisfaction expressed, and I believe there was good cause for the general hatred of them, though the chairman had told me that they were excellent for management and economy. After they were gone, they were found to have purloined quantities of tea and sugar, and very bad practices were discovered; many of which I could have told them, had they been willing to listen.

I happened by chance to visit the union the day they were leaving, and the sounds of rejoicing were great— shouting and hurrahing, discordant enough, no doubt, to

the ears of the departing. It had begun the evening
before, to the matron's great disgust and anger, and she
would willingly have inflicted some punishment. Had
justice been done to them, I believe even the worst of the
inmates would have shown some good feeling at such a
time as this; as it was, it was a melancholy spectacle.

In January the paper I had sent to Birmingham was
published in the *Philanthropist*, and finished in the
February number. I heard from Mr. H—— on the subject, and he mentioned facts concerning the prison at
Wandsworth, and the workhouse.

During my visit to Dawlish I occupied my leisure with
writing what might do for an article in a review, and now
I was looking out for some means of publishing it. I
asked Miss Emily Taylor about the *Edinburgh*, the
editor being her nephew. She thought an article was
already bespoken, but I wrote to Longmans, and from
him I heard that an M.P. was engaged to write in it on
the subject of workhouses. Amongst the persons I had
seen who were much occupied in the cause was Mr. Allen,
who from the first I had occasionally met at the Strand
Union. He visited weekly to take books. He now called
with a note from Mr. C. Buxton, to say that he was going
to write the article, and wished to see me to talk the
matter over. He asked me to dine with them on January
27th. Mr. Allen seemed discouraged, and said he was
now excluded from some workhouses where he used to
visit. I knew that ladies had been turned out from St.
G——'s Workhouse. I heard much about the management of this one from a young girl sent to me, who had
been an inmate. This information came very opportunely
just as I was about to write my paper for Birmingham.

January 27th 1858.—I dined at Mr. C. Buxton's, and met Sir John Nicholson, who was come over from Melbourne, and was negotiating with the Poor Law Board about sending over the children from pauper schools. He said they would be ready to receive any number, and were in the greatest want of girls and women for servants. I found Mr. B. very ready to agree with my views. Mrs. B. visits at the St. James's Workhouse.

February 7th.—I took Mr. and Mrs. Buxton to see the Strand Union. I had with me some coloured Scripture prints, which I had stuck on boards, and gave two to each ward. The old people seemed delighted, and looked at them as if they had not seen a picture for years. Their expressions of genuine pleasure were amusing: " It helps one to imagine it so well," and so forth. All spoke of the new master and matron with pleasure and satisfaction.

February 12th.—This winter I read the short life of Sarah Martin, who was the humble prison visitor at Yarmouth. From her visits to the gaols on Sunday I took the hint, and thought I would propose to go to those who could not attend the chapel service. I mentioned it to the chaplain, and he cordially sanctioned it; and in the ward, when I proposed it, it was joyfully agreed to, the nurse and some saying it would be a great comfort. There was only one Roman Catholic, and she would not be likely to object. I spoke to the porter, and prepared him for it. I went this day for the first time, at three o'clock, and found several still at their private teas, though the usual hour is four. The doors were opened between the two wards, so that more might hear; only two or three were gone to the service. I read the afternoon service and a sermon, and ended with the evening hymn.

Almost all said they could hear. One, whom I asked if she liked it, said, "Like it? I was quite overpowered at hearing those beautiful Church prayers again; it is such a comfort. Thank you for the means of grace!" Next time she said, "It is something to think of after you are gone." Many joined in the responses. At first there was an old man who was allowed to visit his wife at this hour; he was a clerk, and answered most audibly.

February 27th.—I heard from Mr. Butterworth, saying that the inspector of lunatic patients had been at the West London Union, and recommended that cheerful objects should be in the patients' room—pictures, chintz curtains, etc.—and proposing that the ladies should consider the matter, as we had already given coloured prints in the children's nursery. This was a hopeful sign, and may make an opening for ladies' visiting there, which we wish to begin. I have twice taken some flowers, to their great delight; they thoroughly appreciate their beauty, and it is pleasant to hear and see such genuine admiration, some having had and enjoyed gardens formerly.[1]

February 28th.—In the sick ward I visit at the West London, there is a poor girl of sixteen, a cripple, always sitting in a low chair by the fire; she was sometimes doing needlework. I asked her why she did not read, and found that she could not; so I took her a little book,

---

[1] This may be considered to have been the beginning of the now very general "Flower Missions," which send flowers to almost all workhouses and hospitals by ladies. For years I took a Sunday nosegay, which was, by great care, made to last through the week. I found it to be the one gift that could be made without jealousy, as it was common to all,

and the nurse promised to teach her: she knew her letters. In a week, by my next visit. she could read a little story, and made great progress, and seemed anxious to get on. I took her some old prints and a book to stick them in, and cut out an alphabet, etc., with which the nurses seemed as delighted as the poor girl. Must not even such slight gifts be a gleam of sunshine in her dreary life? The walls of that room are her world; sickness and death are ever before her eyes. At one visit I found the woman in the bed close to her chair just dead. Presently she would be washed and laid out, all in full view, for there are neither curtains nor screens in these rooms. What a youthful life must this be! She has no relatives or friends, those that once took care of her being dead.

In a subsequent number of the Journal of the Workhouse Visiting Society, there is the following notice of this case:—"Those readers of the Journal who may remember the case of the poor cripple girl, may be glad to hear that her progress in reading advanced so satisfactorily that this summer she learnt entirely by heart the Church catechism, and was confirmed by the Bishop of London. She has since received the Holy Communion twice, the chaplain being satisfied that she was prepared to do so. She is carried down to the chapel service, and can now make good use of her Bible and Prayer-book. Without the aid and encouragement of a lady visitor, I do not see how this poor girl would ever have been able to read at all." She was afterwards moved into a small, quiet room, with only two or three decent inmates.

March 25th.—Had the first meeting of the sub-com-

mittee, in the Social Economy Department, for the consideration of the Workhouse subject. It consisted of five
members, but only Lord Raynham, Mr. Hastings, and
myself were present. We discussed the matter for an
hour, then arranged another meeting, and proposed more
members, ladies as well as gentlemen. Lord Raynham
still means to bring it forward again in Parliament, and is
strengthening his cause by collecting facts.

Heard from E. S———. Speaking of the workhouse subject, he says, "It is a noble cause, worthy of your best
energies. And sooner or later you will see the fruit; but
if not, remember that one soweth and another reapeth,
and if no one ever sowed there would never be any reap-
ing. The way in which great works and great reforms
are effected in these days is by some person taking up the
subject as their speciality, and pursuing it with unflagging
zeal and energy."

March 31*st.*—Took the manuscript article to the editor
of the *Church of England Monthly Review*, and he promised to get it into one number, which will be best. In
last week's *Guardian* was another letter upon the subject from the union chaplain at Cuckfield, about building
chapels for workhouses. He speaks of the gradually
growing interest in the cause, and alludes to my letters
and the paper I sent to Birmingham. Visited the Strand
Union, the infirm and sick wards, looked into the lying-in
ward, a small one. The nurse said the chaplain never
went there, and they had no books. Even *she* thought
they ought to be visited; that if they had committed " any
little error," they might have an opportunity of amendment. True enough, I thought. I had lent them books
or tracts there, some time ago. In Mrs. S———'s ward they

expressed great gratitude for the books which Mr. A——
was distributing. I spoke to a poor woman seated on a
low stool, whom I found was blind, and had been so
nearly from her birth. She had been here eight years,
and in "such places" all her life. She said she knew the
Bible well, and leads the singing in the services. What
a life must hers be!

April 2nd.—Good Friday. I went to the infirm wards
this afternoon for service. The only one in the chapel
was at nine. I had about thirty-two for congregation,
perfectly quiet and attentive. I proposed to read the
Litany for a change. Many made the responses very
devoutly, and the poor little helpless woman said, "What
a treat it was to hear it again!" I read the Psalms,
chapters, and Gospel. All say they can hear but Mrs.
T——, who is in bed, so I read the two hymns to her
afterwards, and she cried over them. I went afterwards
into the men's sick ward, as I have done for some Sundays
past. One day they said Mr. A—— had been, and one
man said "it was a comfort to hear something read." I
left him some tracts. To-day I read two hymns to them,
then knelt down and read the collect for Good Friday,
and one or two prayers.

April 24th.—Another encouragement to-day. In a note
from J. F——, she says, "Mr. Jackson, of Leeds, wishes
me to tell you that your Workhouse pamphlet went the
round of the Leeds guardians the other day, when a new
workhouse was under discussion, and he has reason
to believe that it had a good share in leading to many
improved arrangements, which have been resolved upon
for the house."

April 25th.—Sunday. I received another encouragement to-day, in the offer of help in visiting the union by one of the medical students of King's College, who has attended in the wards of the hospital to read to the patients. He is willing to go to the sick or infirm men on Sunday afternoon, and thinks there are some students who will go in the week. How much voluntary help is wasted in the world!

May 1*st.*—A meeting of the sub-committee to-day. Lord Raynham and Mr. Monckton Milnes came in, Miss Parkes, her mother, and Miss Craig. Mr. Milnes spoke a good deal about it, and appeared interested. He evidently fears that the prejudices of the guardians will interfere with change and the admission of ladies, and that the increase of expense will be an objection to better superintendence. It was agreed that a deputation should go to Mr. Sotheron Estcourt on Tuesday, previously to Lord Raynham's motion being brought forward, which it may be that evening. It had been suggested that our committee should prepare a report, to be presented to the Poor Law Board; but as there was no time to arrange that, Lord Raynham asked me to write down a short outline of what it was proposed to bring forward. This I did, and sent a copy to him and Mr. Milnes. There is still a prevailing fear of getting ladies to help. Clearly there must be something very radically wrong and imperfect in their education, if none, or few, can be trusted to act with principle and judgment. I always find "benevolent impulses" are dreaded, and till something better is provided, women's help will not be desired as it should be. The deputation consisted of four gentlemen. The President listened patiently to their statement, but nothing was sufficiently clearly made out; the point of ladies' committees being the chief one urged, and that Mr. Sotheron Estcourt said they *did* sanction, and approve. He said also that the Poor Law Board would consider any report that proceeded from the association, and that was encouraging. At this time I wrote a paper in the *Penny Post*, a "Plea for Workhouse Visitors," and the subject was also noticed in the *Literary Churchman*.

May 11*th.*—I called on Mr. Chambers, at the House of Charity; he was formerly chaplain to a union, and takes a great interest in the subject. He considered the want of classification in the country even greater than in London, and consequently the contamination worse. He told me of one man dying in a room full of boys, who were dreadfully frightened all night by his cursing and swearing. There was the old story of farmer guardians in the majority, and the *ex-officio* guardians always endeavouring to introduce reforms, which were always rejected. He quite confirmed my idea that some reformatory discipline was necessary and desirable, yet he seems to think that nothing but a complete separation of the deserving sick and aged can do the work satisfactorily, leaving the able-bodied to be dealt with as subjects for a reformatory; but the expense of fresh establishments will be an objection to this plan. A complete classification and subdivision might do what we require. Half the evils of workhouses Mr. C. attributed to idleness, and want of occupation for hands and head.

As one object of these extracts is to show what improvements have taken place in the course of twenty years, I will give one or two more instances from my own experience.

I visited J. T—— at St. Giles', and found him sitting

6

in the yard. My heart sank, as I stood and talked to him, to hear the language of the men and women—a mother and son abusing each other, and no one in authority near to stop it. Two young women patients were sitting in the corner, where the men were. This court, it seems, is for the sick, whether men or women, and though a gate separates it from the outer part, this was open to-day, and there is never anything to prevent conversation going on. In the downstairs (or, rather, underground) ward was the poor man in the corner, who has been in bed there nine months; he can only see to read when the sun shines. In the next bed is a half-idiot, been in bed there two years. The same Irish old woman is there as nurse, and has never slept out of the ward for nine years! She said how weak and unable to do the work she became. J. T—— has seen the matron once since he came in. It seemed to me a most sad sight to see the court filled with idle women of all ages, sitting and lounging about. . . . I met Mr. R—— at dinner, and spoke to him about the home in Margaret Street, where they have eight infirm women, paid for by out-door allowance from the parish, and rescued from the workhouse. I asked if they did not quarrel. He said, "No; one of the sisters was always with them, at meals and all times. One old woman said 'it was like heaven.'" This is my vision of a workhouse. Why should not superior persons be always with them, to enforce order, and command respect? At the Strand Union they are thankful now for having morning and evening prayers introduced into the wards, and they speak of all the indulgences of the present master and matron with grati-tude . . . .

July 9th.—Had our committee meeting in Waterloo Place to decide on the resolutions for the Workhouse Visiting Society. Mr. W. Cowper (who is to be our president) could not come, so Sir Benjamin Brodie, and then Mr. Monckton Milnes took the chair. Ten ladies were present. Dr. Bence Jones, and Mr. Howson from Liverpool, came in. A few days after I had an interview with Mr. Sotheron Estcourt at Whitehall, in the same room where, five years ago, I saw Mr. Baines and Lord Courtenay. I had a most pleasant visit, and was much encouraged by obtaining his sanction to the clause about Poor Law permission; he said he could not, of course, give his name, but he would subscribe and help us in every way. He spoke of his plans for separating the *worst*, especially when crowded in the winter.* He appears a very benevolent, kind man.

During this year, 1858, I visited many workhouses and district schools, and made notes upon them. Wandsworth, St. James's, City of London, Whitechapel, West Ham, Hampstead, Windsor, Kensington, Bethnal Green, Hackney, St. Geerge's, Hanover Square, and Westminster workhouses; Hanwell, Forest Gate, Plashet, Anerley, Edmonton, and other schools.

In the summer of 1858 I had the opportunity of visiting several distant workhouses, and thus enlarged my experience. At Northampton a lady visitor had already begun to carry out our plans, with the sanction of the chaplain—visiting the sick, the schools, and taking a Sunday class of the young women.

* This referred to a paper Mrs. Sidney Herbert had sent about the classification of women, in Wiltshire.

Besides this I visited Leicester, Barrow-upon-Soar, Loughborough, Derby, Nottingham, Shardlow, Lutterworth, Rugby, Birmingham, Ludlow, Clifton, Stapleton, Bristol; and I saw many other institutions there, in company with Miss Carpenter, whose opinion and evidence on workhouse schools, etc., was most valuable.

On my way home I stopped at Swindon, and spent a few days with Mr. and Mrs. Archer, the authoress of " A Scheme for Befriending Orphan Pauper Girls," 1861, which suggested exactly those " associations " which are now being almost universally carried out. Mr. A. was Chairman of the Board of Guardians at the Highworth and Swindon Union at Stratton, and I visited the workhouse there, gaining much useful information. Then I went to Faringdon and Reading, where there were two workhouses In nearly all these places I found that lady visitors would be gladly welcomed and received.

In October of this year I went to Liverpool for the meeting of the National Association for the Promotion of Social Science, the first of the many annual meetings which I was able afterwards to take part in at Bradford, Edinburgh, Glasgow, and Dublin. I also contributed a paper, on the " Statistics of Workhouses," to the British Association, which met at Manchester in 1861, and another to the Church Congress at Oxford, in 1862. At Liverpool I read a paper, and a special meeting of our society was held. I also visited the enormous workhouse with Mr. John Cropper, one of the guardians, who has since done so much to improve the existing state of things, and to make it one of the first where improved nursing arrangements were carried out. I also visited the Kirkdale Industrial Schools, and the West Derby Union.

At the end of this year I found Mr. Corrie, an excellent guardian of St. Giles', ready to help me in all ways to bring about some improvements which were much needed. In the infirmary especially there were indeed many sad sights and cases; the food was generally, and most justly, complained of—boiled mutton four days a week, rice on some days, meat and butter (none in the morning) often uneatable, tea as bad as could be, with a nauseous smell; and yet it was the last meal, at four o'clock, for the suffering and infirm people till breakfast at 8 the next morning! The light of the one gas-lamp over the door was so imperfect, that it was impossible to see to read or do anything after four o'clock in the winter afternoons. The linen could not be recognized as *white*, the beds were of the poorest flock, and the dirtiest of old Irish nurses in black caps reigned supreme, with only the occasional supervision of the one matron over the whole concern! For years I visited in one of the wards a most sad case of a bedridden and blind man about forty, who had lain there for fourteen years, and for whose comfort, and that of the kind old superior, though pauper, nurse, formerly a ratepayer in the parish, who came over daily to look after him from the other part of the house, I supplied candles to relieve the dreary monotony of the long winter evenings. when she used to read to him for hours the books I lent her. He was entirely helpless from spinal complaint, and suffered at times acutely, yet his patience and cheerfulness were marvellous, as was also his intimate knowledge and remembrance of everything: even the birthdays of myself and some of my family were not forgotten. Poor blind John! it was difficult indeed not to feel the deepes compassion for such a case of entire deprivation of all that, apparently, could make life endurable. Often the only food he could eat was what his kind nurse procured for him with the few pence she earned by needlework; and happily, side by side with all this hardship, there was sufficient laxity for visitors to be able to take in any little comforts and alleviations for the sick. I remember well the feelings of despair that used to come over me at these visits, and I could not help wondering if any other place or institution could present objects of such abject and lifelong misery as this workhouse. I can hardly think that many such cases exist now anywhere.

One of the improvements introduced was a Christmas-tree for the poor children in the schools (long since removed into the country); this was followed by tea and a magic lantern, and the feelings of the children were expressed in the following genuine and amusing letters. Twenty years ago Christmas-trees and treats for schoolchildren and "paupers" were not as common as they are now.

"Ladies and gentlemen, I thank the many kind friends . for the beautiful treat that they provided for us on Monday evening. I am happy to say that the large Christmas-tree which was so beautifully decorated with all kinds of toys and ornaments, looked very handsome. And also, after the Christmas-tree, we were supplied with a very nice tea, plum cake, buns, and cakes; and after tea, nuts, oranges, and sweets, and the magic lantern, which was very nicely performed. And we thank all the kind friends for the beautiful treat they provided for us—for it was such a treat as we never had in the school before. And we hope that God will bless them and repay them for their kindness to us poor children."

"I say, God bless our kind friends for giving us that good treat we had at Christmas. We enjoyed it very much indeed. And may God bless Mrs. Corrie's good cook for making us such plum cakes. And may God bless you all, kind ladies and gentlemen, who paid for the plum cakes, tea, and nuts and oranges. We are thankful to you all, and please receive the thanks of all the boys in the workhouse schools of St. Giles'."

In 1859 I visited Brighton, and the subject of visiting the workhouse was brought forward and discussed in the local papers. I was glad to have the opportunity of bringing it before the excellent Colonel Moorsom. who was thus induced to feel an interest in the cause, so great as to come forward as a guardian, becoming ultimately the chairman of the Board, by which many improvements were effected.

In the autumn of 1859 I went to Leeds, and visited the workhouse and Industrial Schools. A meeting was held, at which Dr. Atlay was present, to establish a visitiug committee for the new workhouse.

Afterwards I went to see the Bradford and Bierley Unions, and attended the Social Science meeting at Bradford, reading a paper on "The Supervision and Training of Workhouse Girls."

The impression left by all these visits was then, as now, the great want of a higher supervision and influence, in the schools as well as for the adults. In nearly every institution I visited I found a class of persons as superintendents who seemed to me utterly incapable of the management and government of large numbers, both of inmates and officials. In confirmation of this opinion I will give one description of a visit to a district school near London, copied from my Diary, and I doubt if matters would be found to be much amended at the present time, in many of the schools, in these respects. "I had received an order from one of the guardians to visit the schools. The son of the superintendent (also an officer there) showed us over them, after keeping us waiting some time. He said there was a mistake about the visiting days, and that the guardians had no power to admit visitors; he evidently would have sent us away if he could. I said, 'But was not Mr. B—— a manager also?' He then owned he was. The schools were in an unfinished state—there might be a day for visiting by-and-by; however, he would show us round now we were there. I thought his manner very unpleasant. By degrees he told us a good deal. He evidently considered their ways were perfect, and they needed no suggestions. I ventured to ask if the number (over 1000) was not too large to be manageable, and to allow of individual care and superintendence? His answer was, 'Lord bless ye, we could manage twice as many just as easily—the expense is the same.' All he said I thought was coarse and disagreeable, as if he had lived amongst 'paupers' all his life. He said, 'What metal we have to deal with! We can't send them out except on fine days; they can't bear the cold, and fall ill directly.' (I could not help thinking whether this bitterly cold and exposed place was suitable for these poor, miserable children, brought out of close London homes.) In the dining-hall he said, 'We must overlook them all; they will pilfer or barter anything—food, and so on. One boy broke into the store-room, and was seen carrying away loaves. For punishment he had to carry them about on his head, walking up and down; he said he would rather have been flogged.' We went through kitchens, with steam-boilers and apparatus of the most approved kind; in another room were fireplaces, where the smaller cooking is done under a good cook. I said, 'I suppose they learn the better sort of cooking in doing things for the superintendents?' His answer was, 'I take good care they don't spoil *my* dinner!' In the infirmary were some in bed, some sitting round the fire, miserable, diseased objects; one with dreadful eyes, who could scarcely see. I asked what would become of him when turned out, at sixteen? He would probably be sent to the 'House,' and remain there for life. For such, then, it ought to be made an *asylum*, not a *work*house. Some were in a hopeless state, and he spoke in a thoughtless way before them, saying they would die, or joking about it. It was touching to hear that the poor things frequently beg for a bit from the superintendent's dinner, asking to have it upon his plate, their own being plain white ones! What a longing of the childish heart for change and beauty does this show! One room was filled with girls at work. They do not learn to cut out—'it would be too wasteful; it would cost threepence a head more if they did.' I did not see why the elder girls should not have been taken in turn, and shown how to do it. I was glad to hear that when the inspectors go down (about every three months) they often take ladies with them, who say they go to put their husbands in mind of what to ask, as there are, of course, many things more in their way. The chaplain undertakes to look after those who leave, for two years. I could not help thinking this was a work far more fit for ladies who, in each parish, might undertake this duty more efficiently for the girls. I much wished to see the matron, but she did not appear. Mr. —— spoke of the scenes they often had with the parents, their parting with the children, and the dreadful language often used; and their accusations if they are ill. One man abused him for having done something to his child's arm; by the next visit it was better, and the man apologized for having been so rude. I said it was a good thing, and satisfactory that he did so. 'Oh,' said he, 'that was nothing. You can't depend on these people; they will say a thing one day and another the next!' It is said that the superintendent is making a good thing of it here—in fact, a fortune! He and his party certainly seem to live on the fat of the land; he talked of his 'souffléts,' in speaking of his dinners, and of their 'parties,' with bits of fowl over, and so on. To be head and ruler over 1200 living souls, about seventy of whom are paid officials, what an office of responsibility and trust—demanding qualities of a high order indeed, yet persons are sought for from a low and uneducated middle-class! Who could fail to draw a comparison between such a tone and management as we found there, and that at the large foreign institutions of Mettray and the Rauhe Haus of Hamburg—contrasting the love, the self-devotion of their managers and founders, the noble De Metz and Wichern, whose spirits have indeed seemed to go forth in holy influence over their whole work, the nature of which was surely as apparently hopeless and arduous as any that our pauper institutions could offer! When shall we even *try* to seek for persons thus supremely and nobly fitted for their work, in our English schools and asylums? "

In April of this year I went one day to the Poor Law

Board to speak to Mr. Farnall (in whose company I visited several of the Metropolitan workhouses), and when I told my name to the attendant, he said he knew it well —he had known and loved my family for forty years— and he added, " I must thank you for all you are doing; it is the greatest kindness!" He added more, but I was so taken by surprise that I hardly knew what to say; and just then we were interrupted by Mr. Farnall coming in, and I had no time to ask for an explanation. But I afterwards learnt his name, and that he was a trusty messenger.

The following is an extract from the Journal of the Workhouse Visiting Society, which I give as showing another example of a sad and deserving "workhouse friend":— [1]

" Amongst nnmerous instances of patience and piety to be met with in the hidden wards of workhouses, I have one especially before my mind, which I wish to record, before its remembrance has faded, and becomes lost in that vast number of those who are continually passing from the sick wards,—many of them, we trust, to a better home above.

" The friend of whom I write had been about ten years in this London workhouse. I cannot remember how long I had seen her there, but it is many years since I first noticed a poor woman, of middle age, who was always sitting on a low stool under a window, and between the turned-up bedsteads of an infirm ward: her two next neighbours beyond had both been bedridden for some years. I found that she was a cripple from an accident, but the particulars of this circumstance I do not remember. I regret now that I did not ask more about her

[1] This is the one named on p. 76.

history, but I always fear to appear inquisitive about what the inmates do not freely communicate. She was then, however, entirely lonely, without relative or friend, but her family had been respectable and tolerably well off. One after another had died, and she spoke frequently of her losses, the death of her sister being the last sorrow; she used to visit her in the workhouse, and after her death her life was lonely indeed. It was chiefly then that I began to notice her, and I believe her affectionate friendship for me was most sincere. She was one of the most earnest Churchwomen I ever knew in her rank of life, and her delight in speaking of the services of the Church was very great. Her especial subject of interest was St. Paul's, and she was always most anxious to hear and read about the meeting of the charity children there. She had also much interest in the Jews, and when at home knew about the society for their conversion. She often asked me about them, and I lately began to take in for her the monthly number of the *Jewish Intelligencer*, which greatly pleased her. About two years ago I proposed to visit her ward on Sunday afternoons, to read the service to those who could not get across the court-yard to attend the services in the house; she was the first to welcome the proposal, and I shall never forget the joy and gratitude with which from the first she joined in the prayers and repeated the alternate verses of the Psalms.

"The first Sunday when we had finished she could not express her joy, saying she had not heard the Church prayers for years, and adding, 'Oh, thank you for the means of grace!' She always welcomed me with delight, saying, 'I look for you as the thirsty land longs for rain;' or, 'I think of your coming all the week; it helps me to bear my trials;' or she would say, 'I long for your coming as the hart for the water-brooks;' and she hardly ever failed to express her admiration of the service and love of the evening hymn with which we always ended, saying it reminded her of former times. I hardly ever left without her expressing a hope that I should go again in the course of the week, which often I was not able to do. She had the truest comfort and support from her religion. At every opportunity she partook of the Holy Communion, and spoke of her joy in doing so. But it often grieved my heart to think of what she endured from the conversation and conduct of some of the ungodly around her. Ah! here is the real trial of the workhouse wards, and one that can never be remedied till some Christian women who are respected are found to be more constantly in them, so as to maintain an influence which will check the language and conduct of those who, amongst such numbers and such various characters, we *must* expect to meet with there.

"Often and often has she told me of wranglings, quarrellings, and language which grieved her very soul, and marred the peace which either our services, or the weekly readings of the chaplain, or the celebration of the Holy Communion, had imparted to her. There was no one whom I so earnestly longed to take away to some place where she could more fully enjoy the religious privileges she so valued and longed for. But her wish and mine are now fulfilled, far better than they could have been here on earth. She felt the cold greatly, but she never went near the fire. I never saw her elsewhere than sitting under the window, and her storehouse was in her turned-up bedstead. She never complained, but was most grateful for any little gifts of tea or lozenges, or for trifling articles, such as cuffs made of list, or mittens. Oh, how my heart used to ache for her and many others when I went out for, or came home from, a country holiday in the summer! I used to fear to tell her I was going, and to her anxious inquiries if I should be gone a fortnight, have to tell her perhaps of a three months' absence. I only mention this to show that there is affection and friendship to be met with in a workhouse.

"She had been very poorly from the cold of this winter, and often said her strength was failing. One Sunday she told me she had been looking out the Psalms she would like me to read to her when she was dying, and I then begged that if she were worse she would send for me at any time. She delighted in the reading of the prayers in the ward, night and morning, by the nurse, a plan intro- duced when the present master and matron came; and once when it was interrupted, on the nurse being changed, said she could not live without them now. The last Sunday I saw her she greeted me with, 'Well, dearly beloved in the Lord, you come as the messenger of peace.' I little thought it was the last time I should be such to her. She looked ill, and said she had been sadly, keeping her bed, but she joined as usual in all the service. Before the next Sunday her place was empty. I heard in the course of the week that she was worse, and was moved into another smaller ward; but it was a week of unusual occupation, and I could not spare an hour to go to see her till Thursday, and then I found she had been dead some hours. I deeply regretted that I had not been to her before, but she had been read to by many persons in the house, who all loved and respected her, and I heard that as long as consciousness remained she was happy and resigned, and, indeed, glad to go. I miss her sadly now on Sundays, for I feel that there is no one left in our little assembly who so heartily and earnestly values and joins in our weekly services."

PARAGRAPH
CONNECTING (AND INTRODUCTORY TO) CHAPTER IV

THE last chapter, giving an account of London Workhouses as they existed in 1853 and following years, is succeeded by one at a distance of 31 years, again offering a picture from personal experience, and it is hoped, shewing some considerable advance, as resulting from the efforts of the previous years. The Kensington Workhouse and Infirmary may be considered in many respects a "model" of what such large Institutions should be, mainly, as I believe all will be compelled to admit, because of the, at least, partial separation of classes, the incompatibility of a united management of which (as has been shewn in previous pages), being, as we think, clearly proved. The sick, the aged and the able-bodied, have in that Parish (for it is not a Union) three distinct abodes, each managed by those who are supposed to be best fitted for their respective posts, requiring different qualifications and capacities. The claim of Kensington to be the first to have the courage of their opinions in electing a woman Guardian in 1875, will ever be considered an honourable one, followed up, as it has been, by a constant succession of women on the Board, up to the present time.

CHAPTER IV

NOTES OF SIX YEARS' WORK AS GUARDIAN OF THE POOR
1884—1890

WHEN I first began my work as Poor Law Guardian there had been one able and efficient lady on the Board for six years, besides the one, who, to the honour of the Electors, had been chosen as the first woman on any Board, in 1875, the foundation being thus laid of the great movement which has since taken root in the Country. What I shall now record, therefore, will shew that there is far more than enough for one woman to do on a Board of over twenty men, and it helps to confirm my opinion that at least six are required in a large Union, if all the different departments of work are to be properly attended to.

In giving publicity to these notes, I earnestly hope it will not be supposed that I desire in any way to speak of my efforts as being remarkable or praiseworthy, but rather such as any woman of average common-sense and experience would have carried out equally well,—an opinion I have expressed in various writings during the last thirty years.

The first thing that struck me was the arrangement for the Nurses of the Infirmary, in number between 40 and

50. They had bed-rooms, mostly separate, but in some, as
many as four or six were together. Their hours off duty
were from 8—10, p.m.; night nurses 8 a.m. to 7 p.m.;
in bed from 11—5, but there was no Room for Recreation
or rest, only a Mess-room for meals, and no resource but
their own bed-rooms, or going out of doors, which was
not possible in all weathers, or, tired as they often were
at the end of the day.

Such matters of a household as servants' rooms and
hours and holidays, do not usually come under the notice
of men, so, naturally, the evils of these arrangements had
not struck the members of the Board. The first objection
to my suggestion was, "there was no room that could
serve the purpose". At this time we held our Committee
Meetings in a pleasant room in the Infirmary, which seemed
to be only used on these occasions, once a week in the
morning. It was therefore agreed to allow the Nurses to
occupy it in the evenings, and furniture was added to
make it comfortable, easy-chairs, tables, and pictures; a
Piano and Sewing Machine were lent, and I got subscriptions to provide books for a Library; curtains and plants
made the room really pleasant and attractive, and though
the (as we think) evil custom of the evening hours (instead
of afternoon) still prevails, notwithstanding repeated efforts on
the part of the Lady Guardians, it is a satisfaction to think that
at least an alternative to the outdoor attractions is possible
for those who will avail themselves of it. Since that time, a
new block of rooms for the Nurses has been built, and as
a matter of course, a Recreation-room formed part of it. [1]

[1] Again changes were made when the new infirmary was built in
1894, and a larger and complete Nurses' Home formed part of the
improvements.

Then I looked into the Dietary of the Nurses, and went to see them at dinner, a step not ventured upon by the gentlemen, and consequently it excited the indignation of the then matron, who had previously declared if I were elected, "everything would be ferreted out."

I found that few could eat the whole allowance of meat, and there was much waste in leavings on the plates. I asked what they would like best, for we must allow for some daintiness of appetite on the part of those who have such distasteful work to do, and it is important that their strength should be kept up by appetising food. I found that more puddings, fruits and vegetables, would be preferred, as well as soup or fish, so when I brought this before the Board, with the kind help of the steward, it was agreed that less meat should be given, and the saving in cost would provide puddings, tarts and vegetables daily. The alternative of coffee with tea was given also, and those on night duty preferred it. Coffee cans were also provided.

And here I cannot help noticing also the great amount of waste in food that is caused by the ample and fixed allowance for every inmate, whether able or not to consume it. It is admitted to be a difficult subject and probably any change would be resented, but it does seem hard that public funds should be thus wasted, and we cannot help thinking some amount of discretion might be allowed, without creating dissatisfaction.[1]

[1] Since this was written, I find that the subject is beginning to attract the attention it deserves, and more than one Board of guardians is considering it; I may give here the following facts and statements.

"It is a most extraordinary thing that for more than a generation

In the sick wards I found the small pillows (or rather
bolsters in shape) were all of horse-hair, not having been
picked for years, besides a very insufficient supply for
those who required to be propped up; after much urging
and writing in the Rota report (of weekly visitors) this
reform has partly been accomplished, though I have not
yet been able to get feather pillows substituted, the cost
being, as is said, £100.[1] Then I found the men were

the hard and fast dietary rules of the Local Government Board have
led to the absurd state of things which is now coming to light.
Each inmate must be supplied, and is supplied, at every meal with
the regulation chunk of bread and the regulation slice of meat,
whether he wants it or not. The result is that, while the workhouse meals are far from plentiful, there is not a single large workhouse in which tons of bread and masses of meat and other food
are not swept off the plates to go to the pigs. In one London
workhouse it is calculated that a very moderate change in the serving
of the pauper meals is producing a saving at the rate of sixteen tons
of bread in the year. Mr. Aveling, who is one of the most practical
of London clerks of guardians, has suggested the idea, which does
not seem hitherto to have occurred to anybody, that it would be
quite possible to put plates of cut bread and butter on the table,
and let people *take* what they want.

" The Hampstead Board was the first in London to promote
reform, and their scheme was to serve out rations of two ounces
of bread instead of four, and to make the remainder into bread-
puddings—a proposal which turned out to be very popular with the
inmates. The Chorlton Guardians and the Poplar Board are moving
in the same direction. At last it is said that the Local Government
Board are going to make some sort of an inquiry. It is not even
so much a matter of humanising the treatment of the poor as of
mere common-sense."

[1] In 1889 100 feather pillows were ordered, being about 3 to
each ward, for extra cases of sick or dying.

without any covering for their shoulders when sitting up in bed, though the women were provided with shawls; it was urged, and there is always an answer ready for every suggestion, that they had flannel shirts and did not require more. But few, if any, in some wards, had these, and now flannel capes are provided, at the further suggestion of the last Matron.

The cans provided for the Infirmary wards were used equally for tea, broth and lemonade. There are now new cans for tea, and marked as such. The tea I found was "stewed" or boiled, in coppers for $1\frac{1}{2}$ hour! This seemed to be considered both in Workhouse and Infirmary as the right and proper time, and was defended by the Committee, but in this matter I found support from some Guardians who had been in China and India, and knew how tea should be made, and so we gained the victory, though I was assured that the inmates would not drink it unless it was long brewed, and all the colour got out. It is proved that no more colour is obtained by a longer time, and the unwholesome extract, or "infusion" is all that is gained.[1] I tried hard to get 2 oz. allowed to the gallon of water, as in many other Unions, but in this I was defeated at the time; the year after, however, the matter was brought up again, and the extra half oz. obtained.

Then I found in my kitchen inspections, that there was one copper for the tea and vegetables, such as cabbage; the cook complained of the great amount of cleaning this involved. I urged a separate copper, but was opposed by steward and guardians; this, however,

[1] Strange to say, I have found this practice of long infusion common in many Institutions.

was brought up again after an interval, and a separate copper was supplied for the tea. I may say that on one of these occasions, being accompanied by a male guardian (three were really necessary for the rota, but could hardly ever be obtained) while I was examining the condition of the sauce-pans, he made the remark, "Ah, I see it is more work for women to do"; with which, I think, we shall most of us agree.

I may say that the introduction of green vegetables for the Infirmary diet, was my suggestion. On going round the wards at dinner-time, I was surprised to find only and always potatoes; the nurses said how much the patients would like "greens," and, indeed, they seemed to me an essential article of food for convalescents. My proposal was, as I expected, objected to at first, and as usual, chiefly on the score of expense. But here the steward again came to my help, and suggested that if bacon were supplied instead of meat, with the cabbage, it would equalise the cost, so this was done, to the great satisfaction of all concerned, and, as I believe, to the improvement in health, and recovery, of the patients.

I also remarked on the large number of persons allowed porter in the Infirmary. Few doctors would give it to their private patients in these days, and to encourage a belief in the necessity of strong stimulants in this class of persons, must be undesirable; the amount has been, and is constantly being, diminished, as the statistics of expenditure for the last few years will shew, especially during the 4 years from 1880.

When my colleague left in the summer of 1887 she wrote to me (during my holiday absence) that she had been told of the great annoyance from the smell of the dust-bins which were opposite the Infirmary and lying-in wards. As this was perceived chiefly at night, and during the summer months, it had not been noticed by me, and I did not even know where the locality was.

I at once made inquiries of the steward, and found that all rubbish was put into one receptacle, with an open grating in the door for ventilation, just below the lying-in ward and other sick wards; and it was emptied twice a week. The cart was on the spot at the time of my visit, and I found that it was already full with other collections, and the smell was intolerable. As the rota visitors can do nothing singly, but three must sign the report, I got two guardians to go with me, as well as the steward, and the doctor joined us; all concurred in the evil arrangements, and the latter said, " I am so glad you are going to bring this forward ". One of the Guardians was very reluctant to join us, but I begged him to do so and really *made* him come, and he now says, "that was a grand bit of work we did with the dust-bin!" But what was to be done? No other site seemed available or possible, but after some days' discussion, the steward suggested an adjoining vacant space which would hold a movable iron tank for the reception of the hogwash, thus separating it from the dust and ashes; the former to be removed *daily*. After the usual lapse of time this was done, and a closed tank on wheels, to be moved out and thoroughly cleansed twice a week, was obtained at comparatively small cost, and the evil is stopped. Once again only was a smell complained of, which puzzled us, till it was discovered that the dead flowers, of which there are many in the wards, were put by the nurses into the wrong pails!

This leads me to speak of a kindred, but even more

important, matter, the lying-in wards. Cases of fever and high temperature often came before us, and in conversation with the nurses and others, I felt convinced that the wards were in far too close proximity to those with various diseases, such as cancer, wounds, etc., though considered well placed at the top of the block, but germs and infection of air, of course, ascended to it. I remembered quite well the occurrences of 25 years ago, in connection with King's College Hospital, when Miss Nightingale and some of the first London doctors planned, as they thought, a perfect lying-in ward, at the top of the building, furnished with every appliance and modern invention. It speedily became a complete failure, and had to be given up, the mortality being alarming, and since then no such attempt has been repeated. I ventured to speak of this and my convictions to some guardians and the doctor, but for some time a deaf ear was turned to all that I urged were existing causes for the results in those wards; cases bringing in fever and so forth, were alleged against the real ones. It was useless for me to contend against these opinions, one of the guardians being a medical man; so all that was then done was to take the two top wards for this purpose and transfer cases from one to the other, emptying and purifying each in turn. Some time after, I was much surprised to hear that the same guardian had been making inquiries, and seeing one of the doctors who was at King's College Hospital at the time I refer to. There was at once a complete change of front; this doctor had written a report in which the whole facts were given, and it was then seen that all which I had stated was true, and that such cases ought never to be in any proximity to general wards. Suffice it

to say, the result has been to build a separate block
of one story in the grounds, wholly detached from the
other buildings, and with rooms for the nurses, who are
not to mix with the others at all.   One may perhaps be
allowed to grudge the expenditure of £3000 for the class
of patients which we have to admit and care for in these
wards, but whoever and whatever they may be, we cannot
and must not punish them by death, and such considerations must not enter into our dealings with them.   If these
wards could have been in the workhouse, as in most
Unions, this outlay would have been avoided, but though
we fully considered the question, it was not possible for
us to make the change, on account of want of room, and
also from the trained nurses and probationers being of
necessity under the Infirmary matron.   From another point
of view it is certainly desirable that these wards should
be in the Workhouse, rather than in a separated Infirmary,
because some idea of a stigma is attached to the former,
which, I fear, is not connected with the latter, though it is
ordered that, if possible, inmates should pass through it on
entering, a rule which is frequently evaded.   I may name
another improvement and novelty adopted at Kensington
for the first time by a Board, at the suggestion of our
"Workhouse Nursing Association", viz., to admit probationers who have been trained in other departments for
a year, for three months training in midwifery, by which
they obtain a certificate and diploma from the Obstetrical
Society to qualify them for practice.

No doubt other Unions will soon follow this good
example, but the progress is slow, though the advantages
are obvious.

When I visited the Paddington Infirmary, I found an

excellent arrangement for night-candles with a shade at one side; our Nurses put newspapers round to protect the light from patients when the gas is out, but it is a dangerous plan, so I got one as a pattern and it is adopted, without *much* objection.

On going round one day I happened to ask the nurse about reading prayers night and morning, and found she had ceased to do so, saying, the men interrupted, etc., etc. I knew that the chaplain had provided cards with prayers for all the wards, so I wrote to him and spoke to the matron, and both said they would see to it, as if it was a rule and order, it should be carried out. It is surprising to find how necessary it is to look into everything, and I would especially recommend that it is well to be present, at least occasionally, at the reading of prayers and saying of 'Grace' before meals, which should, if possible, be done by one of the superior officers. One day I went into the dining-hall at dinner-time, and was distressed to hear the tone in which "Grace" was said by one of the labour masters. I mentioned it to the master, saying it was like speaking to dogs, and utterly unbecoming. He promised he would see to it and speak about it.

One want which was greatly felt, was for more cupboards, which have now been supplied, for the clean linen, used to be heaped on the floor when brought in from the laundry, and also for keeping the nurse's provisions, those for night use having been carried in their pockets! New cupboards have now been placed everywhere, as needed. More lockers have also been supplied to the wards.

The dirty linen used to be kept for some time in the wards, and was also fetched on Sundays; now this is altered, and it is taken down to the basement every week-day morning.

One matter on which my hopes have been set for two years, is the obtaining the publication of Annual Reports, instead of the half-yearly chiefly financial statements now presented to the Guardians, which outsiders would not care to read. When I first brought the matter forward, two years ago, I quoted the authority of Marylebone and Whitechapel, and shewed their Reports. I was supported by a majority, one of the " Ex-Officios " being my chief helper, and I thought the matter settled. Next year, when I was expecting to see and hear of the Report, the matter was, to my surprise, again brought before us as a question, whether the little annual Almanac was to be continued, and "which would be preferred"? Several guardians said they found it useful, and did not wish to give it up; but few of us understood that this implied the reversal of our order for a report. I certainly did not so understand it, but when I made a subsequent inquiry at the Board, I was told it was so. Thus the work had to be begun again, and some time after, I urged it once more, and it was decided by a majority, to issue Annual Reports of both Workhouse and Infirmary, and this has been done since then, interesting, as we hope, the Parishioners and Rate-payers, who have a right to know how their money is spent by their representatives. How can we expect them to be interested in matters of which they know nothing, and are kept in entire ignorance? and why should our large Public Institutions be those alone which give no account of their proceedings and management? The same experienced ex-officio Guardian said, I had been "persistent in season and out of season " to gain my point. When a new Lady Guardian was elected in 1888, (making 4 in all) she stated seven points she should aim at and move for; this was one, and I had the satisfaction of telling her it was already settled. There were then but two matters remaining, one of which has been gained since that time.

When, through resignation, a new matron was required for the Infirmary, I had the satisfaction, in conjunction with the Medical Superintendent, to propose a lady, fully trained and experienced at St. Thomas's Hospital, and already known to me. There was no advertising, though it was greatly urged by some, and she was appointed, at a salary of £80. When she left us after two years, I felt we ought to offer £100 for such an arduous post, which proposal, though, of course, objected to by some, was carried; if otherwise, we should not have obtained a first-rate matron, such as other large Infirmaries have secured. When a night-superintendent had to be replaced, I urged the salary being raised from £26 to £30, which was done, and an officer of superior class was elected.

I found much less to do in the Workhouse, the lady who had been six years on the Board having already made great efforts regarding classification, etc., and for some months I was not on the Rota Committee. I cannot help remarking here that this matter had been extensively carried out at Kensington, long before the Circular of the L. G. B. drew especial attention to it in 1896. I must say I have always met with the cordial co-operation of all the officers in my suggestions. One day I noticed a dust-heap in a corner of one of the buildings, which though cleared, I believe, weekly, looked and seemed objectionable. This I named to the master, as I am always glad to get things done quietly that do not require to be brought before the Committee. The next time I went round, I had the surprise and satisfaction of seeing the corner planted, and flourishing with some shrubs!

I was much struck with the monotony of the food in the workhouse, as in all large institutions; the meat being always boiled, though good of its kind, and I asked if it could not be occasionally roasted; the master fell in with the idea, and has contrived to make an oven, heated without further cost, in which legs of mutton are baked at least once a week; boiled meat is, of course, less expensive, is less trouble, and weighs more.

I also observed that there was no drink provided at dinner, either in the Infirmary or Workhouse; "water could be had, if asked for," but I do not think pauper's askings are much liked or attended to; so I suggested supplying oatmeal drink, in cans, hot in winter, and this was done in the workhouse, and is considered a boon; on suet-pudding days at any rate, it must be desirable to have some drink to "wash it down."

From the Whitechapel Report I found that "Instructors" had been provided for both men and women during the hours between tea and bed time, 6.30 to 8. The master told me he thought more mischief was done by this idle interval than throughout the day. [1] I brought the matter before the Committee, and it was most cordially supported

---

[1] I have always considered the early hours enforced in workhouses are a great evil, at least for the able-bodied, as leading to much demoralisation. When these women go out to places, what can they think of working till 11 o'clock at night, compared with the idleness and long hours of sleep enjoyed in the workhouse? And the same may be said of the men.

by the Chairman, and indeed by all. I believe this was the one and only suggestion to which no opposition was offered. Though attendance is not compulsory, as many as 18 to 25 women have attended to read, write, work, and knit, and the master reports most favourably of the plan; the teacher is also able to hear of situations for those who can be recommended. The same plan was soon after adopted for the men. [1]

No stimulants are given in the workhouse, but on the Jubilee day of 1887 it was proposed to give a pint of porter all round, and to those who *preferred* it, lemonade. As may be supposed, these were the few, and I suggested that no porter should be given, excellent extra food being allowed for all. I may say that ladies carry on Temperance work in the House, and induce all who will listen to join it; therefore, to hold out this temptation of strong drink seemed very undesirable. Only three voted with me, and all I could gain was that the quantity allowed should be reduced to half a pint. But later on, this defeat was turned into a victory, which has been largely followed elsewhere.

In the Workhouse I found linen sheets still in use for the old people, and much disliked. It was said, indeed, that in the winter they took them off and slept in the

[1] Subsequently the male Instructor was transferred to the able-bodied workhouse at Mary Place, where (last year) he had 83 inmates in the winter, a smaller number than usual. But the female Instructor continues her useful labours in the workhouse, with, in the winter, 56 inmates; her Report says that " their conduct continues to be exemplary; situations were found for ten women, and 108 garments were made." I am not aware if other large workhouses adopt these excellent plans. 1897.

blankets, at which I did not wonder, in the large, cold wards. The master agreed with me, and said no more should be ordered when the present stock was used. I believe the former plan was adhered to in the Infirmary, where I should have thought it was even more objectionable.

As considerable trouble was experienced with regard to the bathing arrangements of the women, my colleague and I were asked to look into the matter, which we did, with the attendant and some of the inmates. We recommended that rules should be made and printed, and hung up in the Wards, and thermometers provided, so that there should be no fears and complaints of too hot or too cold water, which was one of the grievances. Of course, there was much to be heard and said on both sides, but we are told that there is great improvement and that all works well, now that the guardians are known to be the authority and the Court of Final Appeal.

Once Miss Donkin and I were asked by the Infirmary Committee to go up to question a girl in the lying-in ward, who had been confined only two or three days, and from whom information was required. Who would have been able to do this had *we* not had the power and the sanction of authority? And here I may say, that I have heard reasons against women guardians having been given because of the unpleasantness of some subjects which must be discussed at the Board; only once during my six years were we asked to leave the room for a short time while such a discussion was going on. It was evident to me that certain matters and persons ought to be referred entirely to a sub-Committee of Women, but of this I shall have to speak later on.

I have no idea how long it is since the plan of "Lady

Visitors" has been carried out here, nor do I remember how many years it is since I went to see the Misses Ryan and went over the workhouse with them, but it is probably over thirty. It is, therefore, a great satisfaction to me to find what I urged 40 years ago, being now so fully carried out by the sanction of a large staff of Visitors, about 60 in number both for Workhouse and Infirmary, and quarterly meetings held with the chaplain;[1] in the beautiful chapel, when I have attended the services for them, I hear the prayer read, which was framed and sanctioned for the "Workhouse Visiting Society" in 1858, by the Rev. A. W. Thorold, the then Rector of St. Giles', and afterwards Bishop of Rochester and Winchester. Little did I think when we began our first humble tea parties in the wards of the Strand Union, then in Cleveland St., each visitor, gentlemen as well as ladies, taking their own provisions, that I should ever see the grand entertainments now given, every Christmas and New Year in all the wards at Kensington and elsewhere. The first Christmas tree and entertainment ever given to children in Workhouse schools, was at St. Georges', Bloomsbury, Workhouse, about 25 years ago, arranged by myself and an excellent guardian who lived in Russell Square, Mr. Malcolm Corrie.

Amongst other matters, one minor point I gained

[1] It may be of interest to my readers to know that the number of inmates certified for the Kensington Workhouse is 1281, and for the Infirmary 667; but two London workhouses exceed it in size, Marylebone being certified for 1841 (Workhouse), and 744 (Infirmary); while St. Pancras is for 1983, and 542 in each department. In both Institutions there is a large staff of appointed Lady-Visitors.

was that the children who had been wearing flannel garments in the Workhouse should not be sent out without them, for it must be bad economy to weaken the health of children in any way. It was objected that all clothes given would be pawned, but it was finally agreed that coarse flannel that had been washed, not looking new, and stamped, should be supplied to them on leaving.

One of our most important duties was to visit annually all the Homes to which adults and children were sent in the country, two guardians going to each; Margate was one place to be inspected and I went several times to a school for children and a convalescent home for adults, as well as to Herne Bay, Homerton and West Kensington. One of the guardians who was a medical man, accompanied me and was a great help in my investigations; we entirely agreed that one was not well managed, though well paid for, and we wrote a strong Report on our return; though other guardians who had visited the Home, concurred in it, nothing was done, the clerk saying there was no other certified Home to which we could send. I declined to visit it again, or make further useless Reports; however, after two years continual protest, and having visited another sea-side Home meantime, I had the satisfaction of getting it settled that all suitable cases should be sent there instead, on the same terms. We have also arranged that clothing should be supplied to those convalescents who have not sufficient, as Pauper clothes would not be allowed.

During these years I have acted on various special sub-committees, where a woman's advice and experience seemed absolutely necessary, such as on laundry matters, bathing arrangements, inspection of nurses' rooms as to

8

furniture, carpets, etc., and other matters concerning the female officers. I often had five mornings a week occupied in Poor Law Work in Marloes Road, and I always attended the weekly out-relief committees. Sometimes I went to the able-bodied Workhouse in Mary Place, North Kensington, and had a talk with the master, a non-commissioned officer, filling a most difficult post, the inmates being received from other workhouses besides Kensington.

I always attended the contracts Committees half yearly, consisting of the whole Board, which I felt to be a most important part of our duties, I used to protest against taking the lowest contracts, especially with regard to fish and other articles of food, intended chiefly for the sick. I never had any difficulty with the officers, and with the nurses I had the best relations; they used to come to tea and supper in detachments, and I had plenty of curiosities from my foreign travels to shew them; at Christmas each had a present. It is evident that some progress has been made in ten years. What would be thought now of an untrained Assistant Matron in the Infirmary? Yet when we had to elect a *Head* one, to look after about 500 people and 50 nurses, it was argued by one guardian that it was " quite unnecessary to have a trained matron, we only wanted a kind housekeeper! " then, I said, " we must give up trained nurses, we cannot have one without the other; " but, as may be supposed, his opinion did not prevail, and we had a succession of excellent, thoroughly trained and educated, matrons.

A remarkable instance of the difficulty of ascertaining facts, or knowing how anything is carried on, in these large Institutions, not actually under our eyes, has just occurred, and it seems to shew that our task is never-ending; the driver of our ambulance was brought up on the accusation that he was not sober on the occasion of taking a woman to the Infirmary at midnight, and she refused to come with him, as he had to carry her down from her room. She and the Mission Woman of the Parish came before us, and we heard all they had to say; she would have been alone but for the Mission Woman, who volunteered to go with her. This circum - stance brought to light what I had never heard or thought of, that there was no arrangement made for any nurse to bring patients from their homes; if it occurred to the District Medical officers who sent them, and they deemed it necessary, there was some woman at Mary Place who could be sent with them, or, a friend or relation might be at hand. I inquired at Marylebone Infirmary as to the practice there, and one of our guardians, a manager on the Metropolitan Asylums Board, explained their arrangements with the Ambulances, which were considered necessary with regard to nurses. The doctor supported me, and I brought it before the Committee, where it was agreed to, with one dissentient, who thought that friends could always be found. It was decided that an assistant nurse should be always ready to fetch and accompany women, and in case of need, and serious cases, men also. The matter was then referred back for further discussion, and to my great disappointment, the additional expense was objected to by one guardian, and the plan was not carried out, though to many of us it seemed to be ab- solutely necessary for safety and decency, the only other person with the driver being a pauper inmate.

One matter of economy in which I took a part, was in condemning the suggested plan of re-erecting the Clock

Turret at the Workhouse, at a cost of over £300; it was decided instead to place the Clock in the front of the building, at far less cost. While speaking of economy, I may say we discussed one day the question, what became of the leavings of certain meals provided for officers at a specified cost. No one knew; it was supposed that they were somebody's perquisite, but whatever the amount, I ventured to suggest that all that was over should be returned to the stores or kitchen; and this was ordered to be done. But who can tell or calculate the amount of waste that goes on in these large establishments? [1] One other matter of, as I considered, unnecessary extravagance, was the custom of the fortnightly Visitors of the Banstead Schools, travelling always first-class,—a short journey of about half an hour, when most of us travel now by third class, even for long distances. I accompanied them one day, and expressed my opinion of this needless expenditure of the rate-payer's money. It was altered then, but I do not know if the change was permanent. Yet women are said to be extravagant! I think I can say that in my experience they are at least conscientious about spending public money.

One discovery I made on going round the workhouse, was, finding boys brought by the Police, sitting in the sheds with the men, picking oakum, indulging, of course, in idle, or worse, conversation. I inquired if no other place could be found for them, and it was agreed to keep them by themselves in a room in the Receiving Block. [2]

A marked progress is perceptible with regard to the

[1] The subject of waste of food is further considered at p. 99 of this chapter.

[2] Since this time attention has been drawn to the matter and separate wards are being built for such cases.

feeling and opinion about drunkenness, one of the four present lady guardians being a staunch Temperance Reformer. Several cases of men and women officers have been condoned after serious offences of intemperance, and I and some others have protested, but mercy (so-called) has hitherto prevailed over justice. I doubt if a case of a *woman* would ever be overlooked again, and as two cases of men have been before us in a fortnight, we have spoken strongly about the matter. The first case was given a second chance, as he denied it on oath, though it was certified by the doctor. I then urged that *no* first offence should be overlooked, but followed by instant dismissal, and one guardian said he would suggest the rule next time. Though the second case was fully proved and admitted, with Police Cell punishment, it was again decided to give the man another chance, *but* it was entered on the minutes, that, "in future no first offence would be overlooked," and this he was told to make known to his fellow-officers. I refrain from narrating the cases of two female officers in important posts (one in the Infirmary), who were brought before the Committee in disgrace, the one at a time when neither of the women guardians were present, but I may mention our astonishment on hearing that her conduct had been condoned, and she was to remain. To my indignant remonstrance to one of the yielding members, his meek and humble reply was, "Well, I think we were rather weak!" Needless to say, the offending party was soon after found incapable of duty in the wards, and was summarily dismissed. The other case was of a very good-looking young woman, who shed floods of tears before us, and was in consequence retained in our service for some months, till another outbreak occurred !

Another case was of a paid cook in the workhouse kitchen, a former inmate, with an illegitimate child; as she was ill (in consequence of her habits) she was granted leave of absence in a Convalescent Home; other persons and inmates, inclined that way, jeering and thinking it a nice plan thus to get a holiday! but she was soon after dismissed, and the tone of the whole establishment is now raised. I wish I had kept a record of all the cases of drink in officers and inmates during the time, and surely it would have been a sad and depressing one in both classes! Women are said to be " hard," but are not men too " soft" in these matters?

This year, finding a difficulty in obtaining admission for a Probationer for the Workhouse Nursing Association, the Hon. Sec. and I agreed that it would be a great help if there were printed rules for them, when advertising for, or engaging, them. I suggested this being done, but it was considered unnecessary, as those for the Infirmary nurses and assistants were said to be quite sufficient; to this I replied that they were not suitable, though there were no less than 44 to be read through, most of which did not apply to this class. I ventured to draw up a few rules, with the help of the matron, and submitted them to the Infirmary Committee, just before I went away for a time. I heard nothing till my return, when I found them printed and in use.

With all the progress, there have been some disappointing and retrograde steps, as I suppose there must always be in ever-changing bodies of managers. The most serious of these has been the appointment of one of our nurses as night superintendent, when the former excellent and thoroughly trained one left for a higher post. This was mainly owing to the action of one Guardian who had been a large employer of labour, and believed in the promotion of his work people, reasoning from his own experience; but such an appointment would not be thought of in Hospitals, and where the authority of a higher class of person is indispensable; but the plan was not of long duration, and has not been repeated. Most of the nurses now provide their own outdoor uniform, which is an advance in the right direction, and shews the growth of a feeling of *esprit de corps*, which is very satisfactory, besides being a great protection in their evening hours.

Improvements have been made as to comfort in the supper arrangements, especially on Sunday evening, when those who came in late sometimes found nothing to eat. Without a personal knowledge of, and interest in, the nurses, all these matters cannot possibly be looked into or understood.

Once, when on the Rota for visiting, I found quantities of discarded linen and clothing lying scattered on the floor of the basement, being looked over every three months; I suggested a cupboard for it to be kept in, which was agreed to.

But while telling of what has been done, I cannot help being struck by the way in which time is wasted in talk and discussion of matters, which, however important, drop, disappear and come to nothing. Such have been numerous Sub-Committees on the management of the laundry, the one point of joint control of Workhouse and Infirmary, and I was strongly of opinion that entire separation, as in other large establishments, was the only solution of the difficulties, the loss of articles being one of the chief grievances, the blame, of course, being equally apportioned between the two; pauper women were employed in the Workhouse (though not allowed to enter the Infirmary), and many paid women besides. Nothing, however, ever came of our investigations; now and then some one asks about it, and there it ends! One such Sub-Committee was remarkable; I and two gentlemen were appointed to consider matters relating to a female officer; in July we all dispersed till October, but nothing was ever said or done; we never reported, and things went on as they had done. One of our Lady Guardians used to make awkward inquiries of this kind, without fear or favour. Another said once that no action had been taken as to giving orders to visitors not to bring in food to inmates, though we passed a decree fifteen months ago! [1] Some years since, we spent hours and weeks in discussing excellent plans for Probationers to be engaged for three years, instead of the present plan of Assistant Nurses, at far greater cost, who may have been in common domestic service, and have often no intention of becoming nurses, thus entailing frequent changes. But nothing came of this at the time. [2]

Another astonishing matter is the important things that are brought to light and to consideration for the first time, which one would have supposed settled years ago. This is one example—the power of persons to take away children, of

---

[1] Such excessive abuses were discovered in connection with this practice that we were obliged to forbid it, the most unsuitable articles being brought, and in such quantities, that they lay in heaps in the Porter's Lodge when at last they were stopped! The Doctor has orders to supply everything that he considers necessary.

[2] It may not have been all wasted time, for in 1891 the whole plan was adopted and is now fully carried out, with all the Rules we recommended.

any age, without permission or inquiry as to identity or relationship. This was brought up by a so-called "Uncle" fetching a little girl from the Infirmary, merely waiting for her till she was dressed. As it has been discovered that he is an utterly unfit person to have charge of her (possibly for begging purposes), we are trying to get the child back again, and have now ordered that none under 16 are to be given up, without inquiry, to any others than actual parents.

It occurred to some members of the Relief Committee that there was great liability of abuse in the distribution of tickets to the out-door poor, from a liberty of choice and a possibility of even having undesirable articles given as "groceries"; so the matter was thoroughly discussed, and lists of articles provided to be chosen from, and accounts to be rendered, specifying the same, which seems likely to prevent evils which no doubt have occurred; the Relieving Officers being, of course, consulted by us.

In 1889, we gained a glorious victory against beer on Christmas Day, by a majority of two, though I failed at the Jubilee. The inmates were given the choice of various drinks, the food, of course, being of the best; no one complained, and the master (with 20 years' experience), came before us on the next Board Day to express his satisfaction, declaring they had never passed so happy and quiet a time; the porter at the gate thanked me most heartily for my efforts, saying that the quarrellings, bickerings, and bartering had been spared, and all were satisfied. The plan is being increasingly adopted by Boards throughout the country, and everywhere with success.

One of my early remembrances is of a matron who used to attend the Committees in a hat and feathers, uniform not having been then adopted. It used to remind me of a

memorable visit I paid, perhaps 30 years ago, to a large
Workhouse in South London, when I found the matron
in the afternoon playing the piano in her smart sitting-
room, and she conducted me through the wards in a
gay hat and feathers, and a sweeping velvet train! We
may well say now, "look on this picture and on that!"

One more of my endeavours which failed at the time,
to my great disappointment, was for the appointment of
a Ladies Committee to deal with all matters connected
with women and girls, instead of their being brought
before large Committees of men, who had to question
them in a way, and on matters, which were not only
painful to the members (I being sometimes the only woman
present), but demoralising to the women, the bold ones
probably liking the publicity, but to the few with any
sense of shame, it was distressing and harmful. It was
however opposed, as a decided innovation, and was
dropped for the time. [1]

I must say something more as to the strong objections
we women guardians felt as to the evening hours for the
nurses, who are almost all quite young, and from the
country, so the plea that they could only visit their
friends and relations at that time, was contradicted by
the fact that they had none living within reach. In those
days there was no out-door uniform, and where could
they spend the hours from 8 to 10, in winter or bad
weather? Besides this, they only got exercise in daylight
or sunshine, so essential to the health of nurses, on their
weekly half-days. I believe all the Hospitals have changed

[1] In 1895, I found this plan had been adopted at the Holborn
Union and elsewhere, and I again suggested it to the Women Guardians of Kensington, and it was unanimously agreed to.

their plans in this respect, as well as the large Infirmaries. [1] The answer of the guardians to us was, " it was quite unnecessary, no harm had even come from the custom," to which I replied, " Can we know or trace the history of all the numerous young women who have left us, even in the last five years? "

Many of these were not recognised Probationers bound for a term, but servants of any class, kitchen or house-maids, who thought they would like nursing, but probably left after a short trial, having changed their minds. I am convinced that in such a matter as this, women are the best and most competent judges of fit arrangements for the young of their own sex. [2]

I used occasionally to visit our excellent intermediate schools at Hammersmith, under good management, though the work must be most difficult and trying, owing to the short time allowed for influencing the children, who are either passed on to Banstead, or belong to the hopeless class of " Ins and Outs," and ever changing. It is surprising that so important a link in the chain of education for pauper children should not be adopted in other Unions, as for us it seems to be quite essential.

The opinion which I have given as to the need of at least six women guardians in such a large sphere of work, was

[1] One matron has written an article in the Westminster Review on this and other matters; since reprinted.

[2] I have now (1897) the satisfaction of hearing that last year a change was made, and the nurses have now two hours on two afternoons in each week as additional leave, and it is believed that this will materially conduce to the health and comfort of the nursing staff, and render the service more attractive. Their dietary has also been again revised and improved.

confirmed by all my further experience of the duties of the
Board.   At first, I had only the one colleague who had
worked indefatigably for six years, and for some time after
she left, from ill health, I was alone. Then three more women
were elected, and one took an interest chiefly in the Infirmary,
as I had hitherto done.   One was a manager at Banstead,
which took up a great deal of time, and was otherwise occupied
by temperance work in the Workhouse.   One other was
connected with Charity organisation work outside, and dealt
chiefly with the able-bodied inmates and applicants, and
out-relief, for it was impossible for any one member to
undertake all departments of this enormous work.

One more fact deserves to be recorded, as I believe it
was a new departure. When a vacancy occurred among
the managers of the Banstead schools, I earnestly desired
that another woman might be appointed, and ventured
to propose Miss Eve (afterwards on the London School
Board), hoping she might one day become a guardian,
but no one hitherto had been chosen as manager who
was not one.   This, therefore, was a complete innovation,
but to my surprise, I succeeded, and Miss Eve became
a manager, till other duties obliged her to resign the post.
But she was followed by another woman, and she also
by another, since that time.   Surely it is a truism to
repeat that women should be mainly employed in this
work concerning 500 children, and the inspection of their
Homes, with all their domestic arrangements. [1]

[1] As is well known, the Banstead Schools, for Kensington and
Chelsea, were amongst the first established on the " Cottage Homes"
principle, the girls (about 30) being under a " Mother," the boys
with a " Father and Mother." Schools, Chapel and Infirmary, forming
a village of considerable size.

I may perhaps conclude with giving a warning to my fellow-guardians, that they must expect to find at least one opponent, not to say enemy, on every Board; such is my experience, and that of many others. They will be fortunate if the opposition is thus limited, but let them work on, in good heart; if only their cause is right and sound, and not made up of imaginary grievances, nor "fads," in due time it will be successful and prevail.

There is one more matter which I must name and point out as deserving of the attention of women guardians. When I found that not unfrequently we were told at the Board that persons, women as well as men, had to be taken before the magistrate at the Police Courts, being removed first by the Police to the local Station, where separate cells are provided, I felt naturally anxious to know some particulars as to their treatment, and how and by whom they were received. This led to my being accompanied to the Hammersmith Police Court by our Assistant Clerk, when I was able to make a thorough inspection and examination of the arrangements.

As I wrote to the Papers of that day a full account of what I saw, and at the same time a small Blue Book of the "Commission" of inquiry, was issued, I need not repeat all that passed, and the results that followed. I can only say I was astonished at the arrangements that then prevailed, and had for years been acquiesced in.

No special provision was made for the women, who had to pass many hours there before being called before the magistrate, numbers of all ages were crowded into one room or cell, and Policemen alone were in attendance; women "searchers" only being called in for that especial purpose. I felt at the time that had I reported such a state of things in Naples or Turkey, English hearers would have been shocked. Suffice it to say that these evils are now remedied with regard, I believe generally, to the Police *Courts*, but in many cases, if not in most, the Police *Stations* remain much as they were, and it is this which it is the duty of women guardians to look into. We are told that it is now in the power of the superintendent to send for a woman, or so-called matron, *when needful*, but this is far from satisfying all our requirements, which are, that a *resident* matron should be placed in every Police Station, to be on the spot, especially at night, when the cases are chiefly admitted, and when it is hardly likely that one would be sent for from a distance. Thus when drunken or disorderly women and girls are taken up, they are received by men, and cared for by men, which, considering the conduct that is likely to prevail, can hardly be considered suitable or even decent; and to their inspection at intervals during the night they are also committed. What is now, and has been frequently, urged, is, that a married couple, such as a Policeman and his wife, should be resident in every Police Court and Station, so that a woman should be on the spot at all hours when required. There would probably be little, if any, cost in this plan and why it is not generally adopted we are unable to understand. I may add that though I made several requests to be allowed to see the Police Station at Kensington, I was not permitted to do so, which, as a guardian of the poor, I considered was a somewhat strange refusal of the authorities. At any rate, it seems to me a part of the duty of women guardians to make themselves acquainted with the treatment which those under their care, receive from the authorities, however low and degraded they may be, but more especially in the case of women and girls. Subsequent instances of such being taken over to a Country Workhouse, a distance of 4 miles from the Police Station, accompanied by policemen alone, confirmed me in these ideas as to the need for women to be employed on all these occasions, where women and girls are concerned.

PARAGRAPH
CONNECTING CHAPTER IV WITH CHAPTER V

THE last chapter recounted the experiences concerning a London Poor Law Institution during a period of 6 years as guardian, giving a practical acquaintance with facts which could not have been otherwise acquired, but which still needed to be supplemented by the knowledge of affairs as carried on in a Country Union, casual visits to such workhouses being all that I had been able to accomplish, although these included a large number in various parts of England. The experience gained during three years at the Tonbridge Union was very valuable and important, containing nine Parishes, with a population of 58,334, in 1891, a rural aspect of affairs being revealed which was wholly new to me, and thus was helpful as confirming many theories and opinions long maintained, as to wants, imperfections, and defects, in the administration of the Poor Law by Local Boards of Guardians.

Such experiences as are narrated in the previous and following chapters were necessary for the formation of any opinions which are given in the chapter concerning the "Present and Future of the Work of the Poor Law", as I have ventured to describe it.

CHAPTER V

THREE YEARS' WORK AND EXPERIENCE IN A COUNTRY UNION
1893—1896

APRIL, 1894. A year being now completed since I began my official work here, I will write a few details concerning it, hoping to shew once more, and in another and different locality, what the work is that a woman can do in Poor Law administration.

It must be remembered that up to the end of 1892 the thought of electing a woman as guardian had never entered the mind of any one here; a contested election hardly seemed to be remembered; the same members had continued in office year after year, or if not, some one filled a vacancy by nomination; no one to whom I spoke had seen a Voting Paper. When I began to ask about matters here, I found a general satisfaction expressed; the workhouse was considered to be perfect, indeed "a model for all England," as I was, and indeed am, repeatedly, told; an excellent master had been there for 27 years, though he had the misfortune to lose his equally excellent wife the year before, and his sister had taken her place as Matron.

9

When hints were first given that I might possibly be induced to stand for a vacant seat, I decidedly declined to do so. I said I had given up public work, and did not intend to resume it. I had been told by friends here that I should find "nothing to do" in Tunbridge Wells, every branch of work being fully occupied, with workers in abundance, which I was glad to hear. Besides this, I said I could not run the risk of an election or a defeat; I had never taken any part in one, and could not think of doing so now, and should not know how to set about it. The result of all this, however, was, the inquiries and requests having become more definite, I felt I could not, and ought not to, put aside what seemed to be a perfectly unsought-for opening, and thus I consented to make a beginning, and open the way for others who might soon be found to follow me. Perhaps what may be said to have decided me, was, the singular circumstance of a vacancy on the Board, owing to the death of one of the members, which was to be filled by a by-lection, there was thus no question of "turning out" any guardian. It was generally believed that there would be no contested election, and that no additional candidate would be nominated. An advertisement with influential names of residents of all parties and opinions, was inserted in the local papers, and kind friends circulated notices of some of my previous work, which seemed to be necessary, as one rather amusing circumstance shewed. The name of one influential and important resident was desired to be added to the list of my supporters, but upon his being asked for this favour, he replied that he had never heard of me and could not conscientiously give it; when I was told of this, I wrote to offer to call, if a personal interview was desired, referring him at the same time to my ever kind and courteous friend, the Vicar of Kensington, who was well acquainted with all my work there as guardian, but I believe my "character" was never asked for, and this little incident afforded much amusement when I related it to him on the occasion of our next meeting. No opposition seemed to be threatened, though when one of the prominent members of the Board had been asked as to the prevailing opinion about electing a lady, they were, he replied, "unanimously against it!" Some threats were rumoured as to the probable unpleasantness of my position, which it was said might be made "hot" by some members, but if there were "barks" there were no "bites", and all such rumours died away. In April, 1893,. I received notice that I was duly elected and was to attend the next Board meeting at the Workhouse at Pembury. I had an engagement in London on the previous day, and arranged to return in time, but through wrong information as to the train, I was obliged to travel by a slow one, and so arrived late, after the meeting had begun. It was an unfortunate and for me, very unpleasant, beginning of my work, but when at last I arrived, the master received me, and ushered me at once into the Board Room, where a formidable circle of over 20 guardians was seated. To my surprise, they all rose when I entered, and I was shewn to a seat on the left of the Chairman, which I ever after occupied. I felt obliged to make an apology and explanation for my late appearance, which, always priding myself on punctuality, seemed the more trying and vexatious. Thus my first words were on this personal matter, and I was glad enough when the business was resumed of the election

of various committees and arrangements of the new Board.
I was much surprised when the appointment of Visitors for
the Lunatic Asylum at Barming was made, to find I was asked
to join it as a member, to which of course I agreed,
though I had always shrunk from this duty at Kensington.
One guardian said something about my being on the
School Committee, but this, it was explained by the clerk,
was, for some reason, impossible. I was also placed on
the "Provisions" committee. I made up my mind that
I would not suggest or say anything till I had had full
time for looking round and understanding the state of
affairs, having been only once to the Workhouse with the
Ladies of the Brabazon Employment scheme, during the
previous summer. There was only one guardian I knew
even by sight, having called upon him once to ask about
the nursing arrangements, some time previously; I then
ventured to inquire if they had ever thought of electing
a lady; he said they did not wish to have one who had
been suggested, but he made no objection to the
principle.

I took several opportunities later of seeing the master,
and talking over a few matters with him; I found him
pleasant and kind, and not adverse to some of my ideas,
but it was evident that he was not in a state of health
or spirits to carry out any new plans, and I did not see
much prospect of this being done. There were then
four ex-officio guardians who were often present, all
gentlemen with country seats near, one more coming
occasionally.[1] I was always glad to see them and they

[1] I for one, much regretted that part of the new order which
abolished "Ex-officios," they in many places, having been of great
assistance.

were always helpful. Five or six of the elected guardians soon became friendly with me and remained so to the end. In the course of the first month I was appointed visitor for the fortnight, each one performing this duty alone, and not as at Kensington. Of course I saw much to notice, but in my report thought it best to make no remarks or suggestions after such a short time of experience. In conversation with the nurses in the Infirmary (a fine building, erected in 1891), I found that none had had any training in Hospitals, such as is now beginning to be thought necessary, one only having learnt a little from a matron in an institution, during a few months.

The absence of screens and lockers in the wards struck me, and there were no blinds in the boys' dormitories in the schools, a remarkable omission which I have found elsewhere, when it is well-known the tendency of all these children is to suffer from weak eyes and ophthalmia.

In June there was a proposal for a " Christmas dinner " of beef and plum-pudding to be given to the inmates on the day of the Royal Wedding; I suggested that it was hardly suitable at that season, and proposed a " tea " instead, but it was opposed by several who objected to any such expenditure of the rates. One of the ex-officio members then proposed to raise a private subscription, which was agreed to and carried out; we spoke together about it after the meeting.

In June, 1893, I was surprised one morning by a note from the matron to tell me of the death of her brother that night, after 2 hours' illness. This was one of the remarkable events connected with the beginning of my work.

In August I proposed that a visitor for the girls in service should be appointed, as is now done in all London, and many Country, Unions, in the former by the " Metropolitan Association" and in the latter by the Workhouse Branch of the "Girls' Friendly Society"; it was impossible that this necessary duty could be carried out by the matron, with all her other heavy work, but my proposal met with strong opposition and it had to be withdrawn, though it was suggested by one guardian, (again an ex-officio), that something might be done without the direct authority of the Board; so I took the hint as a permission, and in the course of the year visited as many as 12 of our former school-girls in service, scattered about in farms or villages, or the neighbouring towns. It was not a duty which I coveted or enjoyed, for I seemed to feel I had had enough of the experiences and histories of girls and their mistresses amongst the 600 we had to deal with in my Home of thirty and more years ago, but as there was no one else allowed to do it I undertook it during my three years of service, and notwithstanding predictions to the contrary, I was received cordially and thankfully everywhere, with the exception of one mistress only.

I next proposed that a lady should be appointed to visit the lying-in-ward, where no one was admitted, as I was anxious to carry out the excellent plans of the Kensington "Workhouse Girls Aid Committee", by which many are saved from life-long sin and misery after their first fall. I never found that it was of any use to quote examples of success and experience elsewhere; that of the present Board seemed always all-sufficient, and of course why should a "Model" need improvement? I was not surprised therefore that numerous objections were, as usual, raised, but the "ayes" prevailed, and a lady living in Tunbridge Wells was appointed visitor, with the view of helping girls into service again, and undertaking the partial boarding-out of their infants, without which help they must remain for months or years burdens on the rates.

My next proposal was to be allowed to introduce musical drill for the school children for which I would provide the dumb-bells, and it would thus cost nothing. This was agreed to and a kind teacher of one of the National Schools at Tunbridge Wells promised to give the necessary instruction for which our teachers were not competent; for this purpose I drove her over on her free afternoons till the plan was understood. [1]

One of the greatest troubles and abuses of this summer was the invasion of tramps, who pretended they came for the hop-picking season; on different nights the numbers amounted to 700 and 800, and once even to 900, tents having to be procured from London for them in the adjoining ground.

Instead of the legal two nights, owing to the enormous number, discrimination and identification were impossible, and many repeated their visits, thus obtaining a nice country outing at the expense of the rate-payers, lying by the roadside, and begging by day, all efforts to check them seeming impracticable. However, by the new master's advent their holiday came to an abrupt close, and in a fortnight the numbers were reduced to fifty, or less, printed notices as to the law for casuals being posted up everywhere, and thus the incursion was stopped.

[1] So successfully has the system been carried out that in 1897 a grand "display" was given by these children at a Public Hall in Tunbridge Wells.

In October I urged the necessity of a receiving ward,
as the children passed at once into the school, with the
great risk of bringing infection, as was the case once with
scarlet fever.

A Branch of the Queen's Nurses having been begun
in Tunbridge Wells, the question of nursing the out-door
poor was started, and we had a correspondence with Sir
David Salomons in November, who wished the Board to
have a nurse for Southborough.   I then took the opportunity
of suggesting a grant should be given to our Branch,
which was agreed to in the following February, thus
ensuring good nursing and more rapid recovery for all
who were attended by the Parish Doctors. [1]

In November I was again visitor, and after an experience of seven months felt able to make sundry suggestions.
Instead of the usual two lines in the Report book, generally
remarking that "everything was satisfactory and in
good order" (which I was tempted to suggest might be
stereotyped, to save trouble), I wrote two pages of suggestions, on the Infirmary, schools, etc.   I feared these
would be met with a storm of opposition, but it was all
referred to a sub-committee for consideration, consisting
of two friendly guardians and myself, and after thus
meeting, we agreed upon the proposed alterations, which
were confirmed, and, after some interval, carried out.
Amongst the suggested improvements were a stove in
the girls' bath-room, in a very cold out-building of the
schools,   and a separate wash-house for the Infirmary,
where some of the worst linen was being washed in one

[1] This payment from the rates being sanctioned by the L. G. B.,
it is satisfactory to find that over 100 Boards now subscribe for
nurses who attend the out-door poor.

of the bath-rooms!—In December the subject of Industrial training for the school-girls was brought forward, and a Committee of five appointed to consider it. This lingered on for four months, owing to the difficulty of getting members to attend from the distance at which they lived, and which we can well imagine is the case when all were busy people, once a fortnight being considered quite often enough. As last, however, I believe all our suggestions will be adopted, even to providing baskets for the girls' clothes to be folded up in at night, instead of being thrown on the floor. I remembered Mrs. Nassau Senior's excellent advice when visiting with her some of our large district schools many years ago, that all the clothes should be hung up to air at night, but owing to want of wall space, or any other, in the dormitories, this was impossible. A specimen of a wire basket to hang on at the foot of the bed (as used in some large district schools), was sent for approval, but we preferred the cheaper and more simple wicker basket. For the boys, training in the workshops and on the land, and military drill, in addition to the musical, were agreed to, and it was decided that girls should not be sent out to service until fourteen years of age, and those who returned from their places were to be sent to a Home, instead of to the Workhouse. Two girls who had been returned with great complaints from their mistresses, I succeeded in getting sent to a good Home at Maidstone for a year, and one to a Preventive Home, by permission of the Board, hoping that they may make a fresh start in life.—In the schools, finding that a brush and comb was shared by several children, the master at my suggestion agreed to give out one to each child; the wet towels used to hang together in a mass, they now have separate pegs on the wall. Surely these are matters to be looked into by women guardians, or by Inspectors, for it does not concern the children alone. In one large Country Infirmary the supply for the old people is 6 brushes and combs to 80 people, or one to each ward. For the sick women more have been supplied, but only 3 combs and no brushes are provided for 40 men, although they may be suffering from various complaints. When Mr. Wyndham Holgate, the L. G. B. School Inspector, came in February, I went over to meet him and spent the day there, hearing him examine the children, and telling him of our suggestions, with all of which he agreed. He strongly deprecated the custom, too prevalent, of the children sleeping in their day flannels, with only the weekly change, as the boys did here, so I asked the matron if she could supply night-shirts for them, which she will do in time. Much of the washing has been taken from the schools, so that the girls can learn to do it better, and all scrubbing-brushes are taken from the laundry, these having been hitherto extensively used; needle-work was only done in the evening, when a little mending was managed, but no afternoons were set apart for it and the mistresses complained about it. All this was afterwards altered, and when a new Industrial teacher came, even cutting-out was taught.

It was surprising to find that in so extensive and com- plete a workhouse no Entrance Lodge had been provided, the gates being far away below the House, so that any or everybody could come and go as they liked, without coming near the porter and his vigilant eye; it can of course only be surmised what may have left the House, or been brought in by inmates. One instance of the latter practice was discovered within a fortnight of the arrival of the new master and matron, in consequence of which a nurse of long standing was dismissed. One old member of the Board was so tender-hearted as to stand up for her, and lamented the disappearance of "a well-known old face"! but as may be supposed, he was in a minority. Other dismissals have taken place, all more or less, through faults of character and drink, five, besides nurses. A pretty new lodge, with high gates, now leads from the road into the grounds, and is inhabited by the porter and his wife, who looks after the women casuals, whose wards adjoin the men's in the separate block, so it is contemplated to move them to another part, and fit up a disused stable for them. The infants under five years have long since been moved from the schools to the House, where they are under the eye of the matron, and can be better cared for; and they are to learn their letters from boards. I found 30 or 40 in the nursery without any playthings, so I wrote to the local papers to ask for toys, new or old, and soon received a plentiful response.

The Library was in a most dilapidated state, consisting of a few books utterly worn-out, and probably having been read over and over again. I first asked the Kyrle Society for a grant, and a parcel was soon sent; the Religious Tract Society gave a free grant, and the S. P. C. K. doubled a subscription of £3 collected from the Guardians; and lastly, the "Rebecca Hussey Book Charity," which gave a Library to my Workhouse Girls' Home in 1861, sent a free gift of £5 worth of books; in all, upwards of £13 worth has been contributed. These are all installed in a good cupboard in the ante-room, accessible to the master and chaplain, and I hope will give much pleasure to the inmates.

In going over the Infirmary and old hospital, I found two idiots, a boy and girl, running about, with no care or supervision, or possibility of training, the latter unable to talk, but both reported by the Doctor to be improvable. Having become aware of the extraordinary fact that no provisision is made for such children under the Poor Law, except in the Metropolitan District at Darenth, I wrote to all the Asylums I knew of to inquire as to the possibility of admission, those on the Election system being, of course, out of the question for paupers. Northampton and Star Cross, near Exeter, seemed to be the only two likely to suit the case. I spoke to several guardians about it, as to the certainty of their being on our hands for life if nothing was done to improve them, and it was decided to send them to Star Cross, at a cost of 12/ a week, 4/ being repaid by the County Council. It is indeed a most strange missing link in our Poor Law arrangements, that no provision for the care or training of either curable or incurable idiots should be made, for the placing of even the latter in the Asylums for adult lunatics is most undesirable, while in Workhouses there can be no efficient care for either class.

One matter I have been pleased to carry out is, having found that Prayers were not read in the Infirmary wards daily, I asked if this could not be done by the nurses, as it seemed a curious exemption that the sick alone should be deprived of this privilege, the rule and order being of course supposed to apply to the whole House. I gave therefore a copy of my book of " Prayers for Workhouses " to the master, who said he would use it, and I asked the nurses who I found one day at dinner, if they thought they could arrange to read them, at least once a day, in the different wards; they all agreed to do so, and each had a copy; they have told me since that the Prayers are liked and appreciated by the patients. Amongst the wants still to be supplied, is the urgent one of a mess or sitting-room for the nurses, who take their meals now in the kitchen, in hot and cold weather, having only their bed-rooms besides.[1] When I named this at our sub-committee for the consideration of my report, I was surprised to find that not one member was aware of the fact, and indeed were unwilling to believe it. It is strange that one of my first experiences at Kensington was a similar one, which proves what I have so often said and wish to enforce, that these "women's wants" are not likely to be understood or thought of, by male perceptions, household economy, and the arrangements for servants, never coming under their cognizance. I ventured to make several suggestions to remedy the omission, but as the change involved some building and other alterations, nothing was done at that time.

Movable baths for the sick were one of my suggestions, to do away with the necessity of patients being carried to the Bath-rooms; twelve screens for the beds were also needed; Lockers were few and far between, and no place for the clothes, as cupboards are scarce, so these are to be made by inmates, if there is time, if not, outside. I have said that the object of obtaining a visitor to the lying-in ward, was to help the girls with their first children, there being about 25 births in the year. We find

[1] This is now remedied by a new arrangement in the old Hospital, by which part is devoted to a "Nurses' Home." 1897.

it extremely difficult to get places for them, even when the infants are provided for by boarding-out. Two have, however, been sent out to service, one whose child died, the other paying 2/6 weekly for hers, private funds finding the rest;[1] if this should prevent their return, as is often the case, a second, third, or even fourth, time, rate-payers as well as others may be glad.

The chief drawback to the comfort and interest of the work, is the hurry in which it has to be done, two hours, from 11 to 1, once a fortnight, being the entire time devoted to Poor Law business, an hour and a half, or three quarters, being generally, in winter at least, taken up with applications for outdoor relief, the cases being considered by three Committees sitting in the Board-room; this is wearisome, the applicants being of course unknown to me, and of very little interest, many of them, to my surprise, being in appearance as well dressed as I am, and wholly unlike all the outdoor paupers I have hitherto seen. We have endeavoured to meet earlier, or defer dinner for half an hour at least, but all our efforts have failed, thus often much that I wish to say or hear has to be deferred, hurried over, or postponed till the afternoon, when I have left. During these Committees I became more and more convinced of the evils of lavish, or even liberal, out-relief, feeling certain that the result was to create any number of paupers, who naturally turned to the Poor Law for help of every kind, with no compunction and no thought of self-help, more especially as regards medical relief; though there is an excellent and well established Provident Dispensary in the town, it was sur-

[1] She is still going on steadily in the same place, and paying more for her child.

prising to find how relief was applied for on every trifling ailment or accident, even by those who were in work; sometimes the question was asked by the chairman if the applicant was in any club (perhaps a young man, with a slight injury to his hand), but the reply was "no"; upon which I could not refrain from saying, "why should he be? he can get immediate relief and all he wants by coming here and asking for it." I repeatedly urged the Relieving officers to make the existence of the Provident Dispensary more widely known amongst their clients. It was indeed surprising to see some of the widows who applied as "destitute" in their new mourning garments, and the conviction was more and more impressed upon me that in such a wealthy place the respectable among them, with their children, should be saved from becoming paupers, and be provided with Pensions, according to the plans of the Charity Organisation Society.[1]

Not only was it a constant matter of surprise to see the respectable persons who applied for relief, but on the approach of winter, the large number of apparently strong and able-bodied men whose invariable answer to the question of why did they come? was, "no work to do."

Again I could not help asking myself, was there any other country that thus offered an ever-open Hotel to all who said they could not find work, and is it wise to do so? Many of these men were offered work by guardians on farms or elsewhere, but rarely, as it seemed, with successful results. The desertion of children by parents was another sad consequence of Poor Law relief, or abuse, that frequently came before us.

[1] This, I rejoice to think, is likely to be done in the near future.

And these abuses are not confined to agricultural districts. In a report of the Camberwell Union (1897) we read of several able-bodied men who had been for months and years in the workhouse, and the verdict of a Coroner was, that the jury "considered it disgraceful that the ratepayers should have to keep such a lot of able-bodied men."

From the beginning of my work here I desired to see the orphan and deserted children boarded out, the others sent to a National School, but that is unfortunately impossible in this Union, as the nearest Schools are already overflowing, and those at Tonbridge much too far off. This was the advice also of our School Inspector, but it cannot be adopted here. I have also urged Emigration for the older boys, who are strong and hearty and fitted for Colonial life, but I was met by the objection that they were wanted on the land here. I had heard that they were only kept on farms for six or nine months of the year, and what was to become of them at other times? But even if put to this work, they will not remain with such poor pay, and thus, in a few years, they will drift into London and other large towns, and help to swell the thousands of "unemployed" there. It is a short-sighted policy that tries to keep them here in over-crowded England, when they are wanted and valued in our Colonies. There is also great difficulty in placing boys out in the towns, as employers and tradespeople can always find those who live at home, and need not be boarded and lodged.

The payment of annual subscriptions to Hospitals by Boards of Guardians always seemed to me an undesirable plan, being either too little or too much for the cases sent; in the matter of the local Ear and Eye Hospital I was glad to be able to suggest that patients sent to it should be paid for at so much a week, which, though at first objected to, was finally agreed to.

In March I attended for the first time the Committee for out-relief held half-yearly in the town to consider and revise applications, when a large number of cases came before us. It was a pitiable sight, and one that filled me with surprise as to the enormous amount of ill-health and incapacity in a thoroughly healthy locality like this, many being by no means old people. The Londoner's idea, which I shared, is, that with fresh country air, and less crowded dwellings, all would be well and healthy, and but little sickness known, but here I am quite undeceived, I am shocked and surprised at the amount of ill-health that prevails, both amongst men and women. I am more than ever convinced of the need of Sanitary teaching for all classes, by lectures, meetings, and in Schools, in order to inculcate the plain truths about the laws of health, of which the poor are entirely ignorant; and I know from experience that such teaching is eagerly welcomed. It is sad and painful to see the helpless condition to which so many of the poor are reduced in their old age by rheumatism and other ailments, and if it is true that they have not been able to save, it must be mainly due to these causes. Many, of course, were unable to attend on these occasions, especially from out-lying villages, and I could not help thinking of the admirable plans of the Elberfeld system of relief, by which a much smaller number of families are regularly visited by some persons appointed for the duty, the present number allotted to each Relieving officer being everywhere far too large. Another unavoidable reflection was, would not some amount of thrift and provision for old age have been possible without the temptations of superfluous drink and tobacco, especially when one thought that in no other country in Europe is a similar liberal provision made from public rates, and may not the reliance on this future help have been at least one inducement to reckless expenditure?

In October I accompanied two guardians, as a visitor to the Barming Lunatic asylum, where 1600 inmates are gathered together. It was a painful and distressing sight, and I must say it struck me as being a visit of form rather than of satisfaction, for what could they know of the real state of things and management, when our paupers, men and women, numbering 120, were ranged in rows before us for inspection and we were only able to say just a word or two to a few of them? They were all collected together for us, the medical superintendent accompanying us all the time; of course several asked to be taken away; I had a message to one from her sister, who spoke reasonably, and seemed to understand it. Two thoughts were impressed upon me by this and a subsequent visit, and not for the first time. I wondered what the nurses really were, when out of sight and hearing, and alone with their poor helpless and speechless charges? Is it a religious work of devotion and love to any of them? I have heard a good deal formerly of some large Lunatic Asylums and I fear that special training is greatly needed for these trying posts (now beginning to be supplied), and a higher class of women is called for, not only as attendants, but as commissioners, inspectors and visitors for the women's departments, where it is not fitting nor desirable that these duties should be performed by men. The wards were cheerful and pretty with pictures, flowers, and pianos,—they have music and entertainments, and the women do all the needlework, washing, and some of the cooking of the establishment, and thus are kept fully occupied. I suggested if the Brabazon employment scheme could be introduced here, as it has been in Workhouses, but it did not appear there would be room or time for it. We were told that a few of the patients are restored and sent to their homes, but the younger ones only. Truly an awful and humiliating aspect of poor human nature, and one that it is worth any effort and trouble to investigate the causes and origin of. [1]

Many other reforms and improvements in the Workhouse have been made in the course of the year, one of the chief being the setting apart of three rooms for old married couples, with a common sitting-room; this although included in the L. G. B. regulations, had never been carried out before.

One unused room has been appropriated as a dining-room for the officers, but a common dining-hall is much needed for the inmates, as the present plan of having the meals served in separate wards causes much trouble.

On making one of my rounds as Visitor, I was surprised to discover that there were no baths in the Workhouse, sinks, buckets, and a few fixed basins, being the only provision for washing, besides a bath in the Receiving Ward, far from the House. When the Inspector came to visit us, this want was made known to him, and was soon after

[1] The total number of Paupers Lunatics on Jan. 1, 1897 was 90,274, and this is increasing year by year.

supplied. An enlarged Annual Report that would interest outsiders and ratepayers is needed, as it was at Kensington, and it is hoped may be supplied in future, many improvements having been made, even in a "Model Workhouse!"

At the end of 1894 the subject of Boarding-out the orphan and deserted children was brought forward as an alternative to the engagement of additional teachers, the former couple having left after many years, and the number of children in the winter months amounting to 120, it was beyond the power of two teachers to deal with them. It was decided that the question could not be dealt with by an expiring Board, but it was not opposed, and for the present it was agreed to employ as a paid assistant a young woman, a respectable inmate who had been helping in the Schools. In January the subject was again brought up, and it was decided that all the eligible children should be placed in families, some having already applied for them. Even after three months' discussion some Guardians maintained that they were far better cared for in the Schools, but at last it was settled, and I obtained leave to take the two first little girls to the care of a couple, with no children, who had asked for some as long ago as last summer, they having moved into another house for this object. Since then, others have been sent to homes in the neighbouring villages, 24 in all, to be supervised by a Local Boarding-out Committee. Other Unions near are discussing the plan, and it is hoped will soon adopt it, if our example succeeds. It is also proposed, after some delay, to send the older boys to the Gordon Homes, to the Warspite, or other Training Ships, as it is difficult to dispose of them here, as I have said, some over fourteen being still in the School.

The new building for the kitchen, with an entire apparatus for steam cooking and heating, was decided upon, and the work began with the New Year, but was not completed till September, 1895, and then did not include the Dining hall. In December, 1895, nine new members were to be elected, and great was my anxiety that at least one woman should be amongst them, a local association for this purpose having been started in Tunbridge Wells. In the autumn a public meeting had been held at the Town-hall to advocate the cause, when the Rev. Brooke Lambert, from Greenwich, Miss Lidgett, from St. Pancras, and Miss Slack, from Belper, attended, and I and Miss Ludlow, the intended candidate, spoke also, the Rev. E. Eardley presiding; it was well attended by a hearty and cordial audience, and this no doubt did much to enlighten public opinion and produce the good results of the election. Two former Ex-officio Guardians were amongst those who were successful, but I confess it was with great surprise that, amongst the six to be chosen for Tunbridge Wells, I found myself at the head of the list, Miss Ludlow being second! I fear it was something more than a surprise to some old members of the Board, but it could not but be a satisfaction to all who valued women's work in this great department, to see so speedy and undoubted a confirmation of their hopes and predictions. One of the greatest improvements made by the new Board, was the addition of a small House Committee to meet in alternate weeks, which enables us to get through a larger amount of work than was possible at the fortnightly Board meetings.

We then see all the new admissions, which was not possible before, and we can discuss matters more fully

without the fear of the Reporters before our eyes. On one
of these occasions a Report was read by the Medical
Officer on the " Nursing System " of the Infirmary, or, as
it was expressed by one Guardian, the " No System ".
During my whole tenure of office this had been my chief
trouble and anxiety, seeing that though a fine building had
been erected with good arrangements, no trained Nurses
had been substituted for those who had been thought
sufficient during all the previous years in the " Old Hospital ".
I therefore was ever looking for an opening and opportunity to introduce the subject, although the difficulty of
realising any distinction between " trained " and " untrained "
women seemed to be almost hopeless,—one idea about the
former being that " they would not do anything ", though
I could not ascertain that those who expressed this opinion
had any experience of Trained Nurses. The recent circular
from the L. G. B. on the subject was sent to all Boards,
and a copy was given to each of our Guardians, but if
with the same result elsewhere as here, not much can be
looked for from it; it was literally " shelved ", and never
named again! It was decided by our Committee to take
no action in the matter (unkindness to the present staff
being one of the reasons given), but let all go on as usual
for a year.[1] I was anxious to advise one improvement in
the Infirmary which seemed to be practicable, a separation
of the children from the Adult Wards, an arrangement
which I have always urged, as boys and girls must hear
and see much that is undesirable, some of the patients
being sometimes brought in from the class of Casuals and
Tramps, and necessarily, a mixture of all characters is found
there. The careful separation of the Schools, now univer-

---

[1] A period which has not yet ended! 1897.

sally advocated, is of little use, while this practice is continued. The arrangement of the Wards rendered complete separation in Children's Wards impossible, but something has been done in this right direction. In order to check, if possible, the constant trouble caused by the " Ins and Outs ", it has been decided that we can legally offer such admission to the Casual Wards, which will be far less attractive to the class which is the trial of all Poor Law Officers, and so greatly abuses the relief given by the rates.

I gave a Report at the end of the year of 17 girls in service who I had visited in the neighbourhood; much trouble has been taken about these, and some also of the older ones, who had left the school for service, and had not kept their situations. One who I took to her first place last year, left it and went to London, we not having been informed of the change, as according to our rule we should have been. I heard of a good situation for her, and sent to meet her at the station, whence she went at once to it, without any intervention of the Workhouse. Some of them come to tea occasionally on Sunday, as they have no friends to go to; five have been confirmed this year, but three had to return to the Workhouse, to my great regret.

In 1895 Mrs. Malden's Training Home was opened, and it was agreed to send the older girls there for a year, when thirteen, in order to learn household work, which is impossible for all in the Workhouse; those temporarily out of place will also be sent there, and provided with situations, and thus we hope the link and attraction of the Workhouse will be done away with, the girls naturally looking upon it as their home, and often gladly returning to it; indeed they are sometimes told, by their kind, but

mistaken, friends there, to return, if they are not happy!
We may therefore hope for better results from the girls
we send out.   One boy is gone to the Warspite Training
Ship, and four others to the Gordon Home at Dover,
which is the best possible opening for them.   By August
30 children were boarded-out, and ten more, over ten
years, will soon follow, but this is of course, a more doubtful experiment at that age.   On the resignation of the
Chaplain who had held the office for some years, the
former plan was happily reverted to by the appointment
of the Vicar of St. James's, assisted by his curates, the
Workhouse being situated in that Parish.   A disused room,
or surgery, in the Old Hospital has been made his Study,
and the Library is removed there; another empty room
has been made the master's office.   A Thursday evening
service is begun, and this and the Sunday ones are well
attended.

After my last visit of inspection, it was decided to
appoint a dentist to visit the Schools, and one from
Tunbridge Wells kindly undertook the office, and tooth
brushes are provided for all the children.   A proposal to
have a Burial ground within the premises met with my
hearty approval, as it would avoid much expense, and
also the scandal, as it seemed to me, of the old men
inmates being sent out as bearers to the funerals of all
who die in the Workhouse, as well as those who are
buried by the Parish outside, tenders being asked for
from several undertakers.   This was, to my regret, refused
by the L. G. B. but a contract has been taken, though
not including bearers, alas !   Another subject taken up by
a special Committee was the Dietary, which much needs
revision.   On Sundays the dinner for all is only bread

and cheese, a fact which did not seem to be known to the Guardians, and other arrangements have been made. It is also proposed to improve the children's food and substitute cocoa for tea, which is quite unsuitable for them, and porridge should be given far more than at present. For the schools there is now one head mistress, and one assistant teacher, with a drill master and industrial trainer for the boys, out of school. The number is now 68, 50 being boarded-out, and the Committee is fully at work. One of the first two girls who I took to their new home had her first known birthday, which had been discovered from a person who once had charge of her; she came to tea here, an illegitimate child of 8, the other, 10. She at once became devoted to her foster-father and used to follow him about everywhere; when he went out for a week's work in the summer, I asked how she would do without him, and was told she said, "What a lot of kisses father will want when he comes home!" This could never be said by a child in a Workhouse, who has no one to kiss, and knows nothing of family affection. The chapel is at last to be heated by hot water, as the present stove scorches some, while the further end is too cold for the old people, and some are not able to find room, so it is to be hoped that the Chapel may some day be enlarged. One of the Guardians resigned at the end of the year, as though re-elected, he had attended only three times, and this neglect of undertaken duties is now happily prohibited by the L. G. B. I could not help thinking what would have been said if a woman guardian had acted thus! Truly there is in more than one department of life, a different standard for men and women!

At the beginning of 1896, I gave notice, privately, that I intended to resign my post in April, when three years would be completed, and in March I wrote to our Clerk to this effect, and my letter was read at the Board. On April 10th I attended for the last time and took a friendly leave of all my Colleagues, with some kind expressions from several of those who had been most opposed to me at first. I had at one time felt that I could not continue at my post in the face of some unreasonable opposition and misrepresentation concerning my dealings with the girls, and in fact I sent in my resignation, but I had been induced to re-consider and withdraw it, by the advice of several who would deeply have regretted it, and even from distant places I received expressions of indignation and regret at the treatment I had met with, but always from a minority. This probably, however unpleasant at the time, may have done good to the cause in the end, and I had little more to complain of.

I was naturally anxious that on my retirement a lady should succeed me, so that one should not again be left alone, which would not be pleasant for a beginner in the work. Every effort was therefore made to find a suitable and competent person, but it was surprising to find the great difficulty of doing so in so large and wealthy and leisurely a place as Tunbridge Wells. One only indeed could be found who was willing to undertake the duties, the distance being an objection to doing so. It was hoped that no contested Election would be needed, but this was prevented by the then vigorous Anti-Vaccination movement which was carried on by some members of the Board, and an advocate of this cause was nominated, so that the day of Election was an anxious one. I need hardly say that great was the rejoicing when the woman guardian was chosen by a large majority to fill my place, and I was thus able to feel that my three years' work had not been in vain for our cause.

I visited the House during my last fortnight, and had seen every part of it. I could not but recall the many improvements that had been made, though there is still much to be done, and the Hospital remains as it was, and will be, till the system of trained nursing is everywhere ordered and introduced.

In the future it is probable that further enlargement will be required, and the Schools may be removed to a distance, the building being occupied by the Sick and Infirm, who seem to be ever increasing in numbers. Every Officer has been changed with the exception of two, and several have been added. Steam is now used in the laundry, as well as in the kitchen.

During the three years, I have been absent from only four Board Meetings, which is, I think, one more proof of the fitness of women to fill these posts, owing to their greater leisure.

Greater interest in the Workhouse is shewn in the neighbourhood, different clergy going there for the Thursday evening addresses, and more visitors being admitted, all being under the control of the Chaplain. None who go there can fail to be struck by the lovely situation, probably unsurpassed by any other in England, and the garden, radiant through the summer with brilliant blossoms, cared for entirely by the aged inmates, cannot but give pleasure to all who visit this last abode of the helpless and destitute.

In 1895 a visit to the Workhouse was paid by the

Commissioner of the British Medical Journal, and a Report was issued with all the recommendations and suggestions for improvements which have been noticed, one of which was the separation of the children from the Adult wards of the Hospital, several, under seven, being found in the waiting wards of the Maternity Department.

The omission of any intermediate wards between the receiving ward and the House and Schools, is also remarked. The system of Fire Escapes and the whole reconstruction of the Brigade is noticed with admiration, and must not be omitted in our list of reforms. But the necessary retention of Pauper help for the sick is one of the most distressing points of the system of inadequate nursing, feeble-minded, or semi-imbecile, men and women being largely employed, not only as assistants to the nurses, but left in sole charge during the many hours that the nurses are absent. It is hardly necessary to ask what treatment the sick, aged and helpless, receive at the hands of such persons, and it grieved and saddened me to think of it ; women with their illegitimate children in their arms, were also employed in the sick wards, for other duties than mere scrubbing and cleaning. I cannot close my remarks and story of three years' work better than by repeating the comments of the Journal I have alluded to, which so ably sum up the whole needs of the Sick in this union.

"The sick department of this union offers a curious example of the want of logic so often displayed by public bodies. The workhouse has a modern, well-appointed infirmary, while the infirm male patients are in the old hospital, distinct from the quarters of the able-bodied. Except in some minor details, noticed by our Commissioner, the structure and arrangements are those of a general hospital. But what would be said of a hospital of 230 beds which was entirely nursed by untrained persons assisted by paupers? Yet this is the state of the case in the Tonbridge Union. The only trained nurse is the temporary night nurse, and she has no assistant, so that, since her charges are in three distinct buildings, her nursing must be merely nominal. This is an anomalous state of things, and one which surely cannot be long maintained by a Board of Guardians who have shown themselves anxious to provide for the comfort of the sick in so many other ways. No merits of structure can ever compensate for the lack of nursing, and much complex machinery is simply thrown away without the skilled management of those who understand it."

On the conclusion of my work as Guardian I wrote "a retrospect of Poor Law Work" in the local papers, which was afterwards reprinted as a Leaflet, in the hope of encouraging Women Guardians in their often uphill efforts for reform.

CHAPTER VI

PRESENT AND FUTURE *(with suggestions)*

THE preceding chapters will have sufficed to trace the history of the past, as it came under my personal knowledge and experience during a period of 44 years, but the retrospect has not been limited to that sphere alone. Facts have been given and quoted from reliable authorities of varied qualifications, whose aim and objects were identical with my own, in endeavouring not only to expose grave social evils and shortcomings, but also to suggest remedies for them. Some of these have already been carried out, but many still remain unfulfilled. It would have been strange had no results been obtained from the labours of so many earnest workers during this long period, and we may thankfully acknowledge all that has been achieved, slow as the process may appear to outsiders to have been. The law of reaction in matters of opinion must be taken into account, in all such considerations. The abuses and iniquities of the old Poor Law, which had been gradually growing and increasing since its establishment in the days of Queen Elizabeth, when "sturdy beggars and vagrants" were the class chiefly considered and provided for, naturally led to the introduction of the "New Poor Law Act", as it is called, which endeavoured to reform the abuses of the past 200 years, in the year 1832. All who have carefully studied the interesting Blue Book which describes the aims and objects of this legislation, will be able to appreciate its value and importance; but now that more than 60 years have elapsed since the alteration of the Law concerning the Poor, the facts and abuses which it sought to remedy are gradually being forgotten, and an inevitable reaction has set in against what are said to be its harsh and over-strict regulations. In this age of general easy philanthropy, charitable and kind impulses are beginning to take the place of just and sound views of poor relief, and the public purse is more and more looked upon as a bottomless one, into which all the needy may, and indeed have a right to, dip. Though the general direction of public opinion is probably tending towards the restriction of out-relief, or at least for a more careful and strict bestowal of it, there is, in many quarters, a decided movement in opposition to this view, and a consequent demoralisation of the Poor, with an increase of pauperism, is perceptible. And in connection with this subject, it is strange to observe the conflicting currents of feeling and action in some Boards of Guardians concerning the matter of expenditure. Deeply as the cost, or increase, of the rates is resented, especially by some rural boards, very often the merest trifle asked for, however great as a needed improvement, being rejected as an "unnecessary expense," we find, at the same time, a general willingness to bestow lavishly out-door relief, very often with no regard to the principles which should regulate its bestowal. A personal acquaintance with individuals, or the fact of a "deserving" character, is frequently the one plea put forward by members of a Committee, in advocating the claims of applicants, even in localities where wealthy neighbours would have gladly shared, or taken the burden of relief upon themselves, had there been any system of co-operation in existence between the legal rates and the charity outside. In connection with this subject I have recently seen a suggestion made that the Poor Law should confine its dealing to the Indoor Poor and the Institutions required for them, leaving the outdoor to voluntary and charitable organisations outside; and surely there is much to commend this to us from the point of view we are considering, as it is apparently hopeless to attain to any degree of uniformity of treatment by Boards of Guardians, or indeed to any right comprehension of the question of out-relief. The sad encouragement of deceit, and the almost impossible endeavour to ascertain the truth concerning applicants, seems to be unrealised by the advocates of it. Considering the vast divergence of opinion and methods existing in different Boards of Guardians, even in the Metropolis, it has long been a matter of surprise and regret that there are no meetings held by them for the purpose of consideration and discussion of various plans, in order to arrive at a greater degree of uniformity in the treatment of the Poor, instead of the present entire lack of system and agreement, which is unjust to them, and leads to comparisons and preferences which are very undesirable. The same may be said with regard to the management and administration of Workhouses, which vary considerably in this respect. The "Society for promoting the return of Women as Poor

Law Guardians ", [1] holds a Conference once a quarter, which is open to any who like to attend it, when the discussion of various practical questions, and the experience of all, is brought forward, with great satisfaction and obvious benefit to those concerned; as I venture to think it would be if the plan were adopted by their fellow guardians. That the Poor should be forward to press their claims for a share of what naturally appears to them an inexhaustible mine of wealth, which they see freely bestowed on others around them, is not surprising, but that those who so readily bestow it, should, at the same time, so jealously guard the expenditure in other directions, is an anomaly that has often puzzled me, even though the amount asked for may help in the end to save a woman or a child from life-long Pauperism and dependence on the rates.

But the facts and suggestions which will be brought forward in this chapter will concern the condition and treatment of the in-door, rather than of the out-door, Poor, as that subject is already being considered by many competent observers, who have made public their opinions upon it. [2]

The two chief divisions, or classes, of the indoor Poor in receipt of legal relief, which we have to consider at the present time, are those comprising the children, and the Sick and Aged, or Chronic Infirm persons of both sexes; but before entering upon this portion of our subject, I would remark on some points which appear to lie at the foundation of all practical considerations of reform.

We have been repeatedly told of late that the delays and shortcomings of the Central, or Local Government, Board, are owing to the enormous, and ever-increasing,

[1] 4, Sanctuary, Westminster.

[2] I would refer my readers to chap. 8 on " Out-door Relief."

11

amount of work, that is laid upon the Department, and this, we, who have known the former condition of things, under the old "Poor Law Board", which dealt with the legal relief of the Poor as its main object, can readily believe; but if this is a reason, we are unable to take it as an excuse, because the obvious remedy would seem to be, as in other cases of increase of business, to enlarge the powers of work, either by sub-division, or addition to the workers who must carry it out.

So strongly has this been felt, even during the present year, that suggestions have been made in several quarters, that sub-departments should be formed for dealing with the two principal classes which I have named. That a "Children's department" should be sanctioned, to deal with the complicated and vexed question of the treatment and education of all who come under the control of the Poor Law, and must be supported by the rates, under the age of sixteen, seems to be so reasonable and practical a suggestion, that we cannot but hope it may yet receive the attention it deserves, for the advantages of the special knowledge and interest of those who devote themselves to the needs of particular classes, and have made them their study, can hardly be overlooked or denied. Were this change, or rather addition to the present organisation, to be carried out, we should probably hear no more of the desire to remove Pauper children from all control of the guardians (under whom the parents and relatives must still remain, with all the complicated circumstances arising from this fact), and we should be satisfied that the best arrangements were being made for their welfare both in health and sickness.

I cannot refrain from quoting here a sentence from the

recently published "Open Letter" on Pauper Children, issued by the Central Committee of Poor Law Conferences and the Metropolitan Association for befriending them, addressed to the President of the "State Children's Aid Association." "Has your Association ever considered the immense difficulty of defining an 'In and out' child? At what point does it become one, and who is to have the care of it till it reaches that point, and then how would the 'Great Central authority' be able to determine whether or not a child should be entirely removed from the care of its parents? Surely only those intimately acquainted with its family history, as the local Guardians are, can decide the question satisfactorily."

At present the suggestion for the further and special care of children has only partially been carried out by the transference of certain classes of the sick and defective to the Metropolitan Asylums Board.

Without entering further into the recent discussions consequent on the Report on Poor Law Schools issued by the Commission of inquiry last year, we may briefly state that the general direction of public opinion is tending more and more towards the great importance of family life for children, and the best means of attaining it, and with this same object, the reduction in size and numbers of the large District Schools; Cottage Homes, either concentrated in communities, or scattered in towns, boarding out in families, or in separate, smaller Cottage Homes (of which over 200 already exist), being the suggested alternatives; the two latter, though no doubt the best in principle, can never be adopted for all the large numbers of Pauper children with whom we have to deal. [1]

[1] In connection with this subject, I am glad to be able to notice

If this special consideration is desirable with regard to the children, how much stronger is the argument concerning that large population of the sick and afflicted, amounting to over 76,000, in all our towns and country districts, those in the Metropolitan area alone being no less than 13,000.[1]

It is surely not unreasonable to ask that those who

the excellent step adopted by the Whitechapel Board of Guardians, in connection with their newly-arranged plans for the children, the large District School having been given up. Their 4 pairs of semi-detached cottages are to be placed under the "general control and government of a Lady Superintendent of administrative capacity, and who should be a trained Nurse." How desirable this will be in view of the appointment of foster-mothers is pointed out, as well as the importance of bringing the best and most refining influences to bear upon them and the children. The appointment of a female Clerk is also named. Thus, two of the hopes expressed in this chapter are being fulfilled,—the separation of children with something like family life, and the appointment of educated women as superintendents.

[1] It may be of interest to give here the following statistics. In the Metropolitan District there were in 1896, 13,428 sick and bed-ridden persons, with 4,117 aged and infirm; while the number of paid officers acting as Nurses was 1,514; of these, 848 had received previous training: while the Pauper inmates who assisted in the personal care of the sick, amounted to 349.

Then for all England and Wales we find the total of sick and bed-ridden to be 39,264, with 19,287 aged and infirm; the number of paid officers acting as Nurses, 3,715, and of these, 1,961 only had received any training; but it is in the following statement that we find the great and striking difference between the Metropolis with its separate Infirmaries, and the Country Workhouses; the Pauper inmates who there assisted in the care of the sick amounting to 3,443, being nearly equal in number to the paid Nurses. The "Pauper inmates" include those who are Convalescent Patients, but this distinction does not seem to be important.

specially understand the needs and requirements of the sick should be appointed to deal with the class we are now considering, but we do not find this to be the case; there are amongst the officers of the Department but a very small minority of medical men and experts in these subjects, and however admirable are, and have been, those who take part in this, which we may call the "Inspector's department" of the Board, we can hardly consider as sufficient the two special members of the medical profession, for the metropolitan district and all England, who are to be found there, with none of the fourteen general Inspectors and two assistants, qualified (besides the two for schools) as medical men. [1]   It is therefore urged, not for the first time, that there should be, besides a "children's department" a "medical and nursing department," which would be competent to consider and control all such matters as would naturally come before them, and which we do not hesitate to say, form as important a sphere of work as that which concerns the children, for does it not comprise the "State Hospitals" which are bound to provide care and accommodation for all the "destitute Sick and Incurables", who cannot be admitted to our voluntary Asylums?   That such a demand is no vain and unnecessary one, I shall endeavour to shew in this chapter, by evidence obtained from trust-

[1] The absence of medical men as Inspectors of the Poor Law Board, was commented on in an able article in the Medical Times as long ago as 1864, which is too long to be quoted here; the Hospitals of the Army and Navy are named as being subject to constant and efficient medical inspection, as well as those for the insane. The Spectator had also an Article to the same effect, at that time.

worthy, undoubted, and varied sources, proving that grave evils and difficulties still exist, which can only be dealt with by those who have a complete and practical knowledge of the treatment of the sick in public Institutions, and possess the experience gained in Hospitals.   Had this been the case and had such persons been appointed in sufficient numbers, I venture to think we should not have to lament, thirty years after the beneficent act of Mr. Gathorne Hardy was passed, that so much still remains to be done in this direction. The separation of the sick from the Workhouse was indeed effected by that legislation for the Metropolitan District, but it is equally needed in the larger towns (in but few of which it has been carried out) as well as in the Country districts, though different measures of doing so may have to be adopted.   It is obviously impossible for the average man, who is not a doctor, however competent and highly educated he may be in other respects, to enter into the needs of Hospital management or to judge of the care and nursing of the sick, and the qualifications and performance of duty of the women who act as nurses, over whom there is, when employed, in *Workhouse* Sick Wards, no competent or trained supervision at present.   If such unqualified persons could never be appointed for the inspection of Hospitals, why should they still be given these posts in Institutions which are, in a large measure, and to all intents and purposes, of the same nature? After all that I have said and written during many years on the subject of women's work in the administration of the Poor Law, [1] I must again repeat my conviction that

[1] In March 1894 I wrote an article in the " Nineteenth Century " on "Women as Official Inspectors", which was reprinted as a pamphlet the following year.

I claim a still larger share of it for them, and would rejoice to see some experienced women allowed to take part, at least as advisers, of the departments which I have already named, in other ways. The success of the experiment of appointing a Lady Inspector of schools and children, as long as 22 years ago, has never been doubted or called in question, and a further extension of the plan is urgently demanded not only in that department, but also for the Infirmaries and Sick Wards, where the work of the nurses can only be fully tested by the inspection of women, trained either in medicine or nursing. For how otherwise can the real state of things be ascertained and corrected, relating as they do chiefly to the personal care and condition of the sick, when those who have the authority and responsibility are themselves unskilled in the details, and the medical attendant is probably, as in many Country Unions, only an occasional visitor, who cannot bestow the time and attention needed for supervision? The state of things at present being so wholly different from that of thirty years ago, when the sick were comparatively few, and trained women, either as doctors or nurses, did not exist, surely points to the need of a revision of all the Rules and Regulations made for the appointment of Inspectors of Workhouses 40 or 50 years ago. I would urge that at least a trial should be made by the appointment of some women, to be called, if so desired, " Sub-Inspectors," and to act in certain departments of work where they are loudly called for; I ask this in the interest not of the sick only, but of all those women who are now carrying on their up-hill and difficult work in Workhouses, not only with various discouragements and hindrances, but with many impediments also in the way of a successful performance of it, for at present there is no one to whom the young, trained nurse, perhaps just entering single-handed on her arduous duties, can look up, or turn to, for sympathy or advice.

Before I leave the subject of Medical Inspection, I cannot refrain from naming one question closely connected with it, viz., the admission of medical men from the outside, to assist the resident Superintendents and assistants in their arduous task, involving in the case of the larger Infirmaries the care and treatment of the Sick, sometimes amounting to 700 or 800 persons. This is no new question, but like most of those already noticed, has been brought forward at intervals during many years, and has been advocated by the Medical Superintendents, who feel and know the help that would be afforded them by the visits and co-operation of additional medical men, and also of advanced Students, who would be able to acquire in these Institutions that knowledge of many cases, especially of a chronic, or incurable nature, which are not to be seen in Voluntary Hospitals, where if of prolonged duration, they cannot remain till death.

During my term of office at Kensington the subject was brought forward, and earnestly was it desired by some of us that the request should be granted, the medical superintendent having already permission to allow some students from a neighbouring Hospital to visit special or interesting cases. But the matter did not meet with approval, and no advance has been made in this direction; one objection raised was the strong dislike of the poor themselves to any such plan for being made objects of examination, or, perhaps, experiment: but surely there are reasonable arguments against this opposition. In the first place, why should those who are receiving entire support and benefit from the rates, be supposed to object to what all those who of their own free will consent to, in entering a voluntary hospital? And that they do so gladly, is also asserted, the fact being mentioned that if a patient is passed by during the visits of the physician and his accompanying students, he feels himself aggrieved and neglected, rather than pleased, by the omission. But surely there is another and even stronger reason in the fact that there are no other such opportunities for students to learn their profession in many departments, as are to be found in these State Institutions, and as this fact has been acknowledged in the case of the Metropolitan Asylums, to which all infectious diseases are now consigned, we cannot but hope that the wall of prejudice which has hitherto excluded this class of institutions from being made more extensively useful, may ere long be broken down, and we should then probably hear less of their enormous cost to the ratepayers.

Some of the foregoing remarks, it will be seen, apply chiefly to the Country Unions, where the sick are still kept amongst many other classes, but even in the wholly different, and fine Institutions known as the "Metropolitan Infirmaries," the arrangements are not wholly satisfactory with regard to the position of the matron and nurses. Again, I must refer to the totally changed circumstances of the present, as compared with past, times, and it is not surprising therefore to find that the existing regulations are quite unsuited to present conditions. The supreme head over all these large Institutions is the medical superintendent, under whose entire control is placed the matron and the nurses, the steward being the other officer next in importance and power. But though in many respects this arrangement is desirable, experience has proved that it requires modification, and a greater amount of power to be given to the matron. The superintendent may be, and in most cases, is, a young and unmarried man, and yet he has the right to grant, or refuse, leave to the nurses as regards holidays, hours of absence, etc., without reference to the matron. We therefore ask that in all matters of domestic management, including the time of absence for the nurses, the matron should have the power of control, as in voluntary Hospitals.[1]

Now that highly trained and educated women are being placed in these posts of importance, with the greatest advantage to all concerned, these matters deserve the consideration which we hope they will receive, and would assuredly do so, had women the influence and voice which we desire they should have, in the rules and regulations of the Local Government Councils, at least as regards the department which deals with the Poor; for of those details affecting women, they alone can be the fitting judges. Some few who are placed in these posts have made public their aims and desires, in which we have reason to believe the majority of those who are still silent will agree; but in such matters, official recognition and reform move slowly.

The position of nurses in Country Unions placed under the control of the authorised heads, the Master and Matron, is one of far greater difficulty and perplexity, for undoubted

---

[1] I have said elsewhere that the position of the matron "is exactly what the superintendent chooses to make it", and this can hardly be a just or desirable state of affairs.

as the grievances and anomalies are, they are recognised by all to be not easy of solution.

The position is an entirely new one since the last twenty years, for before that time hardly any really "trained" nurses were selected for these Institutions, even "paid" women of any kind being few and far between. Thus the rules framed for their guidance thirty years ago, have naturally been, long since, wholly obsolete. The chief qualification required of a "Pauper Nurse" (for no others than inmates were then contemplated) was that she should be able to read the written directions for the giving of medicines, and it is difficult to believe that this has remained in force to the present day.[1] The result, as may naturally be supposed, has been that a state of "friction" has been largely prevalent in those Institutions where the "trained" and the "untrained" elements have come in contact. The subject has attracted a considerable amount of attention, both by speakers and writers of late, for it has become impossible any longer to ignore it as one of no importance. As the sentiments of those chiefly concerned in the question are not, and cannot be, widely expressed through publication, I shall endeavour to give what proofs I can, from authentic and trustworthy sources, of a state of feeling which all must acknowledge to be serious and highly important as regards the questions we are now considering. Unless some greater amount of freedom and independence can be granted to those women who have learnt their

[1] As I write this, the new order for "Nursing of the Sick in Workhouses," is issued, August 1897, and we trust it may be the means of removing (see Appendix), some at least of the difficulties which have been named, though it can hardly be said to apply to the position of the solitary Nurse in a small Country Union.

profession in well-conducted Hospitals and Poor Law Infirmaries, we fear that the number who will qualify and
apply for such posts, will, in the future, be a diminishing,
instead of an increasing, quantity. In cases where the
numbers of the sick do not allow of entire separation from
the other classes in the Workhouse, we would earnestly
suggest that a certain amount of independence should be
granted to the nurse, as regards their treatment, and
that in these matters she should look to the medical
officer alone for authority and instructions; this would in
no way interfere with her subjection to the Master and
Matron in other arrangements concerning her charge,
although as the distribution of linen, and the supply of
food, must still be left in the hands of these officers, we
fear that all sources of friction and disagreement will
hardly be done away with; with regard to the first of
these two important matters, the supply of linen, we consider that the doctor who is responsible for the wellbeing of his patients, might certainly uphold the authority
of the nurse as to these requirements, even as he orders
the quality and amount of their diet.

It is easy to say, as has frequently been urged in the
recent discussions we have alluded to, that all this "friction"
could, and should, be done away with by mutual good
will, courtesy, and forbearance on both sides. But
why should we look for this ideal state of things in this
department of social life more than in any other? A
perfection of temper and tact, and an absence of jealousy
is not found, nor expected, in any classes or bodies of
persons thus thrown into daily contact, and therefore it
is that definite rules and regulations are needed for the
right performance of their duties, if the machinery is to

work harmoniously; and we venture to think that such changes are required, and are possible, as will attain the end we all have in view, viz., a due recognition of the nurses' position. In connection with the fact of placing trained persons under the control and authority of untrained, or unskilled, superiors, it is surely not irrelevant to refer to other professions, and ask, how would it be possible for the disciplined soldier or sailor who had served his time of probation, to be called to serve under an officer who had not done so? And the same question may be asked about any other class of persons who had served an apprenticeship, and were then placed under an unskilled foreman. But if such changes are deemed to be impossible, and an ideal that is unattainable, there is, we believe, only one alternative left for the efficient management of the sick in our Country Unions, and though I am aware it will again be denounced as impracticable, I nevertheless will name it as one of the "suggestions" of this chapter.[1]

The separation of the various and heterogeneous classes of Paupers was begun to be carried out when the schools were removed from Workhouses, and the principle was again affirmed, in 1867, when the establishment of Poor Law Infirmaries for the Metropolitan District was decided upon as a measure necessary for the adequate treatment of the sick. It is strange that in the thirty years which have elapsed, so little advance has been made in the movement, and only two or three of the larger provincial towns

[1] The following suggestion is from an article contributed to "Nursing Notes", in 1888. "If the number of the sick in individual Workhouses is too small to justify the appointment of a trained nurse or nurses, that several Unions should combine in a Central Asylum, as in certain School Districts."

have adopted the plan. The exclusion of all Pauper help from these Institutions is one of the grandest features of recent reform, and has struck a death-blow to that most fatal of all systems of employment in connection with the sick and helpless classes; the women employed even as "scrubbers" being not inmates, but paid workers, engaged for the purpose from the outside.

It has been repeatedly urged that this beneficent system should be extended to all Unions having a number of inmates exceeding 100, or 150, and recently suggestions have been made for smaller "Homes," or Infirmaries, with numbers far less than this, under the charge of a Head nurse, and as the plan has actually been tried with good results, we cannot see what objection there can be to its further development, the connection with the adjoining, or neighbouring, Workhouse being maintained. But, failing this solution of the difficulty, we would once more bring forward the idea of a still further adoption of the plan of "classification," now obtaining a prominent place amongst theories of improvement.

It may be interesting to notice in connection with this question, that attention was called to it as long ago as 1860, when the following question was asked in the House of Commons by Mr. W. Ewart, M.P.: "Whether it might not be advisable to adopt a system of classification of inmates of Workhouses, so that the more respectable might be separated from the worse conducted classes; whether greater separation of the children from the other inmates could not be effected, and a system of industrial training more generally adopted; also whether it might not be beneficial to encourage the introduction of small, but well-assorted libraries in Workhouses?" To these questions a full reply was given by Mr. Villiers. The subject was also discussed in the journal of the Workhouse Visiting Society in 1860, and a paper was read at the Women Guardians' Conference held at Manchester, 1896, by Mrs. Hazzledine, P.L. Guardian at Nottingham.

It is curious to learn from the practical experience of some Guardians that these plans do not always meet with the approval of those for whose benefit they are made, and that the isolation of smaller and more select groups is often resented by the old people who love company and gossip!

But the present suggestion that the buildings themselves should be classified, and appropriated to the various classes which inhabit them, is no recent one, and appears to have the claim of common-sense in its favour. The majority of Country Unions have now populations far below the accommodation provided for them in former days by Workhouses; in some places buildings to contain 800 are tenanted by less than 100, and in no case, we believe, are they fully occupied. But were the sick to be collected, and moved to one central Workhouse, in numbers from the surrounding Unions that would fill it, how easy would be the task of caring for them as they should be cared for!

All arrangements for a Hospital, or a Home for In-curables (which a large proportion of the inmates are) could then be carried out, the medical officer would find attendance and attention worth while (for of course he would receive better remuneration) while the appointment of a qualified and experienced matron would naturally follow, and under her would be a staff of trained nurses who would gladly come forward to fill the posts offered to them. With a woman Inspector added to the staff, this ideal Poor Law Institution would be complete, and "friction" would be for ever done away with. The objection raised to this proposal is, naturally, that it would be highly distasteful to the class of persons to be dealt with. But perhaps we may say, with regard to this, that in these matters of legal relief and support, "beggars must not be" altogether "choosers" and that it is not undesirable to place some check upon a too easy resort to it. It has already been urged, as a warning, that the present greatly improved condition of Poor Law Infirmaries, offers too many inducements to the acceptance of relief, and especially with regard to the older members of a family, who may be conveniently placed out of the way by consigning them to these comfortable Asylums, without any compunction on the part of relatives, even though a small contribution may have to be made. Perhaps therefore the distance to be traversed before a sick or aged person can be thus disposed of, may not be altogether an objection to be lightly dismissed, for the penalties and "disgrace", or "stigma" supposed to be attached to the receipt of relief from the rates, is in some respects, beginning to be thought a tradition of the past, especially as regards the modern Infirmaries. [1] But

[1] It is now being urged by some that all social disabilities should be removed from the recipients of Poor Law relief, but surely this leniency may be carried too far. I have never been able to agree with the suggestion that the distinctive dress should be done away with in the case of adults. The matter was once discussed at the Kensington Board, and I then gave my reasons against it. We are in these, and some other respects, in danger of forgetting the wholesome maxim that the condition of the Pauper must not be

as every centre to be selected would probably be within easy reach by railway, it may be that this objection is one rather of imagination than reality. At any rate it has already been encountered in the departments both of children and lunatics, who in district schools and asylums are necessarily sent far from their homes and relations, and in the Metropolitan Infirmaries asylums, the distance of most of them from the parishes of the patients, is as great as would be the case in the proposed central hospitals, or infirmaries, in which the increased care and attention, and consequent facilities for recovery, might well be supposed to outweigh as in other institutions, and homes for incurables, the objections which have been urged against the plan. [1]

made superior to that of the independent Poor; and from this point of view I believe the distinctive dress to be desirable for all but the children. It may be well to remember the fact that according to the latest statistics, the total number of all classes of Paupers is 836,674, and of these nearly a quarter of a million are children!

[1] It may not be known to some of my readers that the Poor of the Strand Union have their Workhouse at Edmonton, and those belonging to Holborn go to Mitcham, for the Workhouse and Schools, while the Infirmary for these is at Upper Holloway.

I may add that these views are shared by others who are competent judges of these matters, and believe that division and separation is the only solution of the difficulty concerning the sick.

CHAPTER VII

PRESENT AND FUTURE *(continued)*

IN considering these needs of change and extension we must not suppose that the central board alone has power to remedy all existing evils. Much will still remain in the hands of the boards of guardians who have a large amount of independence and control in all the internal arrangements of administration. Till a greater degree of interest and intelligence is inspired into these bodies it is to be feared that even the most beneficent intentions and regulations from without may be little more than a dead letter, to be conveniently laid on the shelf if not acceptable, mere recommendations having certainly often shared this fate. The small interest shewn in the election, or selection, of their representatives by the ratepayers, has been often commented upon, and is surely one of the many shortcomings we have to lament in public matters.[1] The

---

[1] This is evident to all who take the trouble to look into the matter. In the Parish of Kensington, under the old system, about 23,000 persons were entitled to vote; usually about 8000 did so; at the last Election under the new law between 4000 and 5000 voted. But as I have often stated, I believe this result to be mainly caused by the time fixed for the Elections being in April; it thus

good results anticipated from the new law introduced several years ago, are hardly yet apparent, the chief matter for rejoicing being the great increase of women guardians, whose participation in the work was made possible by it, nearly 900 of such members being soon after added to the list.[1] That all these have not been the best and most fully qualified women has been the subject of some comment and criticism, but we must remember that it is just now a fierce light that beats upon women in a public capacity, and every act is keenly watched and scrutinised. We cannot help asking, did any one expect that all the 900 women thus called to new and unexpected duties, would be perfectly capable of performing them, within the first year of their appointments? Rather let us think leniently of their work and their endeavours in a new and untried sphere, and ask about the performances of the 22,000 men who have had the sole power in their hands for the last sixty years, in the 648 Unions of England and Wales.

Surely it is not unreasonable to ask have *they* had no shortcomings, and made no mistakes during all that long period of years?

But whether men or women are called to these posts, it is quite clear that unless some knowledge and study of

frequently occurs in Easter week, when a large number of the inhabitants are absent, and time was not allowed for sending and returning the Voting Papers by post. It is to be regretted that the change to a more convenient season was not made in the last Act of 1894.

[1] It may surprise us to learn that in Finland, with only the small population of two and a half millions, there were (in 1894) no less than 130 women as Poor Law Guardians, and 50 as principals of Workhouses.

the questions, often difficult and complicated, that are brought before them, is possessed or acquired, they will be but little gain to the poor and helpless populations for whom they are called to legislate. A great, I may say, the greater, part of this work, is eminently fitted for women, and their judgment and opinions cannot fail to be most valuable, if carefully considered and given.

But there are still 300 Boards without any woman upon them, and four Counties where they are still wanting. The time is past when arguments were required to enforce the need of their assistance, and the "Communion of labour" has long since been acknowledged as a necessity in all social work; the hope of their help was expressed by me when I gave evidence before the Poor Law Commission of 1861, and it has since been abundantly fulfilled. To those who have worked in London, and on the larger Boards, where public opinion and the more recent ideas concerning Poor Law and charity, have at least in some measure penetrated, it is strange to find how little advance has been made in remoter Country districts, and the question is ever present as to the motives which induce busy men to travel long distances and give up valuable time for a work of which, they, at least some of them, appear to know and care so little. I venture to think that the majority of women who have come forward for this office, have the real interests of the poor at heart, and desire to deal justly and kindly by them, with no drawback of self-seeking, or advantage to themselves.

But it still remains a matter of surprise and regret, why, especially in the Country, where many residents with leisure are to be found, so few come forward to fill these

posts, and now that Ex-Officio members are no longer
admitted, fewer, instead of more, of the upper classes,
are to be found as Guardians. Various reasons have
been assigned for this reluctance, but the fact remains,
and it is much to be lamented. May we hope that the
duties which women of the upper classes do not shrink
from, but are entering upon with increasing interest and
zeal, and are indeed pressing forward to fill, may be
thought worthy of the attention and devotion of the men
of the same class, who have the knowledge and leisure to
bestow upon them?

The whole question of the care and nursing of the sick,
is in the hands of such persons, as well as the education
of the children, and without their help and advocacy
nothing will be effectively done in either direction. The
mysteries of "trained," as distinguished from, "untrained,"
nursing, seem to be impenetrable to those who have long
been accustomed to the one and only method of cheap
and Pauper attendance, and whose conviction appears to
be that "trained nurses will never do anything!"[1] How
soon these delusions of ignorance may be dispelled, we
cannot venture to conjecture, a positive "order" from the
Central authority being the only hope of reform, "recommendations" and advice having proved alike in vain;[2]
but then the question will remain, how and where are the
nurses to be procured? As this cannot now be answered,
we will proceed to the consideration of another class of
difficulties which stands in the way of the improvements
we desire to see carried out. I have no intention of

[1] This remark has been made to me by those who had never
had any experience of the class, and confessed they had not.
[2] See Order issued, August, 1897.

saying anything against the many good officers, both men
and women, who are engaged in carrying on the administration of the Poor Law throughout the country, but
I cannot refrain from alluding to, and repeating, opinions
which I have expressed even in my first writings on these
subjects, and urged ever since that time. It is beginning
to be generally considered desirable, or even necessary,
that a certain amount of training should be given for all
skilled, or professional, work, of whatever kind, and to
this conviction we owe the wonderful and rapid growth
of trained nursing; [1] but there is a form of this conviction

[1] Since this was written these opinions have been confirmed by
the welcome intelligence of the establishment of " Training Schools
for Prison Warders," which are being carried on, for men, at
Chelmsford, and Hull, and for women at Wormwood Scrubs. In
this we are following the example of Italy, Belgium, and France.
The Probationers go through four months' instruction and practice
in the details of Prison duty, besides lectures from the Governors
and Chaplains. It is well said that " the establishment of these Schools
for officers is a very needful step in the right direction, and con-
stitutes one of the most encouraging amongst a number of recent
progressive efforts put forth by the Home Office ". May we venture
to express a hope that other Departments may be inclined to follow
this good example? The class of persons with whom both Prison
and Workhouse officers have to deal, cannot but have demoralising
effects on the character; when considering the cases brought before
us as Guardians, I have often been inclined to wonder how any
reverence or respect for human nature could be maintained by those
who are constantly brought into contact with the Casual and Able-
bodied Paupers.

It can only be possible for those who undertake the work and
carry it out, with high principles and from conscientious motives.
I have often felt inclined to condone cases of apparent harshness
and severity in officers who were brought into daily contact with the

which has, I believe, acted unfavourably in the Poor Law
system, by the tradition which certainly exists, that some
previous experience of it, *and that alone,* is desirable in
applicants for posts; were this to be combined with
training in another, and perhaps, higher, sphere of
work, there would be nothing to be said against it,
although, of course, no consideration should be allowed
to overbalance that of personal character and fitness.
But the fact that a man or woman has filled a much
lower post in a Poor Law Institution cannot surely be
thought to be a sufficient qualification for another, perhaps,
even the highest. For some of the larger Establishments
in London or the country, it has been repeatedly urged
that the superintendence and government of a population
of varied classes, numbered by hundreds, or even a
thousand, should be given to the class of persons from
whom the governors of Prisons are chosen, the task being
surely one of no less importance and difficulty. But the
plea hitherto urged against this desire, is the want of
"previous experience," and thus those who have mounted
up from the lower steps of the ladder are selected, with,
as I venture to think, often doubtful advantage.[1] If this
is true as regards the male officers, still more so is it of

lowest and most degraded of all classes, and sometimes I have been
tempted to exclaim to my neighbour at the Board, "Could we find
more revolting and degraded objects if we were acting in Central
Africa instead of in Christian England?"

[1] Those who have read Dr. Rogers, "Reminiscences" will acknowledge the truth of these remarks, at least as exemplified in the past,
when one couple of notorious characters were passed on successively
to the management of three important London Workhouses, to which
they had mounted from a lower step.

the women. In all countries the care and supervision of the poor and the sick has been confided to those who fulfil domestic duties at home, and have received some training in them on a still larger scale, such women being often, in Roman Catholic countries, of even the highest rank and position. In Ireland alone are such instances to be found within the range of Poor Law Administration, special orders of women being appointed to undertake the duties of superintendence, and attendance on the Poor. [1] But desirable as this may seem to be, one great hindrance, in addition to that already alluded to, is the almost universal desire, and indeed recommendation, of the Central Board, that "married couples" should be employed in workhouses. No doubt this rule in most cases gives less trouble to the Board of Guardians who control the Union, but it is hardly possible that in even a majority of cases, the two fittest persons should happen to be man and wife, and equally qualified for such difficult and comprehensive duties.

The rule has, however, been broken through of late years in the case of the modern Infirmaries, and we may therefore hope to see the innovation still further carried out. The supervision of small Workhouses would be admirable and congenial employment for many widows and single women of education, including as it does, the care of the sick, while it would not furnish a sufficient sphere for a man of equal position and capacities; but such duties as pertained to, and would devolve upon, him, could be well carried out by a Steward, or Labour

[1] These women, members of Religious Orders, we are rejoiced to learn are now to be permitted to go through a training in Public Institutions, to fit them as Nurses for the Sick.

Master, for the comparatively few who are now to be found as "able-bodied", or as tramps and vagrants; the sick and aged, either young or old, forming by far the larger proportion of our present Pauper population.[1]

But if masters and matrons are still to be appointed as at present, I cannot help asking if a greater care in the examination and approval of the candidates might not be exercised by the Central Board, local prejudices in favour of particular persons being too often the ruling motives in an appointment. I have before me some recent instances which I think can hardly be justified as suitable or fitting for the circumstances, with regard to the age of the persons appointed; one who was an officer in the Country Union at the time, writes thus; "The matron died in the winter, and the guardians have appointed her daughter as matron; a girl of not 21 years old, who was cook here; and most incapable of a matron's duties." In another case, on the death of the matron, the master's niece was appointed, at the age of 19; no doubt in both cases the object aimed at was to

[1] In a paper on "Workhouses and Women's Work," in the Church of England Monthly Review, for 1858, I wrote these words:

"Looking forward into the future, we can picture to ourselves a Model Workhouse, but whether the vision will be realised in 10, 20, or 50 years, we cannot say.—At the head of such a Workhouse should be a woman of education, judgment, and above all, of religious devotion to her work, with a heart full of love for young and old, rich and poor, because they are a sacred charge committed to her care. And for this superintendence a woman would seem to be the fittest person."

I have known the case of superior women training as assistant matrons in order to obtain the higher posts, but could not succeed in doing so, owing to the preference for married couples, 1897.

retain the services of valued masters, whose wishes in the matter were paramount with the Board, but should they have prevailed against the undoubted claims of the poor people to be placed under the charge of more experienced and competent persons?

In another case, on the death of the matron, the Master remained only on condition of his sister being appointed, though she had no previous experience or knowledge of the duties, and of course his conditions were complied with. A higher class of superintendents has long been urged for the appointments connected with large schools, where not only hundreds of children have to be cared for, morally, physically and intellectually, but a large staff of educated men and women teachers have also to be governed; in a few instances this plan has been adopted and I can speak from personal observation of the excellent results that followed such appointments of officers and their wives to these posts; that there is no difficulty in obtaining persons of this class, is proved by the applications which in one case numbered many hundreds. It can hardly be denied that Poor Law appointments are at present mainly bestowed on those who have been long employed in the service, and have worked their way upwards through various grades; whether such a system, which may be described as a close and restricted monopoly, is desirable, I leave for others to judge; but that it exists, is, I believe, an undoubted fact, and for the filling of the highest posts of Workhouse administration its expediency may well be doubted.

Before I leave the subject of appointments for service in Poor Law administration, I must allude to the experience I have had during many years of the system, so generally prevailing, of granting testimonials, and the reception of them by Boards of Guardians. The matter was, occasionally, one of considerable amusement, and the remark was made, that if ever "examples of perfection" were desired to be met with, or heard of, they might be found in those who offered themselves for election to a post in Workhouse or Infirmary. Most of us well knew the value (or rather, worthlessness) of such documents as proclaimed their merits, and we paid little heed to them. But there is surely a serious side to the subject, and it is lamentable to think how many undeserving persons are passed on to important posts by this practice so common to the easy conscience of a public body, the excuse being (as I have already stated in connection with this matter) the unkindness of depriving a candidate of gaining a living, the cruelty as concerned the hundreds of helpless persons, having no part in the consideration.

In confirmation of these opinions, I will give some facts from the experience of a Secretary who has to advertise continually for nurses, 17 being recently required for one Institution alone.

"During five weeks we inserted advertisements in the best papers, and out of the large number of applications received, four only were found to be available, all others being thoroughly unsatisfactory, although in many instances holding *good testimonials.* Boards of Guardians, would, I have no doubt, have accepted most who applied, on the strength of them, but our very searching inquiries, in addition, bring out the truth." One might have hoped and expected that the nurse "Gamp" of the past, with her love for her bottle, was long since extinct, but alas! experience shews she is not, and intemperance continues to rank as one of the chief causes of failure in those who apply, especially for posts in a Workhouse, where it is hoped so high a standard as in other Institutions is hardly expected.

In descending to the lowest class of all in the Poor Law service, we come to the Pauper helps, who, if no longer called by the dignified title of "Nurse," still exercise a considerable amount of control in Workhouses throughout the country. It can hardly be necessary to re-capitulate here the oft-told tale of the doings of these persons, so unworthily filling, or abusing, the posts committed to them, but the sooner their powers are limited to the functions of scrubbing the floors and similar menial work, the better for the poor sufferers in the wards. When it is considered that a certain number of these so-called "able-bodied" inmates, are of the semi-imbecile, or, at least, feeble-minded, class, both men and women, the latter too often of immoral character, it is easy to suppose what the result must be during the long hours when, in the nurses' absence, the sick wards are left to their control. As we may hope that their days of influence are numbered, I will not devote further space to the narratives and details which I could give of the doings of those who will ere long be deprived of their powers and opportunities of doing harm; but all who have visited Workhouses, or acted as Guardians of the Poor, must have abundant knowledge of these facts, and the only matter for surprise is that such a system should have been allowed to continue so long in a vast and important Department of the State. The fact that these persons have been, to a great extent, employed as sole attendants on the sick at night (night nurses being, till quite recently, the exception, even when trained women were employed by day) makes the evil only more obvious and censurable.

I will now give a few extracts which will shew that what has been said about appointments is not without foundation. "The Master was a Relieving Officer before he had this post, and so does not understand the work, especially the Hospital, and no matter what we ask for, or try to improve, they say it never used to be so; but we do not want to go backward, but forward, in our nursing. The food has not been as it should be, and the milk has been diluted with water several times. There is constant trouble too about the clean clothes from the Laundry." Another difficulty is the receiving medical orders from, or through, the master, which the trained Nurse naturally resents; sometimes he alone accompanies the Doctor on his rounds, while the Nurse is not asked to do so, and it is added, "If the matron was to do her duty better as to the superintendence of the sick wards and nurses, this trouble would never have happened, as then the Master and Nurse would see less of each other." A Lady Guardian writes as follows about two excellent trained Nurses who had worked in the Infirmary. "I am more grieved than I can say that our two most excellent Nurses have been compelled to resign. I have had ample opportunities of knowing and appreciating the very good work they have done, in the most trying circumstances. Nurse—especially has had to put up with most shameful treatment from the master. We are utterly powerless to do anything, though we know that things are very wrong in the Workhouse, and deeply as it grieves me for the Nurses to leave, for I not only appreciate their work, but look on them as friends, I see no help for it; the low tone of the officials in the Workhouse makes it impossible for respectable women to remain there. We have three Lady Guardians on our Board, and they and some of the gentlemen would do all they could to support the Nurses, but we are completely overpowered by the others and the Master. The only thing I can see to be done is, for all those who are interested in Workhouses, to do their utmost to have the Infirmaries and part of the House for women and children, completely separated, and placed under women alone.—Neither the master nor his wife have had any preparation for the work they are doing; he was a soldier for a few years, then a policeman and afterwards a relieving officer; his wife is an uneducated woman, quite unfit for matron, never having had a servant under her before she was placed in charge of the Workhouse. The object clearly is to get inferior women as nurses, who will not mind the goings on in the Workhouse. The difference that the nurses have made is wonderful; I cannot speak too highly of their kindness and attention to the poor people, and the good they have done in bringing a Christian spirit into the wards. I look on their departure as a very great loss to the sick and the helpless."—"It would be quite possible to have a nursing superintendent at the head, with night and day nurses under her for the infirmary wards, and a nurse under her to take charge of the home life of the children and infants, and another trained nurse in charge of the women imbeciles. This would make entire separation as far as management was concerned, and avoid friction; the master and matron would still be the heads of the body of the house, the housekeeping, cooking and laundry work, all which forms a separate department, and requires a separate superintendent, who would be the matron. If a plan of this sort could be managed, and with a little contrivance and trouble it might be, most of the difficulties would disappear. The master is one with the visiting committee."

These two nurses had to leave at the end of their month, but received no payment from the Guardians, and had to defray their travelling expenses to a distant county.

Such examples of the too frequently existing state of things could be multiplied tenfold, and there can be no question that the condition is owing not solely to faults on either side of those who occupy the respective positions, but to the fact of arrangements having drifted into the present anomalous state, which it is impossible to carry on with success and harmony. I have alluded to the grievances with regard to food, and will now give some facts proving them to be great, and in some cases, incompatible with the health and work of the nurses. "I am writing to you again to tell you that it is impossible to live here. I have been very ill, and in fact have not been free from pain for some days, nor able to leave my room. I have never been ill before, and it is caused by the wretched diet we get; if the meat is not bad, it is so tough we cannot get our teeth into it, and as we have no puddings or anything else, we either have to eat bread and butter, or go without. The doctor ordered me to drink milk, and I have had to buy it all myself, as the matron would not allow it.— I was not ill one day at Birmingham" (where she was trained) "and why should I be ill here?—I did not know what Workhouse Nursing was when I joined."—Another writes from the same Workhouse, "It is impossible for any

Nurse to work here under the Master and Matron. I cannot understand why we should be treated as we are; the food is disgusting, if the meat is not tainted, it is so hard we cannot eat it, the consequence is, we have to send out for different things, which comes to a great expense. The poor inmates have had pork for dinner 4 times this week."

Here is another extract from a letter of recent date from a fully-qualified and conscientious nurse. "My interest in Workhouse Infirmary Nursing is not in the least abating, but alas! it is more hopeless than ever. I have held on for 16 months, struggling with strange difficulties. After above ten years experience, I am compelled to admit the utter uselessness of Nurses fighting for proper administration under untrained management; they are too weak, I mean their position is too obscure to be successful in the contest. We stand so often entirely unsupported!"

In addition to the letters already given, I will quote one from a solitary nurse in a small Country workhouse just returned from her holiday; which will confirm all that has been said as to the difficulties, which we fear will not be met by the New Order. "Though I much enjoyed the change, the time sometimes hung heavy on my hands, having nothing to do, so I came back on the 10th day. It cheers one now to think of the welcome I had from my patients. It had not entered my head that they would be as glad to see me as I would be to get back.—I have my patients to see to, besides the most of my own housework, and often have I had to use my off-duty time in cleaning up and tidying my rooms and then go on duty again. I have said to one or two of the guardians that it would be good for several reasons to have a new nurse; and they say no, I must not think that, I satisfy them, and the patients like me, I must stay; it will be better in many respects for me. It is not 'for me' that I am thinking at all, but for the people; if I cannot get my will for them perhaps a new nurse can. I have been lately, unconsciously of course, getting into the ruts of a small workhouse; fifteen months here have taken something out of me. I have tried for alterations, but what has been the good? But let me get a few things I have set my heart on, a few men's shirts, handkerchiefs, etc., in my store, and I shall think I have scored something, and made it brighter in little things for the patients, and easier, it may be, for the nurse who shall, in the near or distant future, come after me. I am afraid you will find this all grumble or sentiment, but please remember it comes from a small workhouse where there is nothing but small things to talk about. Sometimes, and only sometimes, for I like the country and the quiet when off duty, I feel I would like to be in a larger town, and there only because it would be nice to have a talk with other nurses about what one reads in the nursing papers, etc., besides, one can hide one's ignorance in a small workhouse; one must read up and remember things."

The following extracts have recently appeared in a nursing publication of this year's date, but are added here, being well authenticated, and bearing out all that has been stated on the question, and the difficulties that beset the present system. Another, and not infrequent, grievance is, that the nurses are expected to cook their own food, sometimes in the wards; a fact which requires no comment.

"One of the great difficulties for nurses who first take up infirmary work in country unions is the question of the *diet* for their patients. Most specially is this the case in the eastern counties, where suet dumpling is sometimes the only available dinner for patients who are dying! It is true that many of the cases are suffering principally from 'the disease of old age,' but we cannot feel that the best is done for such when they are only supplied with 'house' gruel, tea and sugar, with *no* milk, for breakfast, suet pudding or broth for dinner. The following is a picture of the diet in a country workhouse, which certainly is not favourable to economics or humanity.

"The house diet is all that is provided for the healthy and for the sick. If the patient is very sick the doctor may put him on tea and sugar (no milk) for breakfast, in addition to the house food.

"I did get for two men (who could not take house diet nor keep down the broth, and who therefore had to go without dinner nearly every day in the week), after several weeks' begging, 'light puddings' for dinner, which means bread soaked in milk and water and baked. They have had it now every day for three months, and they are tired of it, but there is nothing else to hope for if they refuse it. I have repeatedly asked the doctor and the matron to vary it, to send rice or sago for a change, but to no purpose; they fear the patients will fare too well. It is nothing unusual to see others trying to get down a piece of bread and cheese saved from the night before, and the house diet standing untouched on the table.

"I find there are six out of the fifteen men who leave their gruel every morning, there is only bread left (no drink) on which to make their breakfasts. On Tuesdays and Saturdays seven of them go without dinner as they cannot eat the heavy suet pudding. On Mondays and Thursdays four go without dinner, three or four of the others are given broth or soup, they, too, would have to go without, yet the soup must be sent and may not be returned. It is waste to make much, knowing it will be given to the pigs. It would be more economical to make less, and send instead some sago, rice, or even fish, for those who cannot eat the ordinary diet. Of course, one dares not think of chops and eggs that patients get in other infirmaries. One poor old man of eighty-five (one of the two who are on light puddings, and who we fear is 'going home'), when he is lucky enough to have a few pence, sends out for an egg to put in his pudding, or for days he goes without, and I feel so sorry for him and for several others. The inmates are allowed to have half-pence and send out to town sometimes. The women fare a little better, for they do get tea at breakfast, and sometimes some dripping with the bread, though three of them do without a dinner twice a week (suet pudding)."

One nurse adds:—"I cannot feel contented when I look about and see what the patients want that I can't get. Perhaps bye-and-bye I shall get used to it and not notice it, but for their sakes I hope not!"

We may add that as an Association we do not, as a rule, advocate the training of probationers in small country workhouse infirmaries, but we know that the nurse who writes so enthusiastically about her work would carry out the system most conscientiously as far as her surroundings admit.

A recent coroner's inquest held at the Newport Work-

house Infirmary shows the very great need there is for a
larger staff of nurses on night duty. The facts are, that
an infant of seven days old was overlaid by its mother
and found dead by the day nurse when she went on
duty. The infirmary wards contain 133 sick people, and
they are looked after during the night by a woman about
sixty years of age, neither skilled in nursing nor certificated,
but with "a good deal of experience in watching the sick."
In the male wards she has a male pauper help, but no
assistance in the women's wards. To add to the difficulties
there are ten or eleven small wards. The medical officer
at the workhouse, in reply to the coroner's question:—
"Supposing she were the most certificated and most
competent woman in the world, would one woman, even
with the assistance of a man, be able to look after 133
patients?" said, "It is an impossible task; it is under
discussion at the present time; it is a chronic subject."
The jury returned a verdict of "accidental death," and
added a rider that "three or four more night nurses were
necessary to look after the patients."

This is only one more of the distressing revelations
which come to light so frequently.

The following is an extract from a letter written to us
by a nurse, not belonging to the association, but who
knows our interest in the question of nursing in workhouse
infirmaries.

"The last ten months has proved to me how very
ignorant country Guardians are of their duties towards the
sick and infirm.

"I fear the pointed remarks appearing in the *Hospital*
from time to time are seldom if ever seen by their clerks.

"Surely in no other branch of the nursing profession

can the work be so very unsatisfactory and discouraging as in a lonely country Union. How one longs for lady Guardians, knowing how helpful they can be.

"I had no idea so little inspection was given. In ten months an Inspector has only been here once, and then he did not inspect, not having come for that purpose. What a boon a lady Inspector would be in such places as this. But, alas, the urgently needed reform seems far, far away.

"I am seriously thinking of giving up working under the Poor Law."

We cannot help asking, are not all these matters such as could, and would, be naturally looked into by an Inspector who, as a woman, would surely be the fittest person to appeal to, and who the nurses would feel would be able to listen to and, if possible, redress their grievances. It is hardly likely that these young women will have the courage to bring them before the gentleman who is usually accompanied on his rounds by the master.[1] If the argument has been acknowledged to be conclusive in the case of several other Public Departments, and has consequently been carried out in practice, it can hardly be denied that it holds good equally, if not still more strongly, in this instance, where the work concerns exclusively the condition of the sick, aged and helpless, whether men or women, and the supervision and control of those who have the responsibility

[1] Here I would venture to make the suggestion (not for the first time) that the Nurse, or Nurses, should be allowed to communicate directly and independently with the Inspector, as I learn with satisfaction is sometimes the case; and surely the same request may be made with regard to the matrons of separated Infirmaries, who should be allowed to report and confer directly with him.

of caring for them, but who, at present, in a majority of instances, have no one to whom they can look up for instruction and advice in their important duties.

That the present condition of Infirmaries and Sick Wards is in a transition state can hardly be denied, and that it was unavoidable, as consequent upon the vast changes that took place 40 years ago in the nursing profession, and the qualifications required in those who entered upon it; it was natural that the Institutions which contained the lowest classes of the population (amongst which the sick were not considered as the most numerous or important) should receive less thought and attention than Hospitals, which claimed to be first served; but making all due allowance for this consideration, we venture to think that the time for change and reform has been unnecessarily, and too long, delayed, while every year the difficulties are increasing.

With the object of giving still further proof and evidence of all that has been stated, I will now quote the well-weighed and valuable experience of a Superintendent of a large Provincial Infirmary, whose long training and subsequent practical work claim the attention which I am sure will be given to her views. We think it will be seen that to endeavour to introduce partial reforms and modern methods into the old Institutions, with their original rules and regulations unrepealed, governed, more-

---

[1] As I write this, I note with satisfaction, that one more forward step has been taken by the Central Board in this direction, in the appointment of Miss Stansfeld as assistant Inspector of Industrial schools and work. And here I may add that it was in 1892 the first Sanitary Women Inspector was appointed at Nottingham, and since then, 18 others in various localities.

over, by a body of men who have no special knowledge of Hospitals, or the needs of the sick, is, as it ever will be, to attempt to put new cloth into an old garment, with the same inevitable and unsatisfactory results.

With regard to the statements which I will now give concerning two of the principal classes of Institutions to which I have referred, I cannot help asking again the obvious question, whether the state of affairs described in them, would not have been *more* likely to be discovered by an Inspector, and *most* likely by a woman, who was familiar with the conditions and management of hospitals? We can hardly believe it possible that such representations as they would have made, could have been overlooked, either by the central Board, or by the Local Board of guardians and managers.

Those who have been made acquainted with the series of articles on Workhouses in England and Ireland, as given by the "Commissioner" employed by the British Medical Journal, and recently reported in it, will hardly be surprised at the statements which follow, for they have been equalled, if not surpassed, in those reports, but it might have been hoped and expected that the publicity already given as to the condition of things in some country workhouses, would ere now have promoted the extension of reforms, so urgently required and called for in a large number of cases.

As to the following statement, I can only say it is a plain narrative of facts, but I have omitted some details I shrink from giving publicity to in these pages. We can hardly suppose that the conditions described are exceptional, and I may add that the writer has been personally known to me for many years.

"I may divide the evils which I personally met with, into those connected with the nursing staff, and administration generally, and those connected with the inmates. I expect —— is typical of the provincial, unseparated Workhouse Hospital. When I first knew it, just 2 years ago, there had only been a Resident Medical Officer for 2 months; the former one, non-resident, came at irregular times, often not till 8. p.m. The dispensing was done by an inmate, a former house-painter, who sold the pills, etc.! The Workhouse is 2 miles away from the town, so there was great delay in getting a doctor when urgently needed.

"There were 3 Hospital blocks, as distinct from the Workhouse itself, and a very good Infectious Block, recently built, for any such disease that might develop amongst the inmates. These 3 Blocks were each divided by folding doors into two, and men were on one side, women on the other; there was only a wall between the airing courts, and doors at each side, the men's opening into the field on which the cottages for the children are built.

"There are 420 beds, and the staff consisted of one male attendant who was originally Labour Master and failed in that capacity; two quite elderly women, untrained, two charge nurses trained for 12 months by the Northern Workhouse Nursing Association at Birmingham and Sheffield, who from want of supervision and despair at the state of things, were hopeless. Then there were five Probationers so-called, girls from the neighbourhood, one a general servant, one only 19, and one 23 years of age, in charge of 76 male patients, the one of 19 being on night duty to that Block for men and women, 147 beds. It was a joke amongst the men to wake her in the morning lying on the sofa in the kitchen. The nurse of 23 slept in a room in the Male Hospital; in fact the nurses slept anywhere, and when arranging for the Resident Doctor's rooms, the matron did not know the nurse was not sleeping there! There were no baths for the nurses and only 3 for 147 patients, and it was a cause of much sneering to the matron and old officers that nurses wanted baths at all.

"Each nurse had her weekly rations given out raw, so much beef, generally ribs, and hardly ever mutton, but I succeeded in getting it for them alternately; they had also tea, sugar, potatoes, flour, yeast, hardly ever vegetables, and never fruit. They cooked for themselves, or got an inmate to do it, and I found in consequence that tea and bread and butter were the principal food of these girls. The supply of clothing was so short, it was the usual plan to strip a ward of pillow-cases, towels and the patients' clothes, to get them washed through by the wardswoman, and put on again, especially for 'Guardians' days.'

"There were of course Wardsmen and Wardswomen, great lazy, cruel people; many a story have we heard of what used to be done.

"The Lying-in Ward, which, until a short time before I went, was only a General Ward, without even Screens, had an old inmate in it who we discovered to have an ulcerated leg and cancer of the breast; yet she did nearly everything for the women and babies, and often delivered them too. The women's hair was not combed, it was 'not lucky' to do so, and washing was at a discount. The Doctor and myself could not imagine at first, why the temperatures went up, and the babies nearly always got bad eyes and did badly.

"The old and infirm were put to bed and kept there, for there was no one to dress them, and the passive cruelty was general; the bed sores were frequent, though called 'Eczema,' and yet what could one nurse, much less an untrained girl, do with 80 to 90 cases under her care?

"When the nurse on the Female side went out, the male attendant took charge, and often went to the rescue when the women were fighting. One of the Probationers once stayed out all night, but nothing was done about it, they were resigned and helpless, and hating nurses like poison! Such a thing as washing patients between blankets was unknown; it created quite an excitement when 'I blanket-bathed' a tramp, dangerously ill and exhausted. They were formerly put into a bath by an inmate, or, left dirty. It was a tradition never to *carry* a patient into Hospital, so unless they had broken limbs, Typhoids, Pneunonias, any one who could crawl, was walked up the front and up stairs. The Doctor told me he had 3 deaths in one day, owing to this, during the Influenza Epidemic. The friends brought in what they liked for the patients, and literally picniced in the wards. After a great struggle I got this stopped, and the first time this took place, we had pork chops, beefsteaks, tinned salmon, and rabbit, cheese, fruit, cakes, and whisky, at the entrance to each Block. Then there was the inevitable bribing by friends to get them attended to, so that the friendless got no attention at all.

"Inmates gave out clean clothes from what we called the Stores, a sort of Store-room in each division, and gave the nicest dresses and best aprons to those who paid 1d. or 2d. for them. The same thing was done with soap, etc., and inmates served all the meals, which were principally cooked at the Hospitals, also by inmates. The Imbeciles did an immense amount of irregular Laundry-work; and all the dirty wash. The consequence of this was, Lock, Lying-in, babies and ordinary crib-case clothing was washed in common. There were pail closets for men and women, across the airing courts at the back of the Hospital, and as there was no accommodation for Nurses sleeping in the Hospitals, they had locked up two of the few closets, and the Epileptics, old men and women alike, had to go outside, winter and summer to those vilely smelling places, holding 5 or 6 people, and no door. There was only one Mortuary for 350 beds, and the bodies had to be carried from the Female Block round outside the Male one, some 8 or 9 minutes walk in snow or rain, in the night, or at any time. This is all remedied now, needless to say, and the patients are classified in separate buildings, and the new wards, fitted with the latest improvements, are going on rapidly to completion.

"The serving of the food by inmates was awful; they stole quantities, sold the milk of the helpless and dying, and the meat of the bed-ridden, the tea and the sugar; it was like watching monkeys more than human beings at first; they filched in every possible way.

"The matron never actively interfered with me, but she had come from the care of 46 sick persons to this work, and had not the least idea of what nursing meant. I was in the midst of a fight for more clothes both for beds and patients, when I left, but the Lady Guardians will carry it through. I think the latest incident since I left shows most clearly the helplessness of the Nurses' present condition. Two of the charge nurses were leaving, both on account of health; when they resigned, the hospital sub-committee asked them the reason, and after much hesitation they said there was too much to do; they could not cook, mind the clothes, superintend the dirty washing, sort and count the clean clothes, and do what ought to be done for the sick. The sub-committee are really anxious to do what is right, it is the outlying guardians who are obstructive; at the full workhouse committee the question was asked why the nurses were leaving, and the sub-committee gave their statement. Immediately it was proposed that they should be refused a testimonial for making complaints, and this after 3 years and a half of hard work, and it was a battle to get this defeated.

"Nurses have no standing; no one knows that better than the master and matron and old officers, and until their position is defined, and the guardians are made to realise they know their work in the same way as the schoolmaster and schoolmistress, so long will they be helpless. One of the guardians wanted to know why I did not wash the patients and do the dressings myself, as I was paid to do it; they do not understand these matters, and the masters and matrons play on this ignorance, and raise terrible difficulties, with no redress, for the unfortunate nurse.

"The only hope is separation, by order, for all infirmaries over 100 or 150 beds, and a legal standing for the nurse; the latter is really the principal point, and would solve endless small, but very grave practical, difficulties. If the nurse were allowed to do her duty, and not be trammelled by ignorant prejudices, things would be very different. There is to be also a better system of selection of candidates; it is quite a chance at present; you may choose and recommend one, and if a guardian has a private grudge against one who votes for the nurse, he will vote against it, and she will lose the post."

The following statement is made by one who has the experience of a Superintendent in a large Infirmary in the metropolitan district separated entirely from all workhouse management and control.

"The local Government-Board has recently urged on Boards of Guardians the desirability of appointing educated gentlewomen, possessing the skill and experience of trained nurses, as matrons. Now the matrons' position in a Poor Law Infirmary is a very ambiguous one at the present time, and there is no regulation in such urgent need of reform as that which relates to it. A few words on this important point before passing on to other questions will not be inopportune.

"When the General order defining the matron's position was issued there was no such thing as trained nursing. The matron was not infrequently some surbordinate official, who without either training or education had risen from the ranks, and possibly was quite fitted to discharge the duties of an office that merely recognised capacity to superintend the kitchen, laundry, and clothing of the patients and other domestic arrangements. She was, in fact, and still is in the eyes of the law, a housekeeper and nothing else. The medical superintendent was really the only person of any education or nursing knowledge in the establishment, and therefore supreme control of all officers, servants and patients, was placed in his hands. We have changed all this now, and if a matron is required to have *professional* qualifications for her office, it is only right that her responsibility in connection with those qualifications, should be legally recognised and defined. The principle which gives a man, and often a *very young* man, absolute control over a community of women, is neither a very sound nor a very wise one, and endless friction and irritation is caused on both sides by a mutually false position. Right or wrong the Matron has in every trifling detail to submit to the judgment of the Medical Superintendent, though she may be far better qualified from its nature to deal with the matter under discussion. The aim of all large Infirmaries should be to train their own nurses, and one of the most essential conditions of success is, that the head of the female staff should be herself a trained nurse, with power to direct and control her subordinates, and responsible directly to the Board for the management of her own department. There is an impression among Medical Superintendents that any alteration in the present antiquated regulation, would tend to lessen their authority, but there is no more reason for supposing this would be the case in an Infirmary, than it is in a Hospital where the same office exists. It is the *overlapping* of duties that causes so much unnecessary friction and brings out the worst, instead of the best, in two persons who might otherwise co-operate most harmoniously. Where there is no obligation to consult, courtesy would step in, and cheerfully yield a point if it were seen to be appreciated, and not looked on as a right. For a Matron to give an order one day to the nursing staff and the Medical Superintendent to reverse it the next, without any previous consultation with her, simply because she had omitted to ask his permission, is as undignified in him as it is lowering to the authority of the Matron, and such possibilities ought never to exist.

"Perhaps one of the most vexatious complications arising out of the present system is the custom that obtains in most Infirmaries of delegating to the Assistant Medical Officer—often a young man fresh from Hospital, without any previous experience of administration,—the full powers of Medical Superintendent, in the absence of that officer from the Infirmary. Armed with brief authority which he is anxious to display to the utmost, and regardless of consequences which do not affect him, he often interferes with the matron's authority in a wholly unwarrantable manner, and has even been known, in one institution, to go the length of threatening to suspend her! There is a strange irony in the anomalies of a situation which makes it possible for a second class officer, whose engagement could at any time be terminated by the Guardians, to be placed in a position of absolute control over a first class officer holding a permanent appointment. It is abuses of this sort which must be remedied before our great State Hospitals can take the position which is their due.

" A word or two on the tone and qualifications of Infirmary Nurses.

"As a matter of fact there is not the least reason why these should not compare favourably with any who are trained at the present time in our large Hospitals. The old prejudice against being associated with the Poor Law is dying fast, and every year the standard of candidates who offer themselves for the work is improving. The probationary system and its three years curriculum now adopted with most satisfactory results in the more advanced Infirmaries has opened out a wide field to the yearly increasing number of young women who are anxious to embrace nursing as a profession and of which a comparatively limited number only can find admission into Hospitals.

"What a contrast the neat, trim probationer from whom the initial requirements of a good education and unimpeachable moral qualifications are required, presents, to the ignorant, and often times vulgar-minded, assistant nurse of ten years ago! What a difference too in the tone of the wards! This is one of the most beneficent of the results following on the practice which is tacitly adhered to in certain Infirmaries of giving the matron a free hand in the selection of candidates. When the guardians reserve to themselves the power to *select*, as well as appoint, their nurses, many unsuitable women are introduced in the staff. Candidates in such cases are usually appointed on the strength of testimonials *only*, which are often misleading, if—as has sometimes happened,—they be not actual forgeries.

"The facilities that a well managed Infirmary has for turning out good nurses and affording valuable opportunities to those anxious to make use of them, cannot be over-estimated. Tact, patience, management, discernment, are essential in every woman who desires to become a nurse, but especially are these qualities necessary in an Infirmary nurse. Chronic cases—so despised in a Hospital ward—call forth the best and highest attributes in nursing, for neglect speedily brings a terrible Nemesis in the shape of bedsores, which are regarded as a deep disgrace. Surgical cases, as represented by accidents, are in a minority compared with Hospitals, but there is a sufficient amount of minor surgery to give a nurse plenty of experience in the preparation of dressings, and certainly to qualify her very efficiently for 'private or district nursing, should her inclinations tend that way on completion of her training.

"It is usual now to engage nurses for alternate day and night duty, either for 3 or 6 months at a time, which is a superior arrangement in every way to that which prevailed some years ago of employing a permanent night staff. The night staff should always be under the control of a highly trained superintendent whose experience should be wide enough to deal efficiently with any emergency that might arise in the night. It is greatly to be desired that the heads of wards should if possible be educated gentlewomen. In their hands practically lies the moulding of the future career of the probationer, and discipline and obedience is more readily yielded to one whose position commands respect. Furthermore the whole tone of the ward is regulated by the charge-nurses, and it is most important that her influence should be for good.

"Perhaps one of the most refining influences which surrounds the modern Infirmary nurse is that derived from the Nurses' Home to which she can retire in peace and comfort when the day's work is over. It is here that the Home life which a nurse too often has to leave behind her when she enters on her career, can be developed unchecked.

"The convenient little bedroom to which she can retire when she wishes to be alone, the comfortable sitting-rooms, and dining-room, with regular hours for everything, cause the wheels of life to run smoothly for the toiler, and make these refinements possible which under former arrangements had no place. A Home Superintendent is necessary to carry out the scheme successfully and that she should be a gentlewoman, possessed of tact and good management, is most desirable. That she unites with these attributes the further qualification of a trained nurse, is perhaps not so

necessary as it is expedient. The times off duty are usually
liberal in an Infirmary where the working day is considerably shorter than it is in the majority of Hospitals. Until
recently, it was usual for Nurses to have a pass out in the
evening from 8 to 10, but this plan has been altered in
most institutions to more appropriate hours in the afternoon. The plan of allowing young women to wander
about the streets after dark, is a very bad one, and it is
to be hoped it will soon give way to a more enlightened
arrangement. So much for the past and present of
Poor Law Infirmaries, what of the future? Their
advantages as training schools for nurses have been
pointed out with the anomalies that cripple their usefulness. A new general order would right many wrongs,
and is urgently needed to bring the nursing department
into harmony with modern ideas and methods. There
is yet another departure long since contemplated but not
as yet having received the sanction of authority (whether
of Parliament or the L. G. B.) and that is, the introduction
of Medical Students. The immediate benefit to the patients
by the establishment of a medical school, with a highly
qualified Staff of Physicians and Surgeons to check and
control the work, would be incalculable, while it would
have the effect of raising Infirmaries from a medical
point of view by placing them in this respect on a footing
with Hospitals. It seems a pity that with so large an
amount of splendid clinical material as they possess, they
should not be utilized and rendered valuable to a larger
section of the community. The future holds glorious
possibilities in store, and there is a golden age yet for
our Poor Law Infirmaries. The seed is even now being
sown; will any of us be spared to reap the harvest?"

Before leaving the subject of separate Infirmaries, I should like to name one recent and considerable step that has been taken in the admission of a limited number of ladies into the Chelsea Infirmary for periods of not less than six months, on payment of a fee for the privilege of gaining a little insight into practical nursing. The ladies who enter under these conditions are mostly sent by the National Health Society and are training as County Council Lecturers, or as Sanitary and Factory Inspectors, and all are women of education and exceptional ability. The scheme was sanctioned five years ago, and the following is a statement of the success that has attended it. " I cannot speak too highly of the way in which the pupils perform all their duties, and the improvement that has gradually but surely followed in raising the tone of the nursing staff, since their introduction; the indirect influence they have had is enormous. They are exactly on the same footing as the probationers, and no difference is made in their work."

The suggestions which I have ventured to make in this chapter would be incomplete if I did not allude more fully to the question which lies perhaps at the root of all others, that of trained nursing in workhouses and infirmaries, and how it is to be procured? The recent order will, it is presumed, render compulsory what has hitherto been only permissory, and as such, been disregarded in many instances. In the course of these pages reference has been made to the one voluntary effort which has undertaken the endeavour to supply women who have gone through some experience and training in hospitals or infirmaries for the workhouse sick, with the exception of the Nightingale Fund, which, as is well known, has also largely assisted these objects. [1] But after an experience extending now over 18 years, it is becoming every year more obvious that these efforts are, and must increasingly become, quite inadequate to the demand.

The first object of the promoters of the "Workhouse Infirmary Nursing Association" was to draw attention to the subject, of which there was little or no knowledge, and still less interest; but as this knowledge grew and extended, it became evident that to meet all the demands upon the Association for the supply of nurses was an impossible task. In the last Report, for 1896, it is stated that 130 applications had been received

[1] THE WORKHOUSE INFIRMARY NURSING ASSOCIATION was founded in 1879, in order to supply Boards of Guardians with competent and duly trained Nurses, the following resolutions having been agreed upon:—

1. That the present state of Nursing in the majority of Workhouse Infirmaries is capable of improvement.
2. That it is desirable to promote the employment of paid and efficiently Trained Nurses in all such Infirmaries.
3. That the appointment of a Hospital-trained Lady Superintendent to be at the head of each staff of Trained Nurses is essential to the efficiency of the system.

The difficulties which Boards of Guardians experience in obtaining the services of trained Nurses are well known. The Association assists Guardians in such circumstances by defraying the cost of training young women, and by engaging them for a definite period to nurse under the Association in Poor Law Institutions. Such Nurses when trained are recommended to Boards of Guardians. The supply is, however, inadequate to meet the demand, and many applications have had to be refused, owing to the want of suitable women. It is therefore desired to train a far larger number of Probationers, the cost of each being about £20 for one year.

from Boards of Guardians, only 73 nurses having been able to be supplied, and as of this number of applicants 24 were for the first time, it is evident that the demand will continue to grow, with the certainty that disappointment and dissatisfaction must follow upon the refusal, after indeed Guardians have been urged to employ trained, rather than untrained, or even Pauper, women as nurses. When we read further that after advertising in the usual way, many Boards receive no replies, we can hardly wonder at their having resort to a source which offers them what they seek for, without any cost or trouble to themselves, beyond the payment of a small subscription, the amount of which is voluntary. But it may be asked what is the limit of our powers to supply the number asked for? and to this the first reply must be, the inadequacy of our funds, for it must be remembered that the cause is not one that excites interest or sympathy, except in the few; it is frequently said that the rates were intended to supply all such wants, and that voluntary charity has no concern with it; and when we state that an income of £600 a year is what is given for our work, it will be readily granted that our task is an impossible one, seeing that the training of a nurse for a year only, costs at least £20, and to this income the sum contributed by Boards of Guardians amounted to only £112. But the lack of funds is not the only hindrance to our work, the lack of suitable candidates, either as nurses or probationers, being an even greater difficulty. Out of 41 already trained nurses who applied to the association in the year, only 18 were considered sufficiently promising to fill up forms, and of these only 4 were ultimately appointed; this fact may be still further enforced, by the difficulty having increased during the last 2 or 3 years, owing to the growing demand for nurses everywhere; out of 316 applicants for training, only 16 were able to be accepted, in addition to a large number who applied by letter. Since the beginning of our work £3,636 has been expended in training.

As to the conclusions to be drawn from these statements, I cannot do better than quote from the Report already alluded to, with reference to the difficulties we meet with. " It is argued that as Metropolitan Infirmaries now train a much larger number of Probationers than formerly, the smaller workhouses should be well supplied with nurses; the fact is, however, that a very small proportion of nurses continue under the Poor Law for many years, and those whose term of agreement at Infirmaries is completed, generally take up work in other fields of nursing. We must add that if Country Unions are to have a proper supply of trained nurses, the conditions under which they work should be made more in harmony with other departments of nursing.... In order to secure the services of such nurses as are required, it is quite necessary that their position should be more clearly defined."—In addition to the facts and reasons here stated, we cannot help adding our conviction that for the work of providing this most important class of officers for our State Institutions, some more organised and official efforts will have to be made by the Department that is responsible for the administration of the Poor Law, and that public funds will have to be provided for this object. The first step to be taken in this direction would be to require the training of Probationers in all the Infirmaries that are large enough to supply it, and that such nurses when trained, should be bound to continue for a fixed period in the service of the department which trained them, with some provision for the future, instead of, as at present, being free to give their services elsewhere, in posts which, naturally, are preferred, as offering far greater attractions; and thus the smaller country workhouses, where the need is greatest, are left entirely beyond the reach of benefit.

In considering the needs of this Department of the Public service, we cannot help alluding to the analogy offered by the Nursing service arrangements of the Army and Navy, where as it seems to us, the inducements and advantages offered to men, might equally well be granted to women. In both systems, the men for Nursing service are engaged, bound for a term of years, paid salaries during training, receive gratuities at the end of their time, and even also pensions, under certain conditions. Now why should not this system be adopted for women in another Department? It is said that they would not be willing to consent to be bound for such long periods, but if this is the case, let the period be shorter, and we do not believe that seven years, or five, would be objected to, with the prospect of some benefit at the end of the time; the status thus given to a Nurse under the Poor Law would go far towards improving her condition, and we have little doubt that many would enter the service on these terms, and with the increased security of position as belonging to a public body.

These advantages of the Men Nurses are not offered to the women who enter the services, but in the instance we are urging, where at present the inducements are far less, why should it not be tried, at least as an experiment, under the present emergency? Even if the money came from the rates, the expense would hardly exceed the present cost of Probationers and Assistant Nurses in Workhouses, seeing that the so-called cheap "Pauper Nursing" is now to be wholly done away with. But supposing this system to be still objected to, there seems to be but one alternative, viz., to render the profession of Poor Law Nursing more attractive and honourable by a greater independence of untrained control, increased comfort, and privileges, such as are enjoyed in other branches of the work. Results would then be found, as in the Army and Navy services, where the applications for admission far exceed the requirements.

It may seem strange that the recent order should have been issued without any reference to the means by which it can be carried out, in reliance, apparently, upon the one private and voluntary association that has hitherto existed, and which, as has been shewn, is utterly inadequate to supply the demand that will now arise. We can claim indeed to have shewn the way, and to have proved the need, but to supply it throughout England is an impossibility which all must acknowledge. Our failure to do so will, we trust, compel the adoption of measures on a scale which can alone be adequate and successful, by the public and recognised authorities who have now issued the order.

I cannot conclude this chapter of suggestions concerning the future, without naming one of the chief "missing links" in our organisations for various classes of the afflicted and destitute. I allude to those children who belong to what are called the semi-imbecile, or feeble-minded, but who cannot be included in the Asylums for Idiots, or certified as such. It may be a surprise to many, as it was to me, to discover the fact, that no special provision is made for any who form that large class, and are to be found in every country Workhouse. Those who hear of the existence of the vast Asylum which for many years has been working at Darenth, may have supposed that it was open to some children who they may have desired to send there, but they will quickly learn that it is for the reception of children from the Metropolitan District alone, and that no others have as yet been provided for by the Authorities.

Why this preference should be shown, and all others be neglected, who equally need the help and training which might possibly save them from life-long pauperism and dependence on the rates, has long been a subject of wonder and regret to many who work on Country Boards of Guardians, and desire to do something for these poor children, who, if they are to receive any benefit, must be placed under the care and instruction of skilled teachers, who also, can only be provided when the numbers are sufficiently large to justify the outlay and cost. I have already given my experience in my story of work in a Country Union, and that is only a specimen of what is going on everywhere, beyond the Metropolitan District. These children are left to the care of no one in particular, but run about in all the wards, without control or training, even when efficient nurses are to be found, who have no time to bestow on these poor creatures, who in the generality of cases must be left to the care of inmates, too often of the lowest character, whether men or women: thus they grow up to be hopeless Idiots, beyond the reach or possibility of amendment; for to endeavour, here and there, to procure admission into the few existing Asylums, maintained for this class of children, is a task which

Guardians cannot be expected to undertake, with faint hopes of success. It has never been denied that such provision is urgently called for, and the subject has been brought forward repeatedly in the Press, and at Poor Law Conferences, by medical men and others, well qualified to deal with it. If, as we are told, the matter is one for County Councils to undertake (as for Lunatic Asylums), and not the Local Government Board, we can only trust that some practical result may shortly be carried out by them. [1]   But the difficulty of dealing with this class of the semi-imbecile, is not confined to children alone, and is one of the most serious that meets us in our dealings with the inmates of Workhouses, and this too is a subject repeatedly brought forward during many years. The adults of this class form a scandal and a disgrace in every Union throughout the land, for I may venture to say that not one is to be found where they are not present; and as matters now stand concerning them, they are likely to continue and even grow in numbers, without check or hindrance. All who have considered the subject agree in believing that the only real and adequate check to the evils of the present system of unrestrained liberty, would be to grant further powers of detention, and I am quite unable to understand the arguments applied to this matter as to the " liberty of the subject," which surely is a mockery and delusion as regards this class, dependent as it is upon the support of the rates. Discussion has frequently taken place, and opinions stated

---

[1] The consideration of the case of feeble-minded children is now taken up by an Association which provides Homes or Schools for them, but it seems impossible that the work can be carried out by voluntary efforts alone, without a far greater support from public funds.

on the evils which all acknowledge to exist, and in 1889 a paper was written and read by me on " The Abuse of Relief to Unmarried Mothers in Workhouse Wards ", at the South Eastern Poor Law Conference, held at Exeter Hall, but the only arguments urged against increased restrictions of liberty, acknowledging that some remedies are imperative, have been that voluntary efforts are being made in establishing Homes for such feeble-minded women and girls as are to be met with in every Union, without indeed any powers of detention, but with the confident hope and expectation that moral influences and restraints will suffice to do all that is needed. It is too soon at present to be able to judge of the success of so recent a movement, even as regards the numbers to be dealt with, but I venture to foretell that it will be quite inadequate for this class of women, while for the corresponding class of men and boys, it must be absolutely impracticable. The vicious instincts and restless desires which are characteristic of these classes, can never be controlled sufficiently to ensure their detention for any length of time, especially when hard work must be part of the system of treatment, as a means of support and maintenance. Neither do we believe that funds supplied by voluntary sources, even with the small payments from the rates, can ever suffice to meet the needs of so large a class as that we are now considering.

That it may not be supposed that these considerations are based upon theory and abstract opinions, I will give two out of hundreds of cases that could be supplied by all who have a practical knowledge of workhouse inmates. In my narrative as Guardian of a Country Union, I mentioned having at last succeeded in getting a child, who was a semi-imbecile, sent to an Asylum for Idiots, at a cost far greater than that of keeping her in the Work-house; she was considered to be improvable, and only such cases were received; her mother was in the Work-house, and had been maintained there for years, being one of the semi-imbecile class; on my visiting the Union soon after I left the neighbourhood, I was in-formed of the distressing fact that she had, some time since, demanded, and taken, her discharge, and after a short absence had returned to her convenient and ever-open Hotel, or rather, in her case, well-appointed Lying-in Hospital, to add still one more burden on the long-suffering ratepayer; and, apparently, there is no limit to her doings in this direction. The next case is from a large London Workhouse, where such a woman as I have just described returned, for the second time, to bring an idiot child into the world (the first one being a lunatic) she herself being not only an imbecile (as we may well call her) but a dwarf.

Can such persons be considered to be responsible for their actions or moral conduct, any more than those who are detained in Lunatic Asylums, and is not their liberty and freedom of action the cause of endless misery and ruin to others besides themselves?

The desire for further powers of detention is not limited to this class alone; no greater problem of difficulty presents itself to all who are working in Poor Law administration than the perpetual and ever-present one of the "Ins and Outs", for no class of Paupers abuses the relief of the Poor Law in the degree that they do; and the officers are powerless to prevent it. It is true that some few additional restrictions have recently been made with regard to the time required for giving notice of discharge, and of the interval that must elapse before the next "outing" is demanded, but all this is of little avail to check the practice, and the abuse of these occasional absences, productive of gross evils to all concerned, but more especially to be deplored when children are involved in the movements, and must be fetched from the District School to accompany the degraded parent, or parents, too often to scenes of misery and vice, they returning to impart their newly acquired experiences to their schoolfellows. I could tell of circumstance during my London Guardian work that would confirm all that I am now stating, were further proof needed, but it cannot be, for the evil is too well-known. [1] I have said that the children have to accompany the parents, but that is not all; too often, someone is met with outside, or sometimes also an inmate, by appointment, who joins the party, and the nights are spent in a manner and in places I will not venture to describe. I cannot help asking, is there any other country in Europe where legal relief is given, and offered, under such attractive conditions as these, and with such direct encouragement to vice and immorality? The master who refuses to give the permission for a few days' outing, knowing how it will be abused, is defeated in his object, and even mocked, by the immediate demand for "discharge," which cannot be refused, and the only result is the additional trouble to himself and his officers in making the necessary entries, which probably gives satisfaction to the applicants.

[1] This matter was dwelt upon in my Letter to the President in 1887, when I was Guardian at Kensington, and acquainted with all these evils.

I cannot help thinking if those who framed such rules as these could for a time act personally as Guardians, and witness the results of their administration, we should find little difficulty in obtaining an alteration which all practical persons desire.

While thus I have been tracing the progress of events during so many years, it will be seen that my first impressions were for the need of greater care and kindness and discrimination in administering the law which was at least intended to be just and merciful in dealing with the Poor who were to be saved by it from starvation, and the results of absolute destitution. That this object has been at least more fully attained in this year of great national rejoicing, by the issuing of the most important Order ever yet framed for the largest class of persons which has to be dealt with, is a matter of unfeigned rejoicing and thankfulness to all who have worked in the cause for many years, and it opens, we would fain believe, a new era in this direction, both of medical care and nursing.

But, as will have been seen from the facts which I have given, other changes, and modifications of plans, are also needed, some in the direction of greater strictness and repression of liberty, if Pauperism is to be reduced in the wealthiest country of Europe.

Finally, looking back on the years that are passed, and remembering the manifold and beneficent changes that have taken place during that time, I am able to believe that the future will bring still more good things, and that ere long we shall see all our wishes fulfilled, in both the directions I have indicated; and in this sentence I will sum up my "last thoughts about Workhouses."

PARAGRAPH

CONNECTING CHAP. 7 WITH CHAP. 8

ALTHOUGH, as I have said, my object in the preceding chapters, has been to deal with the condition and treatment of the indoor, rather than the outdoor, poor, the question of out-relief as connected with the latter class, is nevertheless so important a matter in the administration of the Poor Law, that I feel justified in adding the following chapter, written some years ago, but now out of print, which gives some statements concerning the condition of things at the time when the new act was introduced. The study of ponderous Blue Books is not attractive, and thus many who ought to be conversant with past history, are wholly ignorant of it as regards these important questions which affect so closely the condition of the poorer classes in this country. I therefore venture to hope that the abstract once again offered to my readers, will be acceptable to many besides guardians of the poor, by whom, of course, the subject should be carefully and diligently studied, if they are in any way to be fitted for the high and responsible duties which they have undertaken; duties which concern not only thousands of our poorer fellow creatures, but the classes above them, who have chosen them for their representatives.

CHAPTER VIII

OUTDOOR RELIEF IN ENGLAND

Extracts from the Report of the Commissioners in 1834, *and from the Writings and Speeches of various Authorities to* 1888.

As the subject of outdoor relief has lately been prominently brought before the public in the discussions on the Local Government Bill, it may be useful to give a few extracts from the Report of the Commission appointed in 1834 to investigate the whole matter, previous to the introduction of the Poor Law Amendment Act of that year.

The evils which had at that time become widespread and flagrant are not known to the present generation, who may not be able or willing to search the annals of Blue Books to discover them.

As there appears to be a tendency at the present time in some quarters to revert to former systems, it cannot but be helpful to give some details of the existing condition of things concerning pauperism more than fifty years ago, forgotten by many and unknown to more.

At the beginning of the Report of the Commissioners we read, "the great source of abuse is the outdoor relief afforded to the able-bodied on their own account, or on that of their families. This is given either in kind or in money; but the latter is still more prevalent."

Instances are then given from various parts of England detailing the abuses of the different systems of relief, and the following remarks are made:—

" Out-relief is that now most extensively given, and it appears to contain in itself the elements of an almost indefinite extension; of an extension, in short, which may ultimately absorb the whole fund out of which it arises. Among the elements of extension are the constantly diminishing reluctance to claim an apparent benefit, the receipt of which imposes no sacrifice, except a sensation of shame, quickly obliterated by habit, even if not prevented by example; the difficulty, often amounting to impossibility on the part of those who administer and award relief, of ascertaining whether any and what necessity for it exists; and the existence in many cases of positive motives on their parts to grant it when unnecessary, or themselves to create the necessity."

" Another evil connected with outdoor relief, and arising from its undefined character, is the natural tendency to award to the deserving more than is necessary, or, where more than necessary relief is afforded to all, to distinguish the deserving by extra allowances . . . It appears that such endeavours to constitute the distributors of relief into a tribunal for the reward of merit, out of the property of others, have not only failed in effecting the benevolent intentions of their promoters, but have become sources of fraud on the part of the distributors, and of discontent and violence on the part of the claimants."

" A common consequence is that, to satisfy the clamours

15

of the undeserving, the general scale of relief is raised; but the ultimate result of such a proceeding appears always to be to augment the distress which it was intended to mitigate, and to render more fierce the discontent which it was intended to appease. Profuse allowances excite the most extravagant expectations on the part of the claimants, who conceive that an inexhaustible fund is devoted to their use, and that they are wronged to the extent of whatever falls short of their claims. Such relief partakes of the nature of indiscriminate almsgiving in its effects as a bounty on indolence and vice; but the apparently legal sanction to this parochial almsgiving renders the discontent on denial the most intense. Wherever, indeed, public charities are profusely administered, we hear from those who are engaged in their administration complaints of the discontent and disorders introduced." "It appears, from all our returns, that in every district the discontent of the labouring classes is proportioned to the money dispensed in Poor's Rates, or in voluntary charities."

Again, "It appears to the pauper that the Government has undertaken to repeal in his favour the ordinary laws of Nature; to enact that the Children shall not suffer for the misconduct of their parents, the wife for that of the husband, or the husband for that of the wife; that no one shall lose the means of comfortable subsistence, whatever be his indolence, prodigality, or vice—in short, that the penalty which, after all, must be paid by some one for idleness and improvidence is to fall, not on the guilty person or on his family, but on the proprietors of the lands and houses encumbered by his settlement."

Let us note the following remarks of fifty years ago on a subject recently dwelt upon as important:—

"Uniformity in the administration of relief we deem essential as a means, first, of reducing the perpetual shifting from parish to parish, and fraudulent removals to parishes where profuse management prevails from parishes where the management is less profuse; secondly, of preventing the discontents which arise among the paupers maintained under the less profuse management, from comparing it with the more profuse management of adjacent districts; and, thirdly, of bringing the management, which consists in details, more closely within the public control. . . . The importance of uniformity in reducing removals appears throughout our evidence. We have found that the confirmed paupers usually have a close knowledge of the detailed management of various parishes (although the managers rarely have), and act upon that knowledge in the choice of workhouses." "The notion generated by the indefiniteness of the existing system of relief is that the Poor's Rates are an inexhaustible fund, from which all who call themselves poor are prevented drawing to the extent of their desires only by the cupidity or partiality of parish officers." *

To these extracts we may add that there was a general consensus of opinion at the Central Conference of Guardians held in 1882, that we should try to return to the state of things in the early part of last century, when (to

* One of the propositions to the Select Committee agreed to by the Charity Organisation Society is as follows:—"The latitude permitted to Guardians has been the source of much mal-administration of the law. Continuity and uniformity of practice have been altogether unattainable. Such success as has been achieved has been the result of the action of individual Guardians; at their retirement, or during their temporary absence, the lax system returns."

use the words of the Royal Commissioners of 1834) "Parochial relief appears to have been given chiefly through the workhouses, and not to have been extended to many beside the impotent. Relief was considered a burden to the payers, and a degradation to the receivers, a remedy for unexpected calamity, and a mitigation of the punishment inflicted by Nature on extravagance and improvidence. The paupers were a small and disreputable minority. All other classes were anxious to diminish the number of applicants, and to reduce the expense of their maintenance."

"One would have thought that all who are aware how nearly the nation was brought to ruin, moral and financial, in the three first decades of this century, must agree that every man should be encouraged to feel that he has descended in the scale of manhood when he gives up the task of independence allotted to him by Providence, and throws himself upon the forced contributions of his neighbours."—GENERAL L. GARDINER.

The following opinions were expressed before the Lords' Committee on Poor Law Relief, 1888:—

"If outdoor relief were abolished, charity would receive such an impetus that it would prove sufficient. He thought it was the business and duty of the rich to take up cases of deserving distress ... It is hopeless to look for much improvement unless the present too wide discretion of the Guardians is curtailed, and by legislation and Orders of the Local Government Board the progress that has already been made is made general and permanent"—MR. A. G. CROWDER, Guardian of St. George's-in-the-East.

"Outdoor relief was a direct and positive injury to the working classes, apart from the moral injury; and he believed that for every penny given in outdoor relief, two pence was taken from wages."—MR. ALBERT PELL, Guardian of St. George's-in-the-East.

The Rev. C. H. Turner, Rector of St. George's-in-the-East, said, "In his opinion, the administration of outdoor relief had a great tendency to make the poor more improvident than they were already, and indisposed them to take advantage of savings banks and provident funds. It was also detrimental to their moral character, in not only making them dependent, but it had a great effect on their relations. It also acted as a stimulus to increasing the population, because of improvident marriages."

Mr. Hedley, Local Government Board Inspector in the Metropolitan District, said, "He would like to see outdoor relief abolished as far as possible. It operated most injuriously on thrift and on the general providence of the labouring classes. Relief ought only to be given to the destitute, and when given, it ought to be adequate. Outdoor relief, as at present administered, was always inadequate to meet destitution, and was mostly given in aid of unknown resources. It also had a very baneful effect on charity, which it stifled."

Mr. J. S. Davy, Poor Law Inspector for Lancashire and Yorkhire, "disapproved labour yards and the labour test, and advocated the entire abolition of outdoor relief."

Mr. W. Vallance, Clerk to the Whitechapel Poor Law Guardians, said. "Their policy up to 1870 was that of meeting apparent existing needs by small doles of outdoor relief. The experience of the winter 1869-70 taught that the system fostered pauperism, improvidence, and imposture, without helping the poor, and the Guardians began by gradually restricting outdoor relief in out-of-work cases, until they were enabled to suspend entirely the Outdoor Relief Regulation Order. No cases of out-relief other than those of sudden and urgent necessity had been added to the list for nearly eighteen years. The change of policy had resulted in a diminution of indoor as well as outdoor pauperism, and in an improvement of the condition of the poor."

Mr. W. H. Long, Parliamentary Secretary to the Local Government Board, in addressing a meeting of his constituents in April, 1888, said, "He had no sympathy for the able-bodied pauper, who ought not to exist. There was no greater mistake than to suppose that because the Poor Rate fell directly upon the occupiers of land or houses they alone felt the weight of the burden. There was nobody upon whom it fell with greater heaviness than upon the thrifty and industrious labourer and the artisan. It was the greatest drain upon the capital of the country, and it was to capital that the working man had to look for his wages, and if by any law or foolish administration of outdoor relief with a lavish hand they brought up the Poor Rate to the extent it reached in the early part of the century, they would bring upon themselves a ruinous burden. The outdoor paupers of England and Wales were as eight to one compared with the indoor paupers."

In a recent paper on the English Poor Rate, by Major P. G. Craigie, he remarked "on the reforms effected in particular Unions, where, without either driving paupers into the house or out of the Union, the cases of out-relief were reduced from 1,100 to 66, and 10d. per pound saved in the annual outlay. The conclusions drawn were that the statistics of pauperism showed it to be a largely preventible disease, which could be restricted with benefit to the poor and relief to the ratepayers at the will of the local authorities... The all-powerful democracy of the day should be impressed with the proved danger of out-relief, and the proved economic benefit of a strictly-administered Poor Law should be insisted on. The single obligation of the Guardians to relieve destitution should not be confounded with the relief of distress and hard cases by charity, which is totally outside the functions of the Poor Rate; nor should it be overlooked that a system of outdoor relief, so far from an advantage to the labourer, exposed the lower working class to an unfair competition on the part of those who, deriving part of their support from the Poor Rate, could afford to sell their labour for an inadequate remuneration."

"Where there is a moderate stringency in enforcing orders for the workhouse, there pauperism, indoor as well as outdoor, diminishes, and the Poor Rate diminishes... One experienced relieving officer, expresses himself thus: 'No relieving officer, no outdoor relief,' the mere existence and presence of the relieving officer originating outdoor relief. The time has arrived for causing outdoor relief to cease altogether—not abruptly, but by gradual and systematic steps ... No doubt it would create much surprise to perceive how easily outdoor relief would disappear without any one being the worse for its disappearance; while the indoor relief would not be increased. By not being able to look forward to outdoor relief as a last resort, a general thriftiness would be created, by which persons would provide for the future needs of themselves and their families. For those who investigate cases know that scarcely a case of destitution arises which is not produced from excessive improvidence or by worse conduct." — Mr. N. A. Rock.

"Labourers earning good wages are to be encouraged to spend them in drink or wastefulness, in place of insuring themselves against the claims of sickness and old age in a sound friendly society, and then to 'cadge' upon their thrifty neighbours in order to protect themselves from the legitimate consequences of their own immoral conduct. Anything more socialistic or demoralising in its effects cannot be conceived. . . . If the drinking, wasteful workman has a right to outdoor relief at all from his thrifty, sober neighbours, he has a right to a very great deal more than he now gets, and his out-relief should feed, clothe, and warm him, besides paying his rent. I need scarcely say that it does nothing of the kind; but all this is done for him in the Union house. When the demoralisation of the labouring classes has been sufficiently effected by well-intentioned but short-sighted philanthropists, and rates raised accordingly, we shall find ourselves in the condition of things which preceded the new Poor law."—Mr. G. R. Portal.

There is a still further expression of opinion by Mr. Albert Pell, whose evidence has been already given: "It would seem that there has never been a time when the object of the Poor Law should be more clearly ascertained, expounded, and strictly observed, than at the present, seeing that it contemplates the relief of destitution, not poverty, and that its proper function is rather one of police than of charity."

"In relieving destitution out of the Poor Rate, a reference to the character of the applicant should not in the Board Room influence the Guardians, whose official duty there is simply to relieve destitution with other people's money.

For the worst character they are bound to do this, adequately and humanely; for the best character ('deserving' is the stock phrase) they should officially do nothing more. If they do, they are relieving, not the so-called 'deserving' pauper (or 'industrial pensioner'), but his neighbours from fulfilling duties which generous feeling and Christian teaching suggest and insist on, and which, if not interfered with, have hitherto proved equal to the occasion. The idea expressed in and out of Parliament, that a strict administration of the Poor Law will fill the workhouses, is contradicted by fact and experience. A withdrawal of outdoor relief acts as a tonic by which the disease (for disease it is) of pauperism is counteracted and subdued; and, with the decline of the disease among outdoor cases, the numbers of indoor cases drop, or at all events are not swelled, while the natural stimulus to industry and self-preservation, so cruelly sapped and hindered by the expectancy of outdoor relief, comes again into action, and the whole tone and circumstances of the poor are slowly but certainly bettered . . . . Experience, to those who have studied the matter, proves beyond doubt that bounty out of the Poor Rate, prompted as it frequently is by the most selfish motives masquerading as charity, is one of those tender mercies which, in its effect on the poor themselves, specially poor children, is cruel in the extreme."

That the amount of pauperism is mainly caused by and mainly dependent upon the encouragement given to it in various localities is a fact beginning to be recognised. The following statistics from a Northamptonshire Union are striking and instructive as to the decrease of pauperism during the last fifteen years. The amount of outdoor relief given in 1873 was £5,618; in 1888 it was £491, while the number of indoor paupers remained the same; the proportion of indoor to outdoor was about 2 to 1, and the proportion of paupers to population was 1 to 74.

We may add the concluding paragraph of the annual report of this Union:—"The moral and social saving, which is of course the most important, cannot be so plainly tabulated; but it may be permissible to note one very gratifying feature of it—viz., that very many who would otherwise have been on the relief list as children with their parents, have, during these last fifteen years, grown up into manhood and womanhood without receiving any sort of help from the Poor Rates; and the general experience is that those persons who as children know nothing of the relieving officer or the parish doctor, and hear nothing of their parents going to the Board of Guardians, do not as men and women make the Poor Law their first resource in times of difficulty and need . . . In 1873 there were on the out-relief lists no less than 254 children, and during the last half-year only two; at the present time there is no child at all receiving out-relief, nor has there been for the last two months. Though there were so many children having out-relief, there were as many in the workhouse then as since—viz., twenty-six in January, 1873, and 1888."

Does not this statement help to prove the fact that the manufacture of paupers and pauperism is both practicable and easy?

The following is from the report of the Bradfield Union:—"Previous to 1876 all widows with children received out-relief as a matter of course, and one of the results was that the sons and daughters of aged or infirm widows made the receipt of it an excuse for not assisting to support them. Impressed with this and other evils, the Guardians in 1876 resolved to give no more out-relief to widows after the first month of their widowhood, except in temporary cases of sickness, but to offer the house to destitute widows with their children; or, if they preferred it, to take all their children except one into the house. . . . Improvident marriages have certainly decreased, and thrift after marriage has certainly increased; this is, however, no doubt, in a great measure, due to the restriction (almost abolition) of all out-relief in the Union and only in part to that of widows able-bodied. Widows can claim, and do obtain, full current wages for their services. Sons and daughters support the aged and infirm widows. Begging by widows' children, once so common, if not yet extinct, has so much decreased that I never hear of it, and they attend school as regurlarly as their neighbours. A long experience has clearly shown that 90 per cent, of the pauperism of the rural districts is *created* by out-relief."

Extracts from speeches in Parliament on the Local Government Bill, 1888 :—

Mr. Ritchie, President of the Local Government Board, said, " As far as he knew, there was no recommendation from any responsible body—any Commission or Committee—to the effect that there should be a contribution towards outdoor relief. There had, however, been a very large number of recommendations in favour of giving some relief from a particular kind of property towards indoor pauperism. Although he was very far from saying that in most cases outdoor relief had been unduly or lavishly given, yet all reformers had striven against the tendency which had existed in some parts of the country towards lavish expenditure on outdoor pauperism. Where outdoor relief had been recklessly administered it had done a great deal of injury to the people."

Mr. Rathbone (Liverpool) " objected to any proposal which would lead to laxity in giving outdoor relief. He maintained that outdoor relief had always had the effect of lowering wages. . . . It was doing away with what was now a bribe or inducement to give outdoor relief with the idea that it was cheaper than indoor relief. They knew, by a most fatal experience, how this idea of the old Poor Law demoralised the whole character of the rural population, and a considerable part of the urban population of this country . . . Cases of deserving poor ought to be dealt with, to a large extent, by private or organised charity, and could alone be advantageously dealt with in that manner. If they bore in mind the immense importance of preserving the independence of character, and encouraging providence in our population, they should seek to put the relative position of indoor and outdoor relief on such a footing as would discourage that laxity which so rapidly encouraged pauperism and demoralisation . . . . The effect of a similar system in the East End of London had not only been to discourage idlers to rely on the rates, but had been also to encourage the action of the wealthier classes in providing adequate relief in its best form to the deserving poor. He wished that all hon. members remembered, as he did, the introduction of the new Poor Law. At that time the state of the country was such that our working classes were paupers, and our working women were becoming prostitutes. The Government of the day had the courage to bring in a Bill which caused such an outcry as few younger men had heard. It would have been possible for the Conservative Party of that day to have raised a great outcry, but what did the Duke of Wellington do? He came forward and said that he had never known a more courageous act than the introduction of the new Poor Law by the Government of that day, and that he and his party would support them through it."

Mr. W. H. Long thought " it would be generally admitted that the administration of the Poor Law by the Boards of Guardians in recent years had shown that they had endeavoured to realise what a wise application of the Poor Law really meant. They had recognised that it was their duty, not to administer the rates as if they were charitable resources placed at their disposal, but a demand on the pockets of the people, the deserving poor included."

Mr. F. S. Powell thought " that a consideration of the Report of the Commission which had inquired into pauperism before the passing of the Poor Law Amendment Act in 1834 would be a warning to those who spoke blindly as to the tests imposed at that time, especially with regard to the condition of the rural districts .... While he did not believe that it was possible entirely to dispense with indoor relief, he thought that legal relief ought to be diminished as far as possible, and that voluntary and charitable relief ought to be increased. When he heard hon. members making speeches in that House about sending poor people to the workhouse he doubted whether the rich classes were doing their duty. Poor people were often relieved at the expense of the ratepayers when they ought to be relieved by their wealthy neighbours. He could not agree that indoor relief manufactured a whole generation of paupers, and it was undoubted that much

mischief was done by outdoor relief. He should like to
see more undertaken by private benevolence and less by
Poor Law relief. The proposal of the Government would
undoubtedly discourage out-door relief, and, so far, it
would be advantageous."

Viscount Ebrington said, "There was a time when
outdoor relief was freely given in this country, and he
supposed the labouring population were never in a more
miserable condition. Wages were almost always lowest in
those localities where outdoor relief was most freely given."

As reference has been made to some Poor Law Unions
where the giving of out-relief has been greatly restricted, if not
done away with, we add an extract from the last report
issued by the Guardians of Whitechapel, to March, 1888:— *

"The policy of relief administration in Whitechapel has
undergone a marked change during the last twenty years.
Up to 1870 the system may be said to have been that
of meeting apparent existing circumstances of need by
small doles of outdoor relief. . . . The experience of the
winter of 1869-70, however, was such as to lead the
Guardians to review their position and earnestly to aim
at reforming a system which was felt to be fostering
pauperism and encouraging idleness, improvidence, and
imposture, whilst the 'relief' in no true sense helped the
poor. It was seen that voluntary charity largely consisted of indiscriminate almsgiving; that it accepted no
definite obligation as distinct from the function of
Poor Law relief; that the Poor Law was relied upon

* It is much to be desired that this example were followed in all
unions, and annual reports published for the enlightenment, not
only of Guardians, but of all ratepayers, who ought to, and might
thus, take an intelligent interest in these matters.

to supplement private benevolence; that the almsgivers too frequently were the advocates of the poor in their demands upon the public rates; and that both Poor Law and charity were engaged in the relief of distress, much of which a thoughtless benevolence and a lax relief administration had created .... They began by gradually restricting outdoor relief in 'out of work' cases, until they were able entirely to suspend the Outdoor Relief Regulation Order, and to apply strictly the principle of the Prohibitory Order .... Thus the door of out-relief became gradually closed, and, as a fact, no cases—other than those of sudden or urgent necessity, relieved by the relieving officers in kind—have now for nearly eighteen years been added to the outdoor relief lists .... These progressive results have not been accompanied by a proportionate, nor even an appreciable, increase in the number of indoor paupers relieved .... This is probably owing, in part, to the discouragement which the system has produced to speculative applications for relief, and, in part, to the concentration of official and voluntary effort upon the dispauperisation of the poor. There is also reason to believe that the policy which has been pursued has resulted in an improvement in the condition of the poor. Rents are said to be better paid, and more money to be deposited in savings and penny banks than formerly; whilst publicans and pawn-brokers are equally lamenting the badness of trade. The poor are certainly more self-respecting than they were ... So uniform and strict has become the administration of legal relief, and so well understood is the system, that an application for prospective outdoor relief is now rarely made to the Guardians. By 'prospective' relief is to be understood relief other than that already afforded by the relieving officer under circumstances of urgent necessity, and submitted to the Guardians for review merely .... The main object and design of the new Poor Law being to relieve destitution, not to do the work of charity, the principle was affirmed that in such relief 'the condition of the pauper ought to be on the whole less eligible than that of the independent labourer,' whilst the relief should be adequate to his wants .... The practice of almost uniform outdoor relief, taken in conjunction with the legal right which exists, amounts to a vast provision of State aid for every ill that flesh is heir to. Superseding, too, as it does, the necessity for the exercise of self-denial or prudent forethought, the poor are educated to dependence, being practically told that every recurring misfortune or contingency of life will be amply met out of the public rates; whilst they are demoralised by the knowledge that the adversity which flows from idleness, intemperance, or improvidence, is rewarded by an eligible form of relief at the expense of the industrious, thrifty, and self-reliant."

In fact, the Poor Law has been claimed as a " National Club," upon which the poor have a claim given them by the law, and which they mean to enforce.

In connection with these extracts we will add some from the Report of the Select Committee of the House of Lords on Poor Relief, 1888:—

" This decrease [of pauperism] must, to a great extent, be ascribed to the more strict and efficient administration of the law by Boards of Guardians, and especially to the restriction of out-relief. While admitting that where no organised method of charity has been established, outdoor relief cannot, without hardship to the poor, be dispensed with in certain cases, we cannot too strongly insist on the disastrous results which are certain to follow from outdoor relief if not very carefully administered, and kept within narrow limits—not only in bringing heavy burdens on the ratepayers, but, what is far more important, in demoralising the working class by the discouragement of thrift and honest industry. . . . In the case of the aged and infirm who are of respectable character, it is a very general practice to give out-relief, which usualy takes the form of small weekly doles, insufficient for the support of the pauper, and which, from the difficulty of ascertaining the true circumstances of the recipient, especially in large towns, are frequently granted to persons who are not really destitute. Such doles are eked out either by private charity or some aid from relatives, or by slender earnings; in which latter case, to the extent to which the person who is assisted in that way obtains employment, there is no doubt a tendency to reduce the rate of wages for services of that particular character . . . . Frequently, also, if the doles were withdrawn, it would be found that there are relatives who are in a position to afford the necessary support, and who would do so when aid was not forthcoming from the rates."

The importance attached to the subject of out-relief is shown by the various Orders and Reports issued from time to time by the Central Board concerning its administration. In 1844 the " Outdoor Relief Prohibitory Order" permitted such relief for able-bodied paupers only " on account of sudden and urgent necessity, of illness, and, with certain restrictions, in the case of widows." Again, in 1852 some alteration was made, and in 1869 an important Report was given by the President of the Local Government Board, in order to induce Boards of Guardians rigidly to

16

insist upon the main principles of the English Poor Law, especially the workhouse test. In 1871 a fresh circular was issued, in which the question of the grant of outdoor relief was specially discussed. Again, in 1878, the chief points of the former Order were recapitulated and enforced. Besides these, the reports of numerous Inspectors bear upon the subject, and Poor Law Conferences took the matter up, with the result that the percentage of outdoor paupers had fallen from 4·6 in 1871 to 3·0 in 1883.

It is the opinion of the learned German Dr. Aschrott, who has made an elaborate study of the English Poor Law, that public relief should be given to the able-bodied, but he adds, " If this is introduced, their labour must be fully employed in return for the relief afforded. If an evil effect on the social life of the nation is to be avoided, this relief must be subject to the condition of shutting up the paupers within the four walls of an institution, and thus limiting their personal freedom. Whether such institution should be a workhouse or a pauper colony is a further question which can only be answered in view of local circumstances. The relief of the able-bodied cannot be carried on without regulations which are to a certain extent penal."

Again, he remarks, " It is significant that in England Poor Law relief is extended to one class of persons to whom it would not be afforded in Continental States, and in whose case serious danger is caused by an ill-considered system of relief. This class is that of the able-bodied poor. In England the obligation exists to relieve the destitute man who prefers to have recourse to the Poor Law rather than maintain himself. . . . The able-bodied class could not be indulgently treated without the exercise of a demoralising influence on the general working population." *

A remarkable investigation was made a few years ago into the "Causes of Pauperism" by the Committee of the Manchester Board of Guardians, and published in the Local Government Chronicle, March, 1884, with the following results:—Ten classes were described, and from the total of each class it was found that more than half, or above 51 per cent, of the cases were caused directly from drinking habits; in men, one-fourth arose from drunkenness, but in women, only one-twentieth of the pauperism was chargeable to this cause. It is a remarkable fact that "want of employment" amounted to only one-fortieth part of the pauperism. And this fact is found to agree with the results arrived at by the Mansion House Committee in 1887, which investigated the case of the unemployed.

It was stated at Manchester that "it is a fact of serious import that the majority of cases which become chargeable from drunkenness are men in skilled employments. . . . Many of the children of drunkards have to be maintained and educated, and the class of widows and children of such persons produces about one fifth of the pauperism." The Report concludes with these words: "We have the very serious fact that almost all the pauperism we have to deal with arises from causes which come into operation during the adult period of the life of those who make application for relief; and that whilst nearly one-half of the destitution arises from sickness, accident, and misfortune, a full half is produced by wilful self-indulgence in vicious

* A law still exists in Prussia for the relief of the able-bodied, but it has completely fallen into disuse.

habits." We cannot help adding the inquiry whether a large portion of the "sickness and accidents" might not also be referred to the same cause? We believe there can be no doubt as to the answer.

The same investigation revealed the fact that pauperism caused by old age and infirmity accounted for one-eighth of the whole number. Were this the case to a still larger extent, how willingly should we all contribute our share towards their comfort and maintenance; but here we must not omit a remark which follows, as regards even this class of inmates, and which is too important to be overlooked, as bearing upon former comments on the results of legal relief;—"The most discouraging aspect of some of these cases is that sons and daughters who have emigrated do not send money to assist their aged parents." Why should they, when they are well cared for from another and a legal source on which they have a claim?

As the argument most frequently used in urging outdoor rather than indoor relief is its economy, we may quote again from the book previously referred to. * The apparent simplicity of outdoor relief, and its advance of costly establishments, with all their attendant expenditure, is at first attractive, especially when the humane side of the question is added to the financial plea. "The objection is one to which we should attach little weight, even admitting its accuracy. It has been often shown that in the case of a Poor Law system the main question is, and must be, what kind of relief is most for the interest of the community, for the advantage of the State; and the question of expense is subordinate to this consideration. The objection is, in truth, very short-sighted. People

* "The English Poor Law" by Dr. Aschrott.

only ask what expense will be incurred by the relief of a given number of paupers in this or the other fashion, and omit to reflect that the tendency of the workhouse, under a proper Poor Law system, is to reduce the number of persons relieved .... Accordingly, any temporary increase in expenditure will be amply balanced in the course of years by the saving consequent on the reduction of pauperism."

With regard to the objection of inhumanity, we may close these remarks with a quotation from the Report of 1834, which bears upon the subject of legislating for extreme cases, instead of on general principles:—"Where cases of real hardship occur, the remedy must be applied by individual charity, a virtue for which no system of compulsory relief can be, or ought to be, a substitute."

The term "legal charity," which was employed by some writers sixty years ago who objected to the action of the Poor Law, was not applicable to the system founded by the Act of Elizabeth, 1601, the object of which was to repress pauperism, and not to indulge humane impulses; and it is somewhat remarkable that nearly all questions of Poor Law reform have been in the direction of reverting to the principles of that Act, the three divisions of which are still adhered to—viz., the relief of the infirm, the needs of the able-bodied, and the education of the pauper children.

In further confirmation of these principles, we add some extracts from the Report of one of the Inspectors for 1887-8, which deals most fully with the subject of outdoor relief—that by Mr. Fleming, comprising the districts of Dorset and Southampton, and parts of Wilts and Surrey. The number of outdoor paupers is more than four times as great as the indoor; and with regard to this he writes:—"The lavish administration of out-relief, to which I referred last year as the unfavourable feature of administration in this district, unfortunately continues. . . . It is not easy to arrive at any sufficient reason why the Guardians choose to give so much outdoor relief in the counties under my observation. Beyond question, there are a great many more out-paupers than there need or should be. In many instances those who need relief do not get it, whilst it is given to those who are not really in distress; or, if real destitution do exist, the amount of relief afforded is cruelly inadequate. . . . So much unsound doctrine with regard to Poor Law administration has of late been suggested as worthy of acceptance, that it seems almost impossible that the true position of the question can have been appreciated by those who now advocate a form of relief which had the fullest trial, and led to such dire misfortune, in the earlier part of this century. The condition of affairs in the days when out-relief was administered without the present salutary checks has been so much lost sight of that Guardians are astonished when they are told that before the introduction of the 'new Poor Law' the Poor Rates in many parishes ranged from 8s. to 21s. in the pound upon the ratable value. Even now many Guardians will argue that out-relief is cheaper than indoor relief, because the applicants will be satisfied with 1s. 6d. out-relief, whereas they would cost 3s. 6d. in the workhouse, regardless of the fact that ten applicants will take out-relief for one who will accept indoor relief. In other words, 14s. will go for out-relief against 3s. 6d. for indoor relief.

"Again, the argument is constantly used that indoor relief is much more disgraceful than out-relief, and the poor would rather die than come into the house. Surely no argument could well be more fallacious. Outdoor relief and indoor relief are equally disgraceful. The one, as fully as the other, implies an admission on the part of the applicant that his means are unequal to his necessities, and that he is therefore obliged to become a burden upon the ratepayers for his support. This entails, as a necessary consequence for the protection of society, a most thorough and minute inquiry into all his private affairs and those of the individuals who are legally liable for his support. The pauper who accepts indoor relief allows the extent of his necessity to be submitted to a complete test, and he gives the best work of which he may be capable in return for the relief afforded to him. The outdoor pauper, in practice, submits to no adequate test of destitution, and gives nothing whatever in return for the burden he places upon the rates. Surely, as a question of disgrace, the man who submits to the workhouse test, and who gives all he can give in return for what he obtains, is far away in a more honourable position than the man who submits to no adequate test, who takes all he can get from the rates, and who gives nothing whatever in return. It is undeniable that an enormous amount of fraud is practised to obtain outdoor relief, and that there can be little fraud in the grant of indoor relief.... It may fairly be assumed that the workhouse inmates represent the tested State pauperism of the country. The outdoor relief, on the other hand, includes an unascertained, and almost unascertainable, amount of imposition.... There is the further argument that out-relief must be given to prevent the breaking-up of the 'happy little homes' of the poor. What relief, however, is given with this object? Too often 1s. or 1s. 6d. and a loaf. And to what homes is this given? Too often to homes where there is known to be habitual drunkenness, where there are illegitimate children, where prostitution (veiled or unveiled) is carried on, where there is overcrowding, where the house is in an unsanitary condition, and in endless other cases where it would be infinitely better both for pauper and ratepayer that the home should be broken up. It is evident that where homes are kept together by the miserable amounts frequently given as relief, either there must be imposition as to the means of the applicants, or it would be very much better that the paupers should go into the house, where their necessities would be wholly provided for.... The hardship of breaking up the very few homes which it might otherwise be desirable to maintain would be very much less than the evil of making the thrifty help to maintain the homes of the unthrifty. Moreover, the support of such homes as might with advantage be maintained is essentially within the province of charity rather than of poor relief.... As to the statement that applicants would rather die than go into the workhouse, and that their independent spirit should be commended for such a determination, it may be questioned whether such independence of spirit is in truth deserving of the smallest encouragement. The objection on their part is, not to become a burden upon their fellow-creatures, but to the receipt of relief in a form which is unacceptable to themselves. The individuals who are too independent to go into the workhouse are perfectly willing to burden the ratepayers with as much out-relief as they can succeed in obtaining from the Guardians. No admiration can be too great for the real independence of spirit which prefers to suffer any extremity rather than admit defeat in the battle of life, or consent to become a burden upon others; but this real independence has no place in the class of case now under consideration .... The remarks I venture to place before the Board on the all-important subject of relief to the poor may be unpopular, and may be miss-called harsh and unfeeling, but all who really understand the problem which Guardians are called upon to solve, will admit that the evils and degradation of pauperism cannot be cured by the fatal policy of doing what is most pleasant and most consonant with the gentler feelings of our nature. It is necessary to look to the effects of administration rather than to the pleasure of giving. Guardians are not the trustees of a benevolent fund. They are the administrators of rates compulsorily levied, and which press most hardly upon those who are often sadly worse off than the paupers to whose support they have to contribute. Whether pleasant or not, the fact remains that the free distribution of out-relief removes the greatest inducement to thrift and independence, and compels the thrifty and independent to provide for those who wilfully fail to provide for themselves."

We will give another quotation, in confirmation of previous and oft-repeated truths, from the Report of Mr. Peel, Inspector:—" The Poor Law was not devised to check the flow of private charity, and were a strict and uniform administration of it adopted throughout the country, it would, I feel confident, result in discouraging pauperism and imposture, and lead to the relief of the thrifty, honest, and deserving, from other quarters."

Mr. Bircham, Inspector of the South Wales District, gives the following remarkable statement:—"The outdoor pauperism in most of the Unions is, in my opinion, still excessive, and might, I think, in time be considerably reduced, were a proper use made of the test of indoor relief. It represents at present nearly 3 per cent. of the total population; whilst the amount spent in the year on out-relief alone represents the interest of 4 per cent. on a capital of 4½ millions."

The total number of paupers in receipt of relief on January 1st, 1888, in 647 Unions and parishes in England and Wales was 831,505, of which total there were 206,286 *indoor*, and 625,219 *outdoor*. This amounted to one out of every thirty-four persons, or 2·9 per cent. of the population.

It may be interesting to observe that the county which contained the largest number of paupers was Dorset, in which no less than 47·4 out of every 1,000 of the population were in receipt of relief, and no less than 41·2 out of every 1,000 receiving *outdoor* relief. In the Metropolis the proportion was 13·4 per 1,000 of outdoor, and Lancashire the next lowest; the total for the Metropolis being 27·8, and for the latter 20·2.

Notwithstanding these still high figures, it is satisfactory to note that the returns for the year 1888 were lower than in any other year since 1885, and the diminution is owing to a decrease in the outdoor paupers. In 1849 the number of such was 55 per 1,000, but had fallen to 21·5 per 1,000 in 1888; while indoor paupers had decreased only from 7·7 per 1,000 to 6·8 per 1,000 in that time—a great decrease having taken place in the able-bodied class.

In nearly all the reports of the Local Government Board

Inspectors there are remarks of satisfaction at the diminution of outdoor relief; but there is an exception, when Mr. Murray Browne " regrets to say that the profuse out-relief which characterises the greater number of the North Wales Unions still continues." In South Wales, also, the Inspector remarks that "the outdoor pauperism is still excessive." In only three counties is the expenditure on out-relief less than on in-relief. The variation in amount is as follows:—The highest expenditure on out-relief being 83·6 in Wales, and the lowest 23·4 in the Metropolis, the nine intervening divisions graduating between the two extremes, that next to the lowest being, however, 50·9 per cent. Notwithstanding the many improvements made in the treatment of indoor paupers, it is satisfactory to observe that the expenditure per head has been less in 1887 than in any of the preceding twenty-five years.

Though not exactly bearing upon the question of out-relief, yet as our object is to enlighten the generally prevailing indifference as to Poor Law management, we may add, what may be a surprise to many, that out of the whole cost of over eight millions (exceeded by nearly £200,000) for relief, that portion spent upon the army of officials which is employed to carry out our machinery, amounts to no less a sum than £1,313,425.

We have given examples of the opinions of some of the officers of the Local Government Board on the question of out-relief, as their wide experience must have the greatest weight in its consideration; but we will add a few extracts from the reports of the Provincial Conferences during the year 1886, as they may be taken to represent the opinions of those who are concerned in carrying out the Poor Law in the different Unions. The following is from a paper by Mr. Bowen Jones, read at the West Midland Conference:—" In 1834 the new Poor Law was passed, the principle of which was to abolish, as far as possible, outdoor relief. How has this statute been administered ? Until quite recently, as a general rule, in a most perfunctory manner. Indiscriminate payment of out-relief has been the rule; and this system, instead of encouraging thrift, has created a premium on improvidence. What incentive existed to exercise the virtue of self-denial on the part of one man, when his frugality would debar him from the benefits received by the reckless, the idle, and extravagant? And what has been the effect of this system of administration as regards the ratepayers? A few years of newborn zeal under the new Poor Law reduced the cost of poor relief very considerably; but then a change took place, for in 1840 the cost was 5s. 9d. per head of population, while in 1884 it had risen to 6s. 6d. per head. . . . The short-comings of 100 years, by which the labouring population were taught to regard the Poor Law Union as a refuge to fly to in case of sickness, or for a pension in old age, cannot be eradicated in a day."

At the Conference held in the Northern District in 1886 a paper was read by Mr. Hodgson, Clerk to the Guardians, Sunderland, in which he said:—" The Poor Law must relieve destitution, and that adequately. . . . It is not an auxiliary existing to eke out insufficient earnings. It cannot supplement the income of the wage-earning classes ... Absolute destitution, then, falls within the immediate and specific operation of Poor Law relief."

At the Conference of the South-Eastern District a paper was read on the administration of out-relief by the Chairman of the St. Neots Union, in which he said:—"The most mischievous of all outdoor relief is permanent relief, or the pension granted to old and infirm persons for life—a style of relief still very common in some Unions; relief given in cases that excite the compassion and pity of Guardians. . . . Every pension granted to an old and infirm person, no longer able to work, is an advertisement encouraging inprovidence and unthrift. You foster the idea in the young that they need make no provision for the future; that, however reckless and improvident they may be, when they are no longer able to maintain themselves, there will be the outdoor relief that will keep them for the rest of their lives. . . . As you can never get to the sources and amount òf a pauper's income, so you never probe the capability of friends to help until you offer the house instead of out-relief; by giving out-relief you stop the flow of that sympathy and willingness to help which it is so important to encourage. . . . We must remember that, with few exceptions, destitution is the consequence of improvidence. It arises, in most cases, from the notion—fostered by the old Poor Law, and kept up by the outdoor relief administered under the present law—that the labouring class are to be helped and provided for, no matter how reckless and improvident they may be. . . . I have only to add one remark— that is, upon the want of uniformity of action amongst Unions in the administration of relief. In one Union out-relief is given in almost every case where want is proved; in another the application in every removable case is met by an offer of the house. This uniformity cannot be obtained unless certain rules be adopted as the basis. . . . Nothing tends to breed discontent so much as want of uuiformity. . . I am quite sure that the more out-relief is restricted, the more the spirit of self-reliance is increased; and the spirit of pauperism, the parent of recklessness and improvidence, is crushed." The following resolution was then adopted by the Conference:—"That outdoor relief, being the chief cause of pauperism, should receive the urgent attention of Guardians, with the object of reducing it to a minimum."

At the same Conference Mr. Fleming, Poor Law Inspector, (whose opinions have been already quoted), read a paper on the same subject, in which he said, "No more sad result has followed the evil administration of the Poor Law than the almost utter obliteration of the obligations of the family tie among a very large section of the working classes. The obligation upon the members of a family for their mutual support, instead of being regarded as a duty and a privilege, is looked upon as a burden and a hardship, which may, without disgrace, be shifted on to the ratepayers. . . . Outdoor relief would very soon be discontinued if Poor Law administrators once realised how completely it works in favour of the improvident and unworthy, at the cost of the thrifty and worthy members of society."

In reviewing the different methods of relief in the various countries of Europe, it cannot fail to have been observed that nothing analogous to our relief of the able-bodied exists, as far as workhouses are concerned. Various institutions provide assistance for nearly every form of misery and distress, but on wholly different lines; nowhere is there to be found the right to enter an asylum at any age, and on the mere plea of destitution, together with the freedom and liberty of discharge. Believing that this freedom of relief is the greatest blot and disadvantage of our Poor Law system, we cannot but add a few remarks on this prevalence of free relief to the classes who are beginning to be known as "ins and outs." It was hoped that the various representations which were made before the House of Lord's Committee of 1888 would have resulted in some recommendation for greater stringency as regards this class, but we regret to find that this was not the case. We cannot but express a wish that those who make our laws should have the opportunity of seeing the working of them in practice as well as in theory. If those who have expressed the opinion that further restriction is not necessary nor desirable as regards this class, could take the place of some of our masters of workhouses for a short period, or could even attend the Committees of Guardians when the cases of these persons are considered, we venture to think that the question of "the liberty of the subject" would not be so often urged against any alteration of the law, which at present allows such freedom of relief to the undeserving, provided by the thrifty and the hard-working.

The liberty to come and go, to take their discharge with the smallest possible restrictions, is the great attraction of the idle and profligate classes to become inmates of our workhouses. To such the "test" becomes no deterrent; it is at their choice to come and go as it suits their own convenience—in fact, the workhouse is an ever-ready, open hotel, and if for good reasons they are refused a day's outing they retaliate by taking their discharge, thus multiplying the trouble of the officers; and if they happen to have children at the schools, they have to be fetched, in order that they may accompany their unnatural parents, too, probably to scenes and haunts of vice. Indeed, where the children are concerned, the freedom of discharge is fraught with even greater and untold evils.

It is no question of those who are able and seeking for work, nor of the more permanent aged or afflicted inmates, for whom some considerations of liberty may be demanded. The cases of all such are easily discriminated, and can be dealt with accordingly. We speak of the idle, the profligate, and habitual "ins and outs," who thus abuse the relief offered by the State, and who, even if possessed of means and pensions sufficient to keep them in comfort out of doors, prefer to spend a few days in wild extravagance and then return to the workhouse as destitute. In accordance with our previous plan, we will proceed to give the opinions of some of those who are most able to judge in this important matter.

Mr. Hedley, Local Government Inspector of the Metropolitan District, said, in giving evidence before the Lords Committee, "he would make it an indispensable condition of the acceptance of indoor relief that the person relieved should not be able to discharge himself under a week ... He did not see that it would be any hardship, and he would make it apply to all classes of the poor." "The facility with which undeserving paupers can now go in and out of the workhouse is an abuse which ought to be remedied."

Even far more restriction than this of the present liberty is desired by many competent judges of the system and its evils, by which a pauper can ensure a holiday every fourth day, if he so chooses.

General Lynedoch Gardiner, fifteen years vice-chairman of the St. Marylebone Board of Guardians, writes thus:—

"A gang of able-bodied men and women, generally fifty in number, give notice every Friday that they will take their discharge on Monday. On that morning they go out, and return, as a rule, on Tuesday afternoon, many of them drowsy with drink. Sunday being a *dies non* as to work, they thus escape work three days consecutively out of the seven. . . . Some years ago the workhouse at Poplar was used by the Marylebone Guardians for able-bodied persons. In 1877 the master said that inmates were in the habit of taking their discharge from Poplar and applying for relief at Marylebone the same day, the object being to avoid the labour and discipline of the house. They walked from Poplar to the Marylebone relieving officer, and asked for an order of admission. One pauper was discharged and re-admitted twenty-three times in ten weeks."

Let us add what the experienced master of that work-house says on this matter:—

"The frequency with which a large number of able-bodied men still continue to leave the house for their weekly holiday, shows, as I have pointed out on former occasions, the necessity for increased powers of detention for dealing with this class. One hundred and fifty-seven returned from leave of absence drunk and disorderly, in most cases on the evening of the day on which they left the house; the charges for disorderly conduct at the gate increased in number, and were twenty-two. Two women have been in prison four times in the year for this."

A relieving officer of large experience in London writes:—"The number that went out and returned the same day in my district from March 1st is 1,482; these were cases sent into our own houses. There should be some method or law so that those who are continually going out should be detained for at least a month or more."

At a meeting of the Bethnal Green Board of Guardians the question was raised respecting the punishment of inmates returning drunk to the workhouse after their weekly outing. Out of some 400 allowed to go out, more than half returned in a condition of drunkenness.

We cannot help asking if a weekly holiday is a necessity for such persons as these, maintained at the expense of thrifty ratepayers? They are not merely individuals who thus use the workhouse as a convenient lodging-house, but whole families do the same, taking their discharge with regularity once a week, spending the day in begging in the most likely places, enjoying themselves on the proceeds, and returning at night to the shelter of the house.

"'Ins and outs' of all sorts are agents of demoralisation, and nothing else, in a workhouse," writes one who has practical experience of this fact.

Men or women demanding their discharge take their children with them, these having to be fetched from one or more of the country schools by officers of the workhouse. One such child was taken thus eleven times in a year, being kept out for longer or shorter periods in scenes of vice by her profligate mother, and then returned to her companions at school. In one workhouse for able-bodied men there were in one fortnight forty-two discharges out of sixty inmates.

"A pauper will enter the house, and at the same time give notice of his discharge, which course would prevent his children being sent away to the school. The case was cited of a woman who had discharged herself forty times in a year, in order to evade the attempts of the Guardians to send her child to school." The Chairman of this Board remarked that "some decision should be come to, not merely affecting the parents of children, but others who made it a practice to run in and out of the house."

At the North Wales District Conference held in 1886 Mr. Murray Browne, Poor Law Inspector, read a paper on the subject of "Increased Powers of Detention and Treatment of Certain Cases," in which he urged its importance as regards inmates of bad character, *especially women* and children. And, surely, we may add, of *Imbeciles* also.

It is difficult to define the line of distinction between these classes and those who apply as casuals for a still shorter period of admission; but we cannot help remarking that great ignorance prevails in the public mind concerning this class, as has been recently shown in London by discussions on the unemployed, and the suggestions made on the subject. Again, we are not aware that other countries provide similar relief for such persons. [1]

A visit to these wards, and an inspection of the inmates, would help to dispel many theories and delusions with regard to their being mainly refuges for honest persons out of work. Truth compels us to state that the most abandoned, and apparently hopeless, portion are the women, and, we may add, the most sad also, as they are often accompanied by children, and sometimes the whole family of six enter with the mother at all hours of

---

[1] In six months of the year 1887, 38,415 casuals were admitted, and of this number 544 were charged at police courts.

the night and morning. A large proportion are said (in some Unions at least) to be the worse for drink on admission. Their behaviour and language can. be better imagined than described; the Superintendent being called up for each arrival, her task is no light or easy one; the vilest names are applied to her, and she is sometimes told by those who well understand the whole meaning and working of the Poor Law, that she is only there because of them, and thus owes her post and her living to their existence (which is true enough)—another instance of what has often been remarked as to the pernicious influence of this claim of right to relief, and the fostering of feelings and conduct which would not be ventured upon where the help is granted as a boon. Many of these casuals are known to procure tickets in one part of London early in the evening, and then wander about (remaining in public-houses as long as they are open) till the early hours of the morning; thus the privileges of admission provided for those in real need and exceptional difficulties are habitually abused by the vagrant and vicious of the lowest classes.

We do not deny that some who need or deserve the relief are to be found amongst the applicants; our object is now to mark the contrast and distinction between our methods and those of other countries, which it cannot but be useful to consider at a time when various theories and suggestions of change are being, and about to be, made on all these questions, especially as regards the casual wards. Signs of increasing interest in all these serious social questions are to be found; and could more frequent opportunities of discussion between various Boards of Guardians be promoted, the best results might ensue, for experience would throw light on many dark and puzzling questions.

The growing importance of thrift and providence was never more deeply felt than at the present time; and this fact forms a significant consideration in connection with Poor Law relief, and especially as regards a laxity in bestowing it on outdoor paupers, the results of which it has been endeavoured to show by the facts and opinions given in these pages.

APPENDIX

To the Guardians of the Poor of the several POOR LAW UNIONS for the time being in ENGLAND and WALES ;—

And to all others whom it may concern.

WHEREAS by certain General and other Orders the Poor Law Commissioners, the Poor Law Board, and the Local Government Board have made Rules and Regulations with regard to the government of the Workhouses of the said several Poor Law Unions, the nursing of the sick poor relieved therein, and as to the appointment of persons to certain offices therein, including the office of Nurse, and the qualification, remuneration, and duties of such persons ;

And whereas it is expedient that further provision should be made in the matter as herein-after mentioned :

NOW THEREFORE, We, the Local Government Board, in pursuance of the powers given to Us by the Statutes in that behalf, do hereby Order that, from and after the Twenty-ninth day of September, One thousand eight hundred and ninety-seven (herein-after referred to as "the commencement of this Order"), the following Regulations shall, except in so far as We may assent to a departure therefrom, be in force in the said several Poor Law Unions :—

ARTICLE I.—(I.) Notwithstanding anything contained in any of the Orders above referred to, no pauper inmate of the Workhouse shall be employed to perform the duties of a Nurse in the Sick or Lying-in Wards of the Workhouse, or be otherwise employed in nursing any pauper in the Workhouse who requires nursing.

(2.) No pauper inmate of the Workhouse shall be employed as an attendant in the Sick or Lying-in Wards of the Workhouse, or upon any pauper in the Workhouse who requires nursing, unless such inmate shall be approved by the Medical Officer of the Workhouse for the purpose, and shall act under the immediate supervision of a paid officer of the Guardians.

ARTICLE II.—No person shall be appointed by the Guardians to the office of Nurse or Assistant Nurse in the Workhouse without having had such practical experience in nursing as may render him or her a fit and proper person to hold such office :

Provided that this Article shall not apply in the case of a female Assistant Nurse in a Workhouse where there is a Superintendent Nurse as required by Article III. of this Order.

ARTICLE III.—(1.) Where at the commencement of this Order the staff of female Nurses and Assistant Nurses in the Workhouse consists of three or more persons, the Guardians shall either appoint a Superintendent Nurse, or, with Our consent, direct that one of the Nurses shall be a Superintendent Nurse.

(2.) Where at the commencement of this Order there is not a staff of three female Nurses and Assistant Nurses in the Workhouse, but the Guardians subsequently propose that there should be such a staff, and also where any Superintendent Nurse ceases to hold office, the Guardians shall appoint a Superintendent Nurse.

(3.) Any Superintendent Nurse appointed after the commencement of this Order shall, unless We dispense with the requirement, be a person qualified for the appointment by having undergone, for three years at least, a course of instruction in the Medical and Surgical Wards of any Hospital or Infirmary being a Training School for Nurses, and maintaining a Resident Physician or House Surgeon.

ARTICLE IV.—(1.) It shall be the duty of the Superintendent Nurse to superintend and control the other Nurses and Assistant Nurses in the Workhouse in the performance of their duties, but such superintendence and control shall, in all matters of treatment of the sick, be subject to the directions of the Medical Officer of the Workhouse, and in all other matters to the directions of the Master or Matron of the Workhouse, so far as the Orders in force in the Poor Law Union and the lawful directions of the Guardians may require or permit.

(2.) The provisions of the Orders in force in the Poor Law Union applicable to the mode of appointment, remuneration, and tenure of office of a Nurse at the Workhouse shall apply to every Superintendent Nurse appointed under this Order:

Provided that no such Superintendent Nurse shall be dismissed without Our consent.

ARTICLE V.—If in an emergency it appears to the Medical Officer of the Workhouse that the employment of a temporary Nurse is required for the proper treatment of any case or cases in the Workhouse, and he informs the Master of the Workhouse in writing accordingly, it shall be the duty of the Master to engage a person to act as Nurse until the next Meeting of the Guardians, and the Guardians shall pay the reasonable remuneration of the person so engaged:

Provided that where there is no Superintendent Nurse appointed under Article III. of this Order, no person shall be engaged under this Article without having had such practical experience in nursing as may render him or her a fit and proper person to hold the office of Nurse.

ARTICLE VI.—This Order shall not apply to any Infirmary or School which is under administration separate from the Workhouse.

This Order may be cited as "The Nursing in Workhouses Order, 1897."

> Given under the Seal of Office of the Local Government Board, this Sixth day of August, in the year One thousand eight hundred and ninety-seven.

HUGH OWEN,
Secretary.

HENRY CHAPLIN,
President.

Nursing of the Sick in Workhouses

Local Government Board,
Whitehall, S.W.,
7th. August 1897.

Sir,

I am directed by the Local Government Board to state that they have had under their consideration the arrangements for the nursing of the sick poor in the Workhouses belonging to Boards of Guardians in England and Wales, together with the representations which have been made to them on the subject, and they have deemed it desirable to issue an Order prescribing further Regulations in the matter. Two copies of the Order are enclosed.

The Board have frequently drawn the attention of Boards of Guardians to the question of the nursing arrangements in Workhouses, and they may refer particularly to the circular which they issued on the 29th of January 1895 on Workhouse administration. The Board in that circular quoted a passage from a previous circular, in which they had pointed out that the office of Nurse was one of very serious responsibility and labour, and that it required to be filled by a person of experience in the care of the sick, and they stated that they considered it of the highest importance that the Assistants to the Nurse should also be paid officers. They further expressed their opinion that the services of pauper inmates as Attendants in sick wards, as distinguished from Nurses, should only be used with the approval of the Medical Officer, and under the supervision at all times of paid officers.

The Board are aware that the employment of pauper Nurses in Workhouses has generally been discontinued, but this is not so in all cases, and they have, therefore, thought it right to provide by

Article I. of the new Order, that no pauper inmate of the Workhouse shall be employed to perform the duties of a Nurse in the Sick or Lying-in Wards, or be otherwise employed in nursing any pauper in the Workhouse who requires nursing. The Article further requires that any pauper who is employed as an Attendant in the Sick or Lying-in Wards, or upon any pauper in the Workhouse who requires nursing shall be approved by the Medical Officer of the Workhouse for the purpose, and shall act under the immediate supervision of a paid officer of the Guardians.

Where the staff of female Nurses and Assistant Nurses in the Workhouse consists of three or more persons, there must, under Article III. of the Order, be a Superintendent Nurse, whose duty it will be to superintend and control the other Nurses and Assistant Nurses in the performance of their duties. This superintendence and control will, in all matters of treatment of the sick, be subject to the directions of the Medical Officer of the Workhouse, and in all other matters to the directions of the Master or Matron of the Workhouse, so far as the Orders in force in the Union and the lawful directions of the Guardians may require or permit.

With a view of providing for existing cases where there is no need for an increase in the staff, and one of the present Nurses is in all respects a suitable person to hold the office of Superintendent Nurse, the Order enables the Guardians, with the consent of the Board, to direct that one of these Nurses shall be a Superintendent Nurse. But, subject to this provision, it will be the duty of the Guardians in all cases in which there is a staff of three or more female Nurses and Assistant Nurses in the Workhouse to appoint a Superintendent Nurse who, unless the Board dispense with the requirement, must be a person qualified for the appointment by having undergone, for three years at least, a course of instruction in the medical and surgical wards of any Hospital or Infirmary being a Training School for Nurses and maintaining a resident physician or house surgeon.

If the Guardians, with the consent of the Board, direct one of the existing Nurses to act as a Superintendent Nurse, the requirements of the Order as to the appointment of a Superintendent

Nurse with the prescribed qualification will still apply when a vacancy takes place in the office.

Under Article II, of the Order it will in future be necessary that every person appointed by the Guardians to the office of Nurse or Assistant Nurse in the Workhouse shall have had such practical experience in nursing as may render him or her a fit and proper person to hold the office. With a view, however, of enabling young women to be instructed as Assistant Nurses under a Superintendent Nurse, it is provided that the requirement above referred to shall not apply in the case of a female Assistant Nurse in any Workhouse where there is a Superintendent Nurse as required by Article III. of the Order.

Provision is made by Article V. for the employment of a temporary Nurse in the case of an emergency.

The new Regulations will come into force from and after the 29th of September next, and the Board are desirous that the Guardians should at once take them into consideration, so that such arrangements as may be necessary may be made immediately the Order takes effect.

The Order will not apply to any Infirmary or School which is under administration separate from that of the Workhouse.

I am, Sir,
Your obedient Servant,
HUGH OWEN,
Secretary.

The Clerk to the Guardians.

PUBLICATIONS ON MATTERS

OF

POOR LAW ADMINISTRATION, BY L. T.

A Few Words about the Inmates of Our Union Workhouses, 1855.

Metropolitan Workhouses and their Inmates, a reprint of letters to the *Guardian*, 1857.

A Paper on the Condition of Workhouses, read at the Association for the Promotion of Social Science at Birmingham, 1857.

A Letter to the *Times* on Workhouse Nurses, 1858.

An Article on Workhouses and Women's work, in the Church of England Monthly Review, 1858.

A Paper on the Management of Workhouses, read at the Meeting of the Association of Social Science at Liverpool, 1858. When the formation of the Workhouse Visiting Society was decided upon.

A Plea for Workhouse Visitors, Penny Post, 1858.

A Paper on the Training and Supervision of Workhouse Girls, read at the Social Science Meeting at Bradford, 1859.

A paper on Workhouse Inmates, read at the Social Science Meeting at Glasgow, 1860.

A Paper on Workhouse Education, read at the Social Science Meeting at Dublin, 1861.

A Paper on Facts and Statistics about Workhouses, read at the meeting of the British Association at Manchester, 1861.

A Paper on Women's Work in Workhouses, read at the Church Congress, at Oxford, 1862.

A Paper on our Poor laws and our Workhouses, 1862.

Preface to Tales of Crowbridge Workhouse by M. A. B. 1863.

A Paper on the Sick, Aged and Incurable in Workhouses, read at the Social Science Meeting at Edinburgh, 1863.

The Supervision of Girls in Service. A Paper in the Reformatory and Refuge Union Journal, 1863.

Readings for Visitors to Workhouses and Hospitals, from various authors, 1865.

A Letter to the President of the Local Government Board, 1866.

Prayers for Workhouses and Hospitals, 1868.

Recollections of Workhouse Visiting and Management during 25 years, 1880.

Suggestions for Women Guardians, 1885.

Thoughts on the diet of Nurses in Hospitals and Infirmaries, read at a Meeting of the Hospitals Association, 1885, and published in the Journal.

State Hospitals, or Nursing in Workhouse Infirmaries, Good Words, 1885, and reprinted in Nursing Notes, 1888.

Workhouse Cruelties—Nineteenth Century, 1886.

Women's Work, Official and Unofficial, National Review, 1887.

Fifty Years of Women's work, do. 1887.

Letter to the President of the Local Government Board, 1887.

Some facts in the Working of the Poor Law, National Review, 1888.

Poor Law Infirmaries and their Needs, do. 1889.

Poor Law Relief in Foreign Countries, and Outdoor Relief in England, 1889.

The Abuse of Relief to Unmarried Mothers in Workhouse Wards; read at the South Eastern Poor Law Conference, Exeter Hall, 1889.

Neglect of the Poor in Workhouse Infirmaries, the Hospital, 1890.

The duty of Workhouse visiting, Monthly Packet, 1890.

Women as Public Servants—Nineteenth Century, 1890.

Thoughts on Poor Law Legislation, Newbery House Magazine, 1891.

Christmas Beer in Workhouses, 1891.

Nursing in Workhouses, a Paper read at the Meeting of the Women Worker's Union, Liverpool, 1891.

Outrelief and charity; a Threefold Cord, 1892.

Leaflet on the Aged Poor, 1893; reprint of a letter to the *Guardian* in 1892 on the question of Old Age Pensions, quoting the first letter of 36 years before, and adding the fact of the newly issued Order of 1893, giving authority to Guardians to appoint Visiting Committees of Ladies; thus carrying out the suggestions of the Workhouse Visiting Society, made in 1858.

Women as official Inspectors, Nineteenth Century, 1894.

Many of these Articles were reprinted as Pamphlets, and some are to be had at the Library of the Women Guardian's Society, 4 Sanctuary, Westminster.

A Retrospect of Poor Law Work, 1894.

The Presidents of the *Poor Law Board*, from 1853, to 1871, were as follows:

1853 Rt. Hon. Matthew Talbot Baines.
   Ed. Pleydell Bouverie.
   T. Sotheron Estcourt.
   The Earl of March.
   T. Milner Gibson.
   C. Pelham Villiers.
   Gathorne Hardy.
   The Earl of Devon.
   J. G. Goschen.
   James Stansfeld.

Presidents of the *Local Government Board*.

1874 G. Sclater-Booth.
   L. G. Dodson.
   Sir C. D. Dilke.
   A. J. Balfour.
   J. Chamberlain.
   J. Stansfeld.
   C. J. Ritchie.
   H. Fowler.
   H. Shaw Lefevre.
   H. Chaplin.

INDEX

P.

R.

S.

T.

U.

V.

A CATALOGUE OF BOOKS
AND ANNOUNCEMENTS OF
METHUEN AND COMPANY
PUBLISHERS : LONDON
36 ESSEX STREET
W.C.

CONTENTS

NOVEMBER 1897

MESSRS. METHUEN'S
ANNOUNCEMENTS

Poetry

SHAKESPEARE'S POEMS. Edited, with an Introduction and Notes, by GEORGE WYNDHAM, M.P. *Crown 8vo. Buckram.* 6s.

This is a volume of the sonnets and lesser poems of Shakespeare, and is prefaced with an elaborate Introduction by Mr. Wyndham.

ENGLISH LYRICS. Selected and Edited by W. E. HENLEY. *Crown 8vo. Buckram.* 6s.

Also 15 copies on Japanese paper. *Demy 8vo.* £2, 2s. *net.*

Few announcements will be more welcome to lovers of English verse than the one that Mr. Henley is bringing together into one book the finest lyrics in our language.

NURSERY RHYMES. With many Coloured Pictures. By F. D. BEDFORD. *Small 4to.* 5s.

This book has many beautiful designs in colour to illustrate the old rhymes.

THE ODYSSEY OF HOMER. A Translation by J. G. CORDERY. *Crown 8vo.* 7s. 6d.

Travel and Adventure

BRITISH CENTRAL AFRICA. By Sir H. H. JOHNSTON, K.C.B. With nearly Two Hundred Illustrations, and Six Maps. *Crown 4to.* 30s. *net.*

CONTENTS.—(1) The History of Nyasaland and British Central Africa generally. (2) A detailed description of the races and languages of British Central Africa. (3) Chapters on the European settlers and missionaries ; the Fauna, the Flora, minerals, and scenery. (4) A chapter on the prospects of the country.

WITH THE GREEKS IN THESSALY. By W. KINNAIRD ROSE, Reuter's Correspondent. With Plans and 23 Illustrations. *Crown 8vo.* 6s.

A history of the operations in Thessaly by one whose brilliant despatches from the seat of war attracted universal attention.

THE BENIN MASSACRE. By CAPTAIN BOISRAGON. With Portrait and Map. *Crown 8vo.* 3s. 6d.

This volume is written by one of the two survivors who escaped the terrible massacre in Benin at the beginning of this year. The author relates in detail his adventures and his extraordinary escape, and adds a description of the country and of the events which led up to the outbreak.

FROM TONKIN TO INDIA. By PRINCE HENRI OF ORLEANS. Translated by HAMLEY BENT, M.A. With 80 Illustrations and a Map. *Crown 4to.* 25*s.*

The travels of Prince Henri in 1895 from China to the valley of the Bramaputra covered a distance of 2100 miles, of whith 1600 was through absolutely unexplored country. No fewer than seventeen ranges of mountains were crossed at altitudes of from 11,000 to 13,000 feet. The journey was made memorable by the discovery of the sources of the Irrawaddy. To the physical difficulties of the journey were added dangers from the attacks of savage tribes. The book deals with many of the burning political problems of the East, and it will be found a most important contribution to the literature of adventure and discovery.

THREE YEARS IN SAVAGE AFRICA. By LIONEL DECLE. With an Introduction by H. M. STANLEY, M.P. With 100 Illustrations and 5 Maps. *Demy 8vo.* 21*s.*

Few Europeans have had the same opportunity of studying the barbarous parts of Africa as Mr. Decle. Starting from the Cape, he visited in succession Bechuanaland, the Zambesi, Matabeleland and Mashonaland, the Portuguese settlement on the Zambesi, Nyasaland, Ujiji, the headquarters of the Arabs, German East Africa, Uganda (where he saw fighting in company with the late Major 'Roddy' Owen), and British East Africa. In his book he relates his experiences, his minute observations of native habits and customs, and his views as to the work done in Africa by the various European Governments, whose operations he was able to study. The whole journey extended over 7000 miles, and occupied exactly three years.

WITH THE MOUNTED INFANTRY IN MASHONALAND. By Lieut.-Colonel ALDERSON. With numerous Illustrations and Plans. *Demy 8vo.* 12*s.* 6*d.*

This is an account of the military operations in Mashonaland by the officer who commanded the troops in that district during the late rebellion. Besides its interest as a story of warfare, it will have a peculiar value as an account of the services of mounted infantry by one of the chief authorities on the subject.

THE HILL OF THE GRACES: OR, THE GREAT STONE TEMPLES OF TRIPOLI. By H. S. COWPER, F.S.A. With Maps, Plans, and 75 Illustrations. *Demy 8vo.* 10*s.* 6*d.*

A record of two journeys through Tripoli in 1895 and 1896. The book treats of a remarkable series of megalithic temples which have hitherto been uninvestigated, and contains a large amount of new geographical and archæological matter.

ADVENTURE AND EXPLORATION IN AFRICA. By Captain A. ST. H. GIBBONS, F.R.G.S. With Illustrations by C. WHYMPER, and Maps. *Demy 8vo.* 21*s.*

This is an account of travel and adventure among the Marotse and contiguous tribes, with a description of their customs, characteristics, and history, together with the author's experiences in hunting big game. The illustrations are by Mr. Charles Whymper, and from photographs. There is a map by the author of the hitherto unexplored regions lying between the Zambezi and Kafukwi rivers and from 18° to 15° S. lat.

History and Biography

A HISTORY OF EGYPT, FROM THE EARLIEST TIMES TO THE PRESENT DAY. Edited by W. M. FLINDERS PETRIE, D.C.L., LL.D., Professor of Egyptology at University College. *Fully Illustrated. In Six Volumes. Crown 8vo. 6s. each.*
VOL. V. ROMAN EGYPT. By J. G. MILNE.

THE DECLINE AND FALL OF THE ROMAN EMPIRE. By EDWARD GIBBON. A New Edition, edited with Notes, Appendices, and Maps by J. B. BURY, M.A., Fellow of Trinity College, Dublin. *In Seven Volumes. Demy 8vo, gilt top. 8s. 6d. each. Crown 8vo. 6s. each. Vol. IV.*

THE LETTERS OF VICTOR HUGO. Translated from the French by F. CLARKE, M.A. *In Two Volumes. Demy 8vo. 10s. 6d. each. Vol. II.* 1835-72.
This is the second volume of one of the most interesting and important collection of letters ever published in France. The correspondence dates from Victor Hugo's boyhood to his death, and none of the letters have been published before.

A HISTORY OF THE GREAT NORTHERN RAILWAY, 1845-95. By C. H. GRINLING. With Maps and Illustrations. *Demy 8vo.* 10s. 6d.
A record of Railway enterprise and development in Northern England, containing much matter hitherto unpublished. It appeals both to the general reader and to those specially interested in railway construction and management.

A HISTORY OF BRITISH COLONIAL POLICY. By H. E. EGERTON, M.A. *Demy 8vo.* 12s. 6d.
This book deals with British Colonial policy historically from the beginnings of English colonisation down to the present day. The subject has been treated by itself, and it has thus been possible within a reasonable compass to deal with a mass of authority which must otherwise be sought in the State papers. The volume is divided into five parts:—(1) The Period of Beginnings, 1497-1650; (2) Trade Ascendancy, 1651-1830; (3) The Granting of Responsible Government, 1831-1860; (4) *Laissez Aller*, 1861-1885; (5) Greater Britain.

A HISTORY OF ANARCHISM. By E. V. ZENKER. Translated from the German. *Demy 8vo.* 7s. 6d.
A critical study and history, as well as a powerful and trenchant criticism, of the Anarchist movement in Europe. The book has aroused considerable attention on the Continent.

THE LIFE OF ERNEST RENAN By MADAME DARMESTETER. With Portrait. *Crown 8vo.* 6s.
A biography of Renan by one of his most intimate friends.

A LIFE OF DONNE. By AUGUSTUS JESSOPP, D.D. With Portrait. *Crown 8vo.* 3s. 6d.
This is a new volume of the 'Leaders of Religion' series, from the learned and witty pen of the Rector of Scarning, who has been able to embody the results of much research.

OLD HARROW DAYS. By J. G. COTTON MINCHIN. *Crown 8vo. 5s.*
A volume of reminiscences which will be interesting to old Harrovians and to many of the general public.

Theology

A PRIMER OF THE BIBLE. By Prof. W. H. BENNETT. *Crown 8vo. 2s. 6d.*

This Primer sketches the history of the books which make up the Bible, in the light of recent criticism. It gives an account of their character, origin, and composition, as far as possible in chronological order, with special reference to their relations to one another, and to the history of Israel and the Church. The formation of the Canon is illustrated by chapters on the Apocrypha (Old and New Testament); and there is a brief notice of the history of the Bible since the close of the Canon.

LIGHT AND LEAVEN : HISTORICAL AND SOCIAL SERMONS. By the Rev. H. HENSLEY HENSON, M.A., Fellow of All Souls', Incumbent of St. Mary's Hospital, Ilford. *Crown 8vo. 6s.*

Devotional Series

THE CONFESSIONS OF ST. AUGUSTINE. Newly Translated, with an Introduction, by C. BIGG, D.D., late Student of Christ Church. With a Frontispiece. *18mo. 1s. 6d.*

This little book is the first volume of a new Devotional Series, printed in clear type, and published at a very low price.
This volume contains the nine books of the 'Confessions' which are suitable for devotional purposes. The name of the Editor is a sufficient guarantee of the excellence of the edition.

THE HOLY SACRIFICE. By F. WESTON, M.A., Curate of St. Matthew's, Westminster. *18mo. 1s.*
A small volume of devotions at the Holy Communion.

Naval and Military

A HISTORY OF THE ART OF WAR. By C. W. OMAN, M.A., Fellow of All Souls', Oxford. *Demy 8vo. Illustrated. 21s.*

Vol. II. MEDIÆVAL WARFARE.

Mr. Oman is engaged on a History of the Art of War, of which the above, though covering the middle period from the fall of the Roman Empire to the general use of gunpowder in Western Europe, is the first instalment. The first battle dealt with will be Adrianople (378) and the last Navarette (1367). There will appear later a volume dealing with the Art of War among the Ancients, and another covering the 15th, 16th, and 17th centuries.
The book will deal mainly with tactics and strategy, fortifications and siegecraft, but subsidiary chapters will give some account of the development of arms and armour, and of the various forms of military organization known to the Middle Ages.

A SHORT HISTORY OF THE ROYAL NAVY, FROM
EARLY TIMES TO THE PRESENT DAY. By DAVID HANNAY.
Illustrated. 2 *Vols. Demy 8vo.* 7*s.* 6*d. each.* Vol. I.

This book aims at giving an account not only of the fighting we have done at sea,
but of the growth of the service, of the part the Navy has played in the development of the Empire, and of its inner life.

THE STORY OF THE BRITISH ARMY. By Lieut.-Colonel
COOPER KING, of the Staff College, Camberley. Illustrated. *Demy
8vo.* 7*s.* 6*d.*

This volume aims at describing the nature of the different armies that have been
formed in Great Britain, and how from the early and feudal levies the present
standing army came to be. The changes in tactics, uniform, and armament are
briefly touched upon, and the campaigns in which the army has shared have
been so far followed as to explain the part played by British regiments in them.

General Literature

THE OLD ENGLISH HOME. By S. BARING-GOULD.
With numerous Plans and Illustrations. *Crown 8vo.* 7*s.* 6*d.*

This book, like Mr. Baring-Gould's well-known 'Old Country Life,' describes the
life and environment of an old English family.

OXFORD AND ITS COLLEGES. By J. WELLS, M.A.,
Fellow and Tutor of Wadham College. Illustrated by E. H. NEW.
Fcap. 8vo. 3*s. Leather.* 4*s.*

This is a guide—chiefly historical—to the Colleges of Oxford. It contains numerous
illustrations.

VOCES ACADEMICÆ. By C. GRANT ROBERTSON, M.A.,
Fellow of All Souls', Oxford. *With a Frontispiece. Fcap. 8vo.*
3*s.* 6*d.*

This is a volume of light satirical dialogues and should be read by all who are interested in the life of Oxford.

A PRIMER OF WORDSWORTH. By LAURIE MAGNUS.
Crown 8vo. 2*s.* 6*d.*

This volume is uniform with the Primers of Tennyson and Burns, and contains a
concise biography of the poet, a critical appreciation of his work in detail, and a
bibliography.

NEO-MALTHUSIANISM. By R. USSHER, M.A. *Cr. 8vo.* 6*s.*

This book deals with a very delicate but most important matter, namely, the voluntary limitation of the family, and how such action affects morality, the individual,
and the nation.

PRIMÆVAL SCENES. By H. N. HUTCHINSON, B.A., F.G.S.,
Author of 'Extinct Monsters,' 'Creatures of Other Days,' 'Pre-
historic Man and Beast,' etc. With numerous Illustrations drawn
by JOHN HASSALL and FRED. V. BURRIDGE. 4*to.* 6*s.*

A set of twenty drawings, with short text to each, to illustrate the humorous aspects
of pre-historic times. They are carefully planned by the author so as to be
scientifically and archæologically correct and at the same time amusing.

THE WALLYPUG IN LONDON. By G. E. Farrow,
Author of 'The Wallypug of Why.' With numerous Illustrations.
Crown 8vo. 3s. 6d.
An extravaganza for children, written with great charm and vivacity.

RAILWAY NATIONALIZATION. By Clement Edwards.
Crown 8vo. 2s. 6d.   [*Social Questions Series.*

Sport

SPORTING AND ATHLETIC RECORDS. By H. Morgan
Browne. *Crown 8vo. 1s. paper ; 2s. cloth.*
This book gives, in a clear and complete form, accurate records of the best performances in all important branches of Sport. It is an attempt, never yet made, to
present all-important sporting records in a systematic way.

THE GOLFING PILGRIM. By Horace G Hutchinson,
Crown 8vo. 6s.
This book, by a famous golfer, contains the following sketches lightly and humorously
written :—The Prologue—The Pilgrim at the Shrine—Mecca out of Season—The
Pilgrim at Home—The Pilgrim Abroad—The Life of the Links—A Tragedy by
the Way—Scraps from the Scrip—The Golfer in Art—Early Pilgrims in the West
—An Interesting Relic.

Educational

EVAGRIUS. Edited by Professor Léon Parmentier of
Liége and M. Bidez of Gand. *Demy 8vo. 7s. 6d.*
                                              [*Byzantine Texts.*

THE ODES AND EPODES OF HORACE. Translated by
A. D. Godley, M.A., Fellow of Magdalen College, Oxford.
Crown 8vo. buckram. 2s.

ORNAMENTAL DESIGN FOR WOVEN FABRICS. By
C. Stephenson, of The Technical College, Bradford, and
F. Suddards, of The Yorkshire College, Leeds. With 65 full-page
plates, and numerous designs and diagrams in the text. *Demy 8vo.*
7s. 6d.
The aim of this book is to supply, in a systematic and practical form, information on
the subject of Decorative Design as applied to Woven Fabrics, and is primarily
intended to meet the requirements of students in Textile and Art Schools, or of
designers actively engaged in the weaving industry. Its wealth of illustration is
a marked feature of the book.

ESSENTIALS OF COMMERCIAL EDUCATION. By
E. E. Whitfield, M.A. *Crown 8vo. 1s. 6d.*
A guide to Commercial Education and Examinations.

PASSAGES FOR UNSEEN TRANSLATION. By E. C. MARCHANT, M.A., Fellow of Peterhouse, Cambridge; and A. M. COOK, M.A., late Scholar of Wadham College, Oxford: Assistant Masters at St. Paul's School. *Crown 8vo.* 3s. 6d.

This book contains Two Hundred Latin and Two Hundred Greek Passages, and has been very carefully compiled to meet the wants of V. and VI. Form Boys at Public Schools. It is also well adapted for the use of Honour men at the Universities.

EXERCISES IN LATIN ACCIDENCE. By S. E. WINBOLT, Assistant Master in Christ's Hospital. *Crown 8vo.* 1s. 6d.

An elementary book adapted for Lower Forms to accompany the shorter Latin primer

NOTES ON GREEK AND LATIN SYNTAX. By G. BUCKLAND GREEN, M.A., Assistant Master at the Edinburgh Academy, late Fellow of St. John's College, Oxon. *Cr. 8vo.* 3s. 6d.

Notes and explanations on the chief difficulties of Greek and Latin Syntax, with numerous passages for exercise.

A DIGEST OF DEDUCTIVE LOGIC. By JOHNSON BARKER, B.A. *Crown 8vo.* 2s. 6d.

A short introduction to logic for students preparing for examinations.

TEST CARDS IN EUCLID AND ALGEBRA. By D. S. CALDERWOOD, Headmaster of the Normal School, Edinburgh. In a Packet of 40, with Answers. 1s.

A set of cards for advanced pupils in elementary schools.

HOW TO MAKE A DRESS. By J. A. E. WOOD. Illustrated. *Crown 8vo.* 1s. 6d.

A text-book for students preparing for the City and Guilds examination, based on the syllabus. The diagrams are numerous.

Fiction

LOCHINVAR. By S. R. CROCKETT, Author of 'The Raiders,' etc. Illustrated by FRANK RICHARDS. *Crown 8vo.* 6s.

BYEWAYS. By ROBERT HICHENS. Author of 'Flames,' etc. *Crown 8vo.* 6s.

THE MUTABLE MANY. By ROBERT BARR, Author of 'In the Midst of Alarms,' 'A Woman Intervenes,' etc. *Crown 8vo.* 6s.

THE LADY'S WALK. By Mrs. OLIPHANT. *Crown 8vo.* 6s.

A new book by this lamented author, somewhat in the style of her 'Beleagured City.'

TRAITS AND CONFIDENCES. By The Hon. EMILY LAW-
LESS, Author of ' Hurrish,' ' Maelcho,' etc. *Crown 8vo. 6s.*

BLADYS. By S. BARING GOULD, Author of 'The Broom
Squire,' etc. Illustrated by F. H. TOWNSEND. *Crown 8vo. 6s.*
A Romance of the last century.

THE POMP OF THE LAVILETTES. By GILBERT PARKER,
Author of ' The Seats of the Mighty,' etc. *Crown 8vo. 3s. 6d.*

A DAUGHTER OF STRIFE. By JANE HELEN FINDLATER,
Author of ' The Green Graves of Balgowrie.' *Crown 8vo. 6s.*
A story of 1710.

OVER THE HILLS. By MARY FINDLATER. *Crown 8vo. 6s.*
A novel by a sister of J. H. Findlater, the author of ' The Green Graves of Balgowrie.'

A CREEL OF IRISH STORIES. By JANE BARLOW, Author
of ' Irish Idylls.' *Crown 8vo. 6s.*

THE CLASH OF ARMS. By J. BLOUNDELLE BURTON,
Author of ' In the Day of Adversity.' *Crown 8vo. 6s.*

A PASSIONATE PILGRIM. By PERCY WHITE, Author of
' Mr. Bailey-Martin.' *Crown 8vo. 6s.*

SECRETARY TO BAYNE, M.P. By W. PETT RIDGE.
Crown 8vo. 6s.

THE BUILDERS. By J. S. FLETCHER, Author of 'When
Charles I. was King.' *Crown 8vo. 6s.*

JOSIAH'S WIFE. By NORMA LORIMER. *Crown 8vo. 6s.*

BY STROKE OF SWORD. By ANDREW BALFOUR. Illustrated by W. CUBITT COOKE. *Crown 8vo. 6s.*
A romance of the time of Elizabeth

THE SINGER OF MARLY. By I. HOOPER. Illustrated
by W. CUBITT COOKE. *Crown 8vo. 6s.*
A romance of adventure.

KIRKHAM'S FIND. By MARY GAUNT, Author of 'The
Moving Finger.' *Crown 8vo. 6s.*

THE FALL OF THE SPARROW. By M. C. BALFOUR.
Crown 8vo. 6s.

SCOTTISH BORDER LIFE. By JAMES C. DIBDIN. *Crown
8vo. 3s. 6d.*

A 2

A LIST OF

MESSRS. METHUEN'S

PUBLICATIONS

———◆———

Poetry

RUDYARD KIPLING'S NEW POEMS

Rudyard Kipling. THE SEVEN SEAS. By RUDYARD KIPLING. *Third Edition. Crown 8vo. Buckram, gilt top.* 6s.
'The new poems of Mr. Rudyard Kipling have all the spirit and swing of their predecessors. Patriotism is the solid concrete foundation on which Mr. Kipling has built the whole of his work.'—*Times.*
'Full of passionate patriotism and the Imperial spirit.'—*Yorkshire Post.*
'The Empire has found a singer; it is no depreciation of the songs to say that statesmen may have, one way or other, to take account of them.'—*Manchester Guardian.*
'Animated through and through with indubitable genius.'—*Daily Telegraph.*
'Packed with inspiration, with humour, with pathos.'—*Daily Chronicle.*
'All the pride of empire, all the intoxication of power, all the ardour, the energy, the masterful strength and the wonderful endurance and death-scorning pluck which are the very bone and fibre and marrow of the British character are here.'
—*Daily Mail.*

Rudyard Kipling. BARRACK-ROOM BALLADS; And Other Verses. By RUDYARD KIPLING. *Twelfth Edition. Crown 8vo.* 6s.
'Mr. Kipling's verse is strong, vivid, full of character. . . . Unmistakable genius rings in every line.'—*Times.*
The ballads teem with imagination, they palpitate with emotion. We read them with laughter and tears; the metres throb in our pulses, the cunningly ordered words tingle with life; and if this be not poetry, what is?'—*Pall Mall Gazette.*

'Q.'' POEMS AND BALLADS. By "Q.," Author of 'Green Bays,' etc. *Crown 8vo. Buckram.* 3s. 6d.
'This work has just the faint, ineffable touch and glow that make poetry 'Q.' has the true romantic spirit.'—*Speaker.*

"Q." GREEN BAYS: Verses and Parodies. By "Q.," Author of 'Dead Man's Rock,' etc. *Second Edition. Crown 8vo.* 3s. 6d.
'The verses display a rare and versatile gift of parody, great command of metre, and a very pretty turn of humour.'—*Times.*

E. Mackay. A SONG OF THE SEA. By ERIC MACKAY, Author of 'The Love Letters of a Violinist.' *Second Edition. Fcap. 8vo.* 5s.
'Everywhere Mr. Mackay displays himself the master of a style marked by all the characteristics of the best rhetoric. He has a keen sense of rhythm and of general balance; his verse is excellently sonorous.'—*Globe.*

Ibsen. BRAND. A Drama by HENRIK IBSEN. Translated by WILLIAM WILSON. *Second Edition. Crown 8vo.* 3s. 6d.

'The greatest world-poem of the nineteenth century next to "Faust." It is in the same set with "Agamemnon," with "Lear," with the literature that we now instinctively regard as high and holy.'—*Daily Chronicle.*

"A. G." VERSES TO ORDER. By "A. G." *Cr. 8vo.* 2s. 6d. *net.*

A small volume of verse by a writer whose initials are well known to Oxford men.
'A capital specimen of light academic poetry. These verses are very bright and engaging, easy and sufficiently witty.'—*St. James's Gazette.*

Belles Lettres, Anthologies, etc.

R. L. Stevenson. VAILIMA LETTERS. By ROBERT LOUIS STEVENSON. With an Etched Portrait by WILLIAM STRANG, and other Illustrations. *Second Edition. Crown 8vo. Buckram.* 7s. 6d.

'Few publications have in our time been more eagerly awaited than these "Vailima Letters," giving the first fruits of the correspondence of Robert Louis Stevenson. But, high as the tide of expectation has run, no reader can possibly be disappointed in the result.'—*St. James's Gazette.*

Henley and Whibley. A BOOK OF ENGLISH PROSE. Collected by W. E. HENLEY and CHARLES WHIBLEY. *Crown 8vo.* 6s.

'A unique volume of extracts—an art gallery of early prose.'—*Birmingham Post.*
'An admirable companion to Mr. Henley's "Lyra Heroica."'—*Saturday Review.*
'Quite delightful. A greater treat for those not well acquainted with pre-Restoration prose could not be imagined.'—*Athenæum.*

H. C. Beeching. LYRA SACRA : An Anthology of Sacred Verse. Edited by H. C. BEECHING, M.A. *Crown 8vo. Buckram.* 6s.

'A charming selection, which maintains a lofty standard of excellence.'—*Times.*

"Q." THE GOLDEN POMP : A Procession of English Lyrics from Surrey to Shirley, arranged by A. T. QUILLER COUCH. *Crown 8vo. Buckram.* 6s.

'A delightful volume : a really golden "Pomp."'—*Spectator.*

W. B. Yeats. AN ANTHOLOGY OF IRISH VERSE. Edited by W. B. YEATS. *Crown 8vo.* 3s. 6d.

'An attractive and catholic selection.'—*Times.*

G. W. Steevens. MONOLOGUES OF THE DEAD. By G. W. STEEVENS. *Foolscap 8vo.* 3s. 6d.

A series of Soliloquies in which famous men of antiquity—Julius Cæsar, Nero, Alcibiades, etc., attempt to express themselves in the modes of thought and language of to-day.
The effect is sometimes splendid, sometimes bizarre, but always amazingly clever —*Pall Mall Gazette.*

Victor Hugo. THE LETTERS OF VICTOR HUGO. Translated from the French by F. CLARKE, M.A. *In Two Volumes. Demy 8vo. 10s. 6d. each. Vol. I.* 1815-35.

This is the first volume of one of the most interesting and important collection of letters ever published in France. The correspondence dates from Victor Hugo's boyhood to his death, and none of the letters have been published before. The arrangement is chiefly chronological, but where there is an interesting set of letters to one person these are arranged together. The first volume contains, among others, (1) Letters to his father; (2) to his young wife; (2) to his confessor, Lamennais; a very important set of about fifty letters to Sainte-Beauve; (5) letters about his early books and plays.

'A charming and vivid picture of a man whose egotism never marred his natural kindness, and whose vanity did not impair his greatness.'—*Standard.*

C. H. Pearson. ESSAYS AND CRITICAL REVIEWS. By C. H. PEARSON, M.A., Author of 'National Life and Character.' Edited, with a Biographical Sketch, by H. A. STRONG, M.A., LL.D. With a Portrait. *Demy 8vo.* 10s. 6d.

'Remarkable for careful handling, breadth of view, and knowledge.'—*Scotsman.*
'Charming essays.'—*Spectator.*

W. M. Dixon. A PRIMER OF TENNYSON. By W. M. DIXON, M.A., Professor of English Literature at Mason College. *Crown 8vo.* 2s. 6d.

'Much sound and well-expressed criticism and acute literary judgments. The biblio graphy is a boon.'—*Speaker.*

W. A. Craigie. A PRIMER OF BURNS. By W. A. CRAIGIE. *Crown 8vo.* 2s. 6d.

This book is planned on a method similar to the 'Primer of Tennyson.' It has also a glossary.
'A valuable addition to the literature of the poet.'—*Times.*
'An excellent short account.'—*Pall Mall Gazette.*
'An admirable introduction.'—*Globe.*

Sterne. THE LIFE AND OPINIONS OF TRISTRAM SHANDY. By LAWRENCE STERNE. With an Introduction by CHARLES WHIBLEY, and a Portrait. *2 vols.* 7s.

'Very dainty volumes are these; the paper, type, and light-green binding are all very agreeable to the eye. *Simplex munditiis* is the phrase that might be applied to them.'—*Globe.*

Congreve. THE COMEDIES OF WILLIAM CONGREVE. With an Introduction by G. S. STREET, and a Portrait. *2 vols.* 7s.

'The volumes are strongly bound in green buckram, are of a convenient size, and pleasant to look upon, so that whether on the shelf, or on the table, or in the hand the possessor is thoroughly content with them.'—*Guardian.*

Morier. THE ADVENTURES OF HAJJI BABA OF ISPAHAN. By JAMES MORIER. With an Introduction by E. G. BROWNE, M.A., and a Portrait. *2 vols.* 7s.

Walton. THE LIVES OF DONNE, WOTTON, HOOKER, HERBERT, AND SANDERSON. By IZAAK WALTON. With an Introduction by VERNON BLACKBURN, and a Portrait. 3s. 6d.

Johnson. THE LIVES OF THE ENGLISH POETS. By SAMUEL JOHNSON, LL.D. With an Introduction by J. H. MILLAR, and a Portrait. 3 *vols.* 10*s.* 6*d.*

Burns. THE POEMS OF ROBERT BURNS. Edited by· ANDREW LANG and W. A. CRAIGIE. With Portrait. *Demy 8vo,* *gilt top.* 6*s.*

This edition contains a carefully collated Text, numerous Notes, critical and textual, a critical and biographical Introduction, and a Glossary.

'Among the editions in one volume, Mr. Andrew Lang's will take the place of authority.'—*Times.*

F. Langbridge. BALLADS OF THE BRAVE: Poems of Chivalry, Enterprise, Courage, and Constancy. Edited, with Notes, by Rev. F. LANGBRIDGE. *Crown 8vo. Buckram.* 3*s.* 6*d. School Edition.* 2*s.* 6*d.*

'A very happy conception happily carried out. These "Ballads of the Brave" are intended to suit the real tastes of boys, and will suit the taste of the great majority.' —*Spectator.* 'The book is full of splendid things.'—*World.*

Illustrated Books

Jane Barlow. THE BATTLE OF THE FROGS AND MICE, translated by JANE BARLOW, Author of 'Irish Idylls,' and pictured by F. D. BEDFORD. *Small 4to.* 6*s. net.*

S. Baring Gould. A BOOK OF FAIRY TALES retold by S. BARING GOULD. With numerous illustrations and initial letters by ARTHUR J. GASKIN. *Second Edition. Crown 8vo. Buckram.* 6*s.*

'Mr. Baring Gould is deserving of gratitude, in re-writing in honest, simple style the old stories that delighted the childhood of "our fathers and grandfathers." As to the form of the book, and the printing, which is by Messrs. Constable, it were difficult to commend overmuch. —*Saturday Review.*

S. Baring Gould. OLD ENGLISH FAIRY TALES. Collected and edited by S. BARING GOULD. With Numerous Illustrations by F. D. BEDFORD. *Second Edition. Crown 8vo. Buckram.* 6*s.*

'A charming volume, which children will be sure to appreciate. The stories have been selected with great ingenuity from various old ballads and folk-tales, and, having been somewhat altered and readjusted, now stand forth, clothed in Mr. Baring Gould's delightful English, to enchant youthful readers.'—*Guardian.*

S. Baring Gould. A BOOK OF NURSERY SONGS AND RHYMES. Edited by S. BARING GOULD, and Illustrated by the Birmingham Art School. *Buckram, gilt top. Crown 8vo.* 6*s.*

'The volume is very complete in its way, as it contains nursery songs to the number of 77, game-rhymes, and jingles. To the student we commend the sensible introduction, and the explanatory notes. The volume is superbly printed on soft, thick paper, which it is a pleasure to touch; and the borders and pictures are among the very best specimens we have seen of the Gaskin school.'—*Birmingham Gazette.*

H. C. Beeching. A BOOK OF CHRISTMAS VERSE. Edited by H. C. BEECHING, M.A., and Illustrated by WALTER CRANE. *Crown 8vo, gilt top.* 5s.

A collection of the best verse inspired by the birth of Christ from the Middle Ages to the present day. A distinction of the book is the large number of poems it contains by modern authors, a few of which are here printed for the first time.

'An anthology which, from its unity of aim and high poetic excellence, has a better right to exist than most of its fellows.'—*Guardian.*

History

Gibbon. THE DECLINE AND FALL OF THE ROMAN EMPIRE. By EDWARD GIBBON. A New Edition, Edited with Notes, Appendices, and Maps, by J. B. BURY, M.A., Fellow of Trinity College, Dublin. *In Seven Volumes. Demy 8vo. Gilt top.* 8s. 6d. each. Also crown 8vo. 6s. each. Vols. I., II., and III.

'The time has certainly arrived for a new edition of Gibbon's great work. . . . Professor Bury is the right man to undertake this task. His learning is amazing, both in extent and accuracy. The book is issued in a handy form, and at a moderate price, and it is admirably printed.'—*Times.*

'The edition is edited as a classic should be edited, removing nothing, yet indicating the value of the text, and bringing it up to date. It promises to be of the utmost value, and will be a welcome addition to many libraries.'—*Scotsman.*

'This edition, so far as one may judge from the first instalment, is a marvel of erudition and critical skill, and it is the very minimum of praise to predict that the seven volumes of it will supersede Dean Milman's as the standard edition of our great historical classic.'—*Glasgow Herald.*

'The beau-ideal Gibbon has arrived at last.'—*Sketch.*

'At last there is an adequate modern edition of Gibbon. . . . The best edition the nineteenth century could produce.'—*Manchester Guardian.*

Flinders Petrie. A HISTORY OF EGYPT, FROM THE EARLIEST TIMES TO THE PRESENT DAY. Edited by W. M. FLINDERS PETRIE, D.C.L., LL.D., Professor of Egyptology at University College. *Fully Illustrated. In Six Volumes. Crown 8vo.* 6s. each.

Vol. I. PREHISTORIC TIMES TO XVI. DYNASTY. W. M. F. Petrie. *Third Edition.*

Vol. II. THE XVIITH AND XVIIITH DYNASTIES. W. M. F. Petrie. *Second Edition.*

'A history written in the spirit of scientific precision so worthily represented by Dr. Petrie and his school cannot but promote sound and accurate study, and supply a vacant place in the English literature of Egyptology.'—*Times.*

Flinders Petrie. EGYPTIAN TALES. Edited by W. M. FLINDERS PETRIE. Illustrated by TRISTRAM ELLIS. *In Two Volumes. Crown 8vo.* 3s. 6d. each.

'A valuable addition to the literature of comparative folk-lore. The drawings are really illustrations in the literal sense of the word.'—*Globe.*

'It has a scientific value to the student of history and archæology.'—*Scotsman.*

'Invaluable as a picture of life in Palestine and Egypt.'—*Daily News.*

Flinders Petrie. EGYPTIAN DECORATIVE ART. By W. M. FLINDERS PETRIE, D.C.L. With 120 Illustrations. *Crown 8vo.* 3*s.* 6*d.*

'Professor Flinders Petrie is not only a profound Egyptologist, but an accomplished student of comparative archæology. In these lectures, delivered at the Royal Institution, he displays both qualifications with rare skill in elucidating the development of decorative art in Egypt, and in tracing its influence on the art of other countries.'—*Times.*

S. Baring Gould. THE TRAGEDY OF THE CÆSARS. The Emperors of the Julian and Claudian Lines. With numerous Illustrations from Busts, Gems, Cameos, etc. By S. BARING GOULD, Author of 'Mehalah,' etc. *Fourth Edition. Royal 8vo.* 15*s.*

'A most splendid and fascinating book on a subject of undying interest. The great feature of the book is the use the author has made of the existing portraits of the Caesars, and the admirable critical subtlety he has exhibited in dealing with this line of research. It is brilliantly written, and the illustrations are supplied on a scale of profuse magnificence.'—*Daily Chronicle.*
'The volumes will in no sense disappoint the general reader. Indeed, in their way, there is nothing in any sense so good in English. . . . Mr. Baring Gould has presented his narrative in such a way as not to make one dull page.'—*Athenæum.*

H. de B. Gibbins. INDUSTRY IN ENGLAND : HISTORICAL OUTLINES. By H. DE B. GIBBINS, M.A., D.Litt. With 5 Maps. *Second Edition. Demy 8vo.* 10*s.* 6*d.*

This book is written with the view of affording a clear view of the main facts of English Social and Industrial History placed in due perspective. Beginning with prehistoric times, it passes in review the growth and advance of industry up to the nineteenth century, showing its gradual development and progress. The book is illustrated by Maps, Diagrams, and Tables.

A. Clark. THE COLLEGES OF OXFORD : Their History and their Traditions. By Members of the University. Edited by A. CLARK, M.A., Fellow and Tutor of Lincoln College. *8vo.* 12*s.* 6*d.*

'A work which will certainly be appealed to for many years as the standard book on the Colleges of Oxford.'—*Athenæum.*

Perrens. THE HISTORY OF FLORENCE FROM 1434 TO 1492. By F. T. PERRENS. Translated by HANNAH LYNCH. *8vo.* 12*s.* 6*d.*

A history of Florence under the domination of Cosimo, Piero, and Lorenzo de Medicis.
'This is a standard book by an honest and intelligent historian, who has deserved well of all who are interested in Italian history.'—*Manchester Guardian.*

J. Wells. A SHORT HISTORY OF ROME. By J. WELLS, M.A., Fellow and Tutor of Wadham Coll., Oxford. With 4 Maps. *Crown 8vo.* 3*s.* 6*d.*

This book is intended for the Middle and Upper Forms of Public Schools and for Pass Students at the Universities. It contains copious Tables, etc.
'An original work written on an original plan, and with uncommon freshness and vigour.'—*Speaker.*

E. L. S. Horsburgh. THE CAMPAIGN OF WATERLOO. By E. L. S. HORSBURGH, B.A. *With Plans. Crown 8vo.* 5s.

'A brilliant essay—simple, sound, and thorough.'—*Daily Chronicle.*
'A study, the most concise, the most lucid, the most critical that has been produced. —*Birmingham Mercury,*

H. B. George. BATTLES OF ENGLISH HISTORY. By H. B. GEORGE, M.A., Fellow of New College, Oxford. *With numerous Plans. Third Edition. Crown 8vo.* 6s.

'Mr. George has undertaken a very useful task—that of making military affairs intelligible and instructive to non-military readers—and has executed it with laudable intelligence and industry, and with a large measure of success.'—*Times.*

O. Browning. A SHORT HISTORY OF MEDIÆVAL ITALY, A.D. 1250-1530. By OSCAR BROWNING, Fellow and Tutor of King's College, Cambridge. *Second Edition. In Two Volumes. Crown 8vo.* 5s. *each.*

VOL. I. 1250-1409.—Guelphs and Ghibellines.
VOL. II. 1409-1530.—The Age of the Condottieri.

'A vivid picture of mediæval Italy.'—*Standard.*
'Mr. Browning is to be congratulated on the production of a work of immense labour and learning.'—*Westminster Gazette.*

O'Grady. THE STORY OF IRELAND. By STANDISH O'GRADY, Author of 'Finn and his Companions.' *Cr. 8vo.* 2s. 6d.

'Most delightful, most stimulating. Its racy humour, its original imaginings, make it one of the freshest, breeziest volumes.'—*Methodist Times.*

Biography

S. Baring Gould. THE LIFE OF NAPOLEON BONAPARTE. By S. BARING GOULD. With over 450 Illustrations in the Text and 12 Photogravure Plates. *Large quarto. Gilt top.* 36s.

'The best biography of Napoleon in our tongue, nor have the French as good a biographer of their hero. A book very nearly as good as Southey's "Life of Nelson."'—*Manchester Guardian.*
'The main feature of this gorgeous volume is its great wealth of beautiful photogravures and finely-executed wood engravings, constituting a complete pictorial chronicle of Napoleon I.'s personal history from the days of his early childhood at Ajaccio to the date of his second interment under the dome of the Invalides in Paris.'—*Daily Telegraph.*
'The most elaborate account of Napoleon ever produced by an English writer.'—*Daily Chronicle.*
'A brilliant and attractive volume. Never before have so many pictures relating to Napoleon been brought within the limits of an English book.'—*Globe.*
'Particular notice is due to the vast collection of contemporary illustrations.'—*Guardian.*
'Nearly all the illustrations are real contributions to history.'—*Westminster Gazette.*
'The illustrations are of supreme interest.'—*Standard.*

Morris Fuller. THE LIFE AND WRITINGS OF JOHN
DAVENANT, D.D. (1571-1641), President of Queen's College,
Lady Margaret Professor of Divinity, Bishop of Salisbury. By
MORRIS FULLER, B.D. *Demy 8vo.* 10s. 6d.

'A valuable contribution to ecclesiastical history.'—*Birmingham Gazette.*

J. M. Rigg. ST. ANSELM OF CANTERBURY : A CHAPTER
IN THE HISTORY OF RELIGION. By J. M. RIGG. *Demy 8vo.* 7s. 6d.

'Mr. Rigg has told the story of the great Primate's life with scholarly ability, and
has thereby contributed an interesting chapter to the history of the Norman period.'
—*Daily Chronicle.*

F. W. Joyce. THE LIFE OF SIR FREDERICK GORE
OUSELEY. By F. W. JOYCE, M.A. With Portraits and Illustrations. *Crown 8vo.* 7s. 6d.

'This book has been undertaken in quite the right spirit, and written with sympathy
insight, and considerable literary skill.'—*Times.*

W. G. Collingwood. THE LIFE OF JOHN RUSKIN. By
W. G. COLLINGWOOD, M.A., Editor of Mr. Ruskin's Poems. With
numerous Portraits, and 13 Drawings by Mr. Ruskin. *Second
Edition.* 2 vols. *8vo.* 32s.

'No more magnificent volumes have been published for a long time.'—*Times.*
'It is long since we had a biography with such delights of substance and of form.
Such a book is a pleasure for the day, and a joy for ever.'—*Daily Chronicle.*

C. Waldstein. JOHN RUSKIN : a Study. By CHARLES
WALDSTEIN, M.A., Fellow of King's College, Cambridge. With a
Photogravure Portrait after Professor HERKOMER. *Post 8vo.* 5s.

'A thoughtful, impartial, well-written criticism of Ruskin's teaching, intended to
separate what the author regards as valuable and permanent from what is transient
and erroneous in the great master's writing.'—*Daily Chronicle.*

W. H. Hutton. THE LIFE OF SIR THOMAS MORE. By
W. H. HUTTON, M.A., Author of 'William Laud.' *With Portraits.*
Crown 8vo. 5s.

'The book lays good claim to high rank among our biographies. It is excellently,
even lovingly, written.'—*Scotsman.*   'An excellent monograph.'—*Times.*

Clark Russell. THE LIFE OF ADMIRAL LORD COL-
LINGWOOD. By W. CLARK RUSSELL, Author of 'The Wreck
of the Grosvenor.' With Illustrations by F. BRANGWYN. *Third
Edition. Crown 8vo.* 6s.

'A book which we should like to see in the hands of every boy in the country.'—
St. James's Gazette.   'A really good book.'—*Saturday Review.*

Southey. ENGLISH SEAMEN (Howard, Clifford, Hawkins, Drake, Cavendish). By ROBERT SOUTHEY. Edited, with an Introduction, by DAVID HANNAY. *Second Edition. Crown 8vo. 6s.*

'Admirable and well-told stories of our naval history.'—*Army and Navy Gazette.*
'A brave, inspiriting book.'—*Black and White.*

Travel, Adventure and Topography

R. S. S. Baden-Powell. THE DOWNFALL OF PREMPEH. A Diary of Life with the Native Levy in Ashanti, 1895. By Colonel BADEN-POWELL. With 21 Illustrations and a Map. *Demy 8vo. 10s. 6d.*

'A compact, faithful, most readable record of the campaign.'—*Daily News.*
'A bluff and vigorous narrative.'—*Glasgow Herald.*

R. S. S. Baden-Powell. THE MATEBELE CAMPAIGN 1896. By Colonel R. S. S. BADEN-POWELL. With nearly 100 Illustrations. *Second Edition. Demy 8vo. 15s.*

'Written in an unaffectedly light and humorous style.'—*The World.*
'A very racy and eminently readable book.'—*St. James's Gazette.*
'As a straightforward account of a great deal of plucky work unpretentiously done, this book is well worth reading. The simplicity of the narrative is all in its favour, and accords in a peculiarly English fashion with the nature of the subject.' *Times.*

Captain Hinde. THE FALL OF THE CONGO ARABS. By SIDNEY L. HINDE. With Portraits and Plans. *Demy 8vo. 12s. 6d.*

'The book is full of good things, and of sustained interest.'—*St. James's Gazette.*
A graphic sketch of one of the most exciting and important episodes in the struggle for supremacy in Central Africa between the Arabs and their European rivals. Apart from the story of the campaign, Captain Hinde's book is mainly remarkable for the fulness with which he discusses the question of cannibalism. It is, indeed, the only connected narrative—in English, at any rate—which has been published of this particular episode in African history.'—*Times.*
'Captain Hinde's book is one of the most interesting and valuable contributions yet made to the literature of modern Africa.'—*Daily News.*

W. Crooke. THE NORTH-WESTERN PROVINCES OF INDIA: THEIR ETHNOLOGY AND ADMINISTRATION. By W. CROOKE. With Maps and Illustrations. *Demy 8vo. 10s. 6d.*

'A carefully and well-written account of one of the most important provinces of the Empire. In seven chapters Mr. Crooke deals successively with the land in its physical aspect, the province under Hindoo and Mussulman rule, the province under British rule, the ethnology and sociology of the province, the religious and social life of the people, the land and its settlement, and the native peasant in his relation to the land. The illustrations are good and well selected, and the map is excellent.'—*Manchester Guardian.*

W. B. Worsfold. SOUTH AFRICA : Its History and its Future. By W. BASIL WORSFOLD, M.A. *With a Map. Second Edition. Crown 8vo.* 6s.

'An intensely interesting book.'—*Daily Chronicle.*
'A monumental work compressed into a very moderate compass.'—*World.*

General Literature

S. Baring Gould. OLD COUNTRY LIFE. By S. BARING GOULD, Author of 'Mehalah,' etc. With Sixty-seven Illustrations by W. PARKINSON, F. D. BEDFORD, and F. MASEY. *Large Crown 8vo.* 10s. 6d. *Fifth and Cheaper Edition.* 6s.

"Old Country Life, as healthy wholesome reading, full of breezy life and movement, full of quaint stories vigorously told, will not be excelled by any book to be published throughout the year. Sound, hearty, and English to the core.'—*World.*

S. Baring Gould. HISTORIC ODDITIES AND STRANGE EVENTS. By S. BARING GOULD. *Third Edition. Crown 8vo.* 6s.

'A collection of exciting and entertaining chapters. The whole volume is delightful reading.'—*Times.*

S. Baring Gould. FREAKS OF FANATICISM. By S. BARING GOULD. *Third Edition. Crown 8vo.* 6s.

'Mr. Baring Gould has a keen eye for colour and effect, and the subjects he has chosen give ample scope to his descriptive and analytic faculties. A perfectly fascinating book.'—*Scottish Leader.*

S. Baring Gould. A GARLAND OF COUNTRY SONG : English Folk Songs with their Traditional Melodies. Collected and arranged by S. BARING GOULD and H. FLEETWOOD SHEPPARD. *Demy 4to.* 6s.

S. Baring Gould. SONGS OF THE WEST : Traditional Ballads and Songs of the West of England, with their Traditional Melodies. Collected by S. BARING GOULD, M.A., and H. FLEETWOOD SHEPPARD, M.A. Arranged for Voice and Piano. In 4 Parts (containing 25 Songs each), *Parts I., II., III.,* 3s. each. *Part IV.,* 5s. *In one Vol., French morocco,* 15s.

'A rich collection of humour, pathos, grace, and poetic fancy.'—*Saturday Review.*

S. Baring Gould. YORKSHIRE ODDITIES AND STRANGE EVENTS. *Fourth Edition. Crown 8vo. 6s.*

S. Baring Gould. STRANGE SURVIVALS AND SUPER-STITIONS. With Illustrations. By S. BARING GOULD. *Crown 8vo. Second Edition. 6s.*

'We have read Mr. Baring Gould's book from beginning to end. It is full of quaint and various information, and there is not a dull page in it.'—*Notes and Queries.*

S. Baring Gould. THE DESERTS OF SOUTHERN FRANCE. By S. BARING·GOULD. With numerous Illustrations by F. D. BEDFORD, S. HUTTON, etc. *2 vols. Demy 8vo. 32s.*

'His two richly-illustrated volumes are full of matter of interest to the geologist, the archæologist, and the student of history and manners.'—*Scotsman.*

G. W. Steevens. NAVAL POLICY: WITH A DESCRIPTION OF ENGLISH AND FOREIGN NAVIES. By G. W. STEEVENS. *Demy 8vo. 6s.*

This book is a description of the British and other more important navies of the world, with a sketch of the lines on which our naval policy might possibly be developed. It describes our recent naval policy, and shows what our naval force really is. A detailed but non-technical account is given of the instruments of modern warfare—guns, armour, engines, and the like—with a view to determine how far we are abreast of modern invention and modern requirements. An ideal policy is then sketched for the building and manning of our fleet; and the last chapter is devoted to docks, coaling-stations, and especially colonial defence.

'An extremely able and interesting work.'—*Daily Chronicle.*

W. E. Gladstone. THE SPEECHES AND PUBLIC ADDRESSES OF THE RT. HON. W. E. GLADSTONE, M.P. Edited by A. W. HUTTON, M.A., and H. J. COHEN, M.A. With Portraits. *8vo. Vols. IX. and X. 12s. 6d. each.*

J. Wells. OXFORD AND OXFORD LIFE. By Members of the University. Edited by J. WELLS, M.A., Fellow and Tutor of Wadham College. *Crown 8vo. 3s. 6d.*

'We congratulate Mr. Wells on the production of a readable and intelligent account of Oxford as it is at the present time, written by persons who are possessed of a close acquaintance with the system and life of the University.'—*Athenæum.*

L. Whibley. GREEK OLIGARCHIES : THEIR ORGANISATION AND CHARACTER. By L. WHIBLEY, M.A., Fellow of Pembroke College, Cambridge. *Crown 8vo. 6s.*

'An exceedingly useful handbook : a careful and well-arranged study of an obscure subject.'—*Times.*

'Mr. Whibley is never tedious or pedantic.'—*Pall Mall Gazette.*

L. L. Price. ECONOMIC SCIENCE AND PRACTICE. By L. L. PRICE, M.A., Fellow of Oriel College, Oxford. *Crown 8vo.* 6s.

'The book is well written, giving evidence of considerable literary ability, and clear mental grasp of the subject under consideration.'—*Western Morning News.*

C. F. Andrews. CHRISTIANITY AND THE LABOUR QUESTION. By C. F. ANDREWS, B.A. *Crown 8vo.* 2s. 6d.

'A bold and scholarly survey.'—*Speaker.*

J. S. Shedlock. THE PIANOFORTE SONATA: Its Origin and Development. By J. S. SHEDLOCK. *Crown 8vo.* 5s.

'This work should be in the possession of every musician and amateur, for it not only embodies a concise and lucid history of the origin of one of the most important forms of musical composition, but, by reason of the painstaking research and accuracy of the author's statements, it is a very valuable work for reference.' —*Athenæum.*

E. M. Bowden. THE EXAMPLE OF BUDDHA: Being Quotations from Buddhist Literature for each Day in the Year. Compiled by E. M. BOWDEN. With Preface by Sir EDWIN ARNOLD. *Third Edition.* 16mo. 2s. 6d.

Science

Freudenreich. DAIRY BACTERIOLOGY. A Short Manual for the Use of Students. By Dr. ED. VON FREUDENREICH. Translated from the German by J. R. AINSWORTH DAVIS, B.A., F.C.P. *Crown 8vo.* 2s. 6d.

Chalmers Mitchell. OUTLINES OF BIOLOGY. By P. CHALMERS MITCHELL, M.A., F.Z.S. *Fully Illustrated. Crown 8vo.* 6s.

A text-book designed to cover the new Schedule issued by the Royal College of Physicians and Surgeons.

G. Massee. A MONOGRAPH OF THE MYXOGASTRES. By GEORGE MASSEE. With 12 Coloured Plates. *Royal 8vo.* 18s. net.

'A work much in advance of any book in the language treating of this group of organisms. It is indispensable to every student of the Myxogastres. The coloured plates deserve high praise for their accuracy and execution.'—*Nature.*

Philosophy

L. T. Hobhouse. THE THEORY OF KNOWLEDGE. By L. T. HOBHOUSE, Fellow and Tutor of Corpus College, Oxford. *Demy 8vo.* 21s.

'The most important contribution to English philosophy since the publication of Mr. Bradley's "Appearance and Reality." Full of brilliant criticism and of positive theories which are models of lucid statement.'—*Glasgow Herald.*

'An elaborate and often brilliantly written volume. The treatment is one of great · freshness, and the illustrations are particularly numerous and apt.'—*Times.*

W. H. Fairbrother. THE PHILOSOPHY OF T. H. GREEN. By W. H. FAIRBROTHER, M.A., Lecturer at Lincoln College, Oxford. *Crown 8vo.* 3s. 6d.

This volume is expository, not critical, and is intended for senior students at the Universities and others, as a statement of Green's teaching, and an introduction to the study of Idealist Philosophy.

'In every way an admirable book. As an introduction to the writings of perhaps the most remarkable speculative thinker whom England has produced in the present century, nothing could be better.'—*Glasgow Herald.*

F. W. Bussell. THE SCHOOL OF PLATO : its Origin and its Revival under the Roman Empire. By F. W. BUSSELL, M.A., Fellow and Tutor of Brasenose College, Oxford. *Demy 8vo.* 10s. 6d.

'A highly valuable contribution to the history of ancient thought.'—*Glasgow Herald.*
'A clever and stimulating book, provocative of thought and deserving careful reading.'—*Manchester Guardian.*

F. S. Granger. THE WORSHIP OF THE ROMANS. By F. S. GRANGER, M.A., Litt.D., Professor of Philosophy at University College, Nottingham. *Crown 8vo.* 6s.

'A scholarly analysis of the religious ceremonies, beliefs, and superstitions of ancient Rome, conducted in the new instructive light of comparative anthropology.'—*Times.*

Theology

E. C. S. Gibson. THE XXXIX. ARTICLES OF THE CHURCH OF ENGLAND. Edited with an Introduction by E. C. S. GIBSON, D.D., Vicar of Leeds, late Principal of Wells Theological College. *In Two Volumes. Demy 8vo.* 15s.

'The tone maintained throughout is not that of the partial advocate, but the faithful exponent.'—*Scotsman.*

'There are ample proofs of clearness of expression, sobriety of judgment, and breadth of view. . . . The book will be welcome to all students of the subject, and its sound, definite, and loyal theology ought to be of great service.'—*National Observer.*

'So far from repelling the general reader, its orderly arrangement, lucid treatment, and felicity of diction invite and encourage his attention.'—*Yorkshire Post.*

R. L. Ottley. THE DOCTRINE OF THE INCARNATION. By R. L. OTTLEY, M.A., late fellow of Magdalen College, Oxon., Principal of Pusey House. *In Two Volumes. Demy 8vo.* 15*s.*
'Learned and reverent: lucid and well arranged.'—*Record.*
'Accurate, well ordered, and judicious.'—*National Observer.*
'A clear and remarkably full account of the main currents of speculation. Scholarly precision . . . genuine tolerance . . . intense interest in his subject—are Mr. Ottley's merits.'—*Guardian.*

F. B. Jevons. AN INTRODUCTION TO THE HISTORY OF RELIGION. By F. B. JEVONS, M.A., Litt.D., Principal of Bishop Hatfield's Hall. *Demy 8vo.* 10*s.* 6*d.*

Mr. F. B. Jevons' 'Introduction to the History of Religion' treats of early religion, from the point of view of Anthropology and Folk-lore; and is the first attempt that has been made in any language to weave together the results of recent investigations into such topics as Sympathetic Magic, Taboo, Totemism. Fetishism, etc., so as to present a systematic account of the growth of primitive religion and the development of early religious institutions.
'Dr. Jevons has written a notable work, and we can strongly recommend it to the serious attention of theologians, anthropologists, and classical scholars.'—*Manchester Guardian.*
'The merit of this book lies in the penetration, the singular acuteness and force of the author's judgment. He is at once critical and luminous, at once just and suggestive. It is but rarely that one meets with a book so comprehensive and so thorough as this, and it is more than an ordinary pleasure for the reviewer to welcome and recommend it. Dr. Jevons is something more than an historian of primitive belief—he is a philosophic thinker, who sees his subject clearly and sees it whole, whose mastery of detail is no less complete than his view of the broader aspects and issues of his subject is convincing.'—*Birmingham Post.*

S. R. Driver. SERMONS ON SUBJECTS CONNECTED WITH THE OLD TESTAMENT. By S. R. DRIVER, D.D., Canon of Christ Church, Regius Professor of Hebrew in the University of Oxford. *Crown 8vo.* 6*s.*
'A welcome companion to the author's famous 'Introduction.' No man can read these discourses without feeling that Dr. Driver is fully alive to the deeper teaching of the Old Testament.'—*Guardian.*

T. K. Cheyne. FOUNDERS OF OLD TESTAMENT CRITICISM: Biographical, Descriptive, and Critical Studies. By T. K. CHEYNE, D.D., Oriel Professor of the Interpretation of Holy Scripture at Oxford. *Large crown 8vo.* 7*s.* 6*d.*
This book is a historical sketch of O. T. Criticism in the form of biographical studies from the days of Eichhorn to those of Driver and Robertson Smith.
'A very learned and instructive work.'—*Times.*

C. H. Prior. CAMBRIDGE SERMONS. Edited by C. H. PRIOR, M.A., Fellow and Tutor of Pembroke College. *Crown 8vo.* 6*s.*
A volume of sermons preached before the University of Cambridge by various preachers, including the Archbishop of Canterbury and Bishop Westcott.
A representative collection. Bishop Westcott's is a noble sermon.'—*Guardian.*

E. B. Layard. RELIGION IN BOYHOOD. Notes on the Religious Training of Boys. With a Preface by J. R. ILLINGWORTH. By E. B. LAYARD, M.A. 18*mo.* 1*s.*

W. Yorke Faussett. THE *DE CATECHIZANDIS RUDIBUS* OF ST. AUGUSTINE. Edited, with Introduction, Notes, etc., by W. YORKE FAUSSETT, M.A., late Scholar of Balliol Coll. *Crown 8vo. 3s. 6d.*

An edition of a Treatise on the Essentials of Christian Doctrine, and the best methods of impressing them on candidates for baptism.

'Ably and judiciously edited on the same principle as the ordinary Greek and Latin texts.'—*Glasgow Herald.*

Devotional Books.

With Full-page Illustrations. Fcap. 8vo. Buckram. 3s. 6d. Padded morocco, 5s.

THE IMITATION OF CHRIST. By THOMAS À KEMPIS. With an Introduction by DEAN FARRAR. Illustrated by C. M. GERE, and printed in black and red. *Second Edition.*

'Amongst all the innumerable English editions of the "Imitation," there can have been few which were prettier than this one, printed in strong and handsome type, with all the glory of red initials.'—*Glasgow Herald.*

THE CHRISTIAN YEAR. By JOHN KEBLE. With an Introduction and Notes by W. LOCK, D.D., Warden of Keble College, Ireland, Professor at Oxford. Illustrated by R. ANNING BELL.

'The present edition is annotated with all the care and insight to be expected from Mr. Lock. The progress and circumstances of its composition are detailed in the Introduction. There is an interesting Appendix on the MSS. of the "Christian Year," and another giving the order in which the poems were written. A "Short Analysis of the Thought" is prefixed to each, and any difficulty in the text is explained in a note.'—*Guardian.*

'The most acceptable edition of this ever-popular work.'—*Globe.*

Leaders of Religion

Edited by H. C. BEECHING, M.A. *With Portraits, crown 8vo.*

A series of short biographies of the most prominent leaders of religious life and thought of all ages and countries.

3/6

The following are ready—

CARDINAL NEWMAN. By R. H. HUTTON.
JOHN WESLEY. By J. H. OVERTON, M.A.
BISHOP WILBERFORCE. By G. W. DANIEL, M.A.
CARDINAL MANNING. By A. W. HUTTON, M.A.
CHARLES SIMEON. By H. C. G. MOULE, M.A.
JOHN KEBLE. By WALTER LOCK, D.D.
THOMAS CHALMERS. By Mrs. OLIPHANT.
LANCELOT ANDREWES. By R. L. OTTLEY, M.A.
AUGUSTINE OF CANTERBURY. By E. L. CUTTS, D.D.
WILLIAM LAUD. By W. H. HUTTON, B.D.

JOHN KNOX. By F. M'CUNN.
JOHN HOWE. By R. F. HORTON, D.D.
BISHOP KEN. By F. A. CLARKE, M.A.
GEORGE FOX, THE QUAKER. By T. HODGKIN, D.C.L.
Other volumes will be announced in due course.

Fiction

SIX SHILLING NOVELS

Marie Corelli's Novels

Crown 8vo. 6s. each.

A ROMANCE OF TWO WORLDS. *Sixteenth Edition.*

VENDETTA. *Thirteenth Edition.*

THELMA. *Seventeenth Edition.*

ARDATH. *Eleventh Edition.*

THE SOUL OF LILITH *Ninth Edition.*

WORMWOOD. *Eighth Edition.*

BARABBAS: A DREAM OF THE WORLD'S TRAGEDY. *Thirty-first Edition.*

'The tender reverence of the treatment and the imaginative beauty of the writing have reconciled us to the daring of the conception, and the conviction is forced on us that even so exalted a subject cannot be made too familiar to us, provided it be presented in the true spirit of Christian faith. The amplifications of the Scripture narrative are often conceived with high poetic insight, and this "Dream of the World's Tragedy" is, despite some trifling incongruities, a lofty and not inadequate paraphrase of the supreme climax of the inspired narrative.'—*Dublin Review.*

THE SORROWS OF SATAN. *Thirty-sixth Edition.*

'A very powerful piece of work. . . . The conception is magnificent, and is likely to win an abiding place within the memory of man. . . . The author has immense command of language, and a limitless audacity. . . . This interesting and remarkable romance will live long after much of the ephemeral literature of the day is forgotten. . . . A literary phenomenon . . . novel, and even sublime.'—W. T. STEAD in the *Review of Reviews.*

Anthony Hope's Novels

Crown 8vo. 6s. each.

THE GOD IN THE CAR. *Seventh Edition.*

'A very remarkable book, deserving of critical analysis impossible within our limit; brilliant, but not superficial; well considered, but not elaborated; constructed with the proverbial art that conceals, but yet allows itself to be enjoyed by readers to whom fine literary method is a keen pleasure.'—*The World.*

A CHANGE OF AIR. *Fourth Edition.*

'A graceful, vivacious comedy, true to human nature. The characters are traced with a masterly hand.'—*Times.*

A MAN OF MARK. *Fourth Edition.*

'Of all Mr. Hope's books, "A Man of Mark" is the one which best compares with "The Prisoner of Zenda."'—*National Observer.*

THE CHRONICLES OF COUNT ANTONIO. *Third Edition.*
'It is a perfectly enchanting story of love and chivalry, and pure romance. The outlawed Count is the most constant, desperate, and withal modest and tender of lovers, a peerless gentleman, an intrepid fighter, a very faithful friend, and a most magnanimous foe.'—*Guardian.*

PHROSO. Illustrated by H. R. MILLAR. *Third Edition.*
'The tale is thoroughly fresh, quick with vitality, stirring the blood, and humorously, dashingly told.'—*St. James's Gazette.*
'A story of adventure, every page of which is palpitating with action and excitement.' —*Speaker.*
'From cover to cover "Phroso" not only engages the attention, but carries the reader in little whirls of delight from adventure to adventure.'—*Academy*

S. Baring Gould's Novels
Crown 8vo. 6s. each.
'To say that a book is by the author of "Mehalah" is to imply that it contains a story cast on strong lines, containing dramatic possibilities, vivid and sympathetic descriptions of Nature, and a wealth of ingenious imagery.'—*Speaker.*
'That whatever Mr. Baring Gould writes is well worth reading, is a conclusion that may be very generally accepted. His views of life are fresh and vigorous, his language pointed and characteristic, the incidents of which he makes use are striking and original, his characters are life-like, and though somewhat exceptional people, are drawn and coloured with artistic force. Add to this that his descriptions of scenes and scenery are painted with the loving eyes and skilled hands of a master of his art, that he is always fresh and never dull, and under such conditions it is no wonder that readers have gained confidence both in his power of amusing and satisfying them, and that year by year his popularity widens.'—*Court Circular.*

ARMINELL : A Social Romance. *Fourth Edition.*

URITH : A Story of Dartmoor. *Fifth Edition.*
'The author is at his best.'—*Times.*

IN THE ROAR OF THE SEA. *Sixth Edition.*
'One of the best imagined and most enthralling stories the author has produced. —*Saturday Review.*

MRS. CURGENVEN OF CURGENVEN. *Fourth Edition.*
'The swing of the narrative is splendid.'—*Sussex Daily News.*

CHEAP JACK ZITA. *Fourth Edition.*
'A powerful drama of human passion.'—*Westminster Gazette.*
'A story worthy the author.'—*National Observer.*

THE QUEEN OF LOVE. *Fourth Edition.*
'You cannot put it down until you have finished it.'—*Punch.*
'Can be heartily recommended to all who care for cleanly, energetic, and interesting fiction.'—*Sussex Daily News.*

KITTY ALONE. *Fourth Edition.*
'A strong and original story, teeming with graphic description, stirring incident, and, above all, with vivid and enthralling human interest.'—*Daily Telegraph.*

NOÉMI : A Romance of the Cave-Dwellers. Illustrated by R. CATON WOODVILLE. *Third Edition.*
'"Noémi" is as excellent a tale of fighting and adventure as one may wish to meet. The narrative also runs clear and sharp as the Loire itself.'—*Pall Mall Gazette.*
'Mr. Baring Gould's powerful story is full of the strong lights and shadows and vivid colouring to which he has accustomed us.'—*Standard.*

THE BROOM-SQUIRE. Illustrated by FRANK DADD. *Fourth Edition.*
'A strain of tenderness is woven through the web of his tragic tale, and its atmosphere is sweetened by the nobility and sweetness of the heroine's character.'—*Daily News.*
'A story of exceptional interest that seems to us to be better than anything he has written of late.'—*Speaker.*

THE PENNYCOMEQUICKS. *Third Edition.*

DARTMOOR IDYLLS.
'A book to read, and keep and read again; for the genuine fun and pathos of it will not early lose their effect.'—*Vanity Fair.*

GUAVAS THE TINNER. Illustrated by Frank Dadd. *Second Edition.*
'Mr. Baring Gould is a wizard who transports us into a region of visions, often lurid and disquieting, but always full of interest and enchantment.'—*Spectator.*
'In the weirdness of the story, in the faithfulness with which the characters are depicted, and in force of style, it closely resembles "Mehalah."'—*Daily Telegraph.*
'There is a kind of flavour about this book which alone elevates it above the ordinary novel. The story itself has a grandeur in harmony with the wild and rugged scenery which is its setting.'—*Athenæum.*

Gilbert Parker's Novels

Crown 8vo. 6s. each.

PIERRE AND HIS PEOPLE. *Fourth Edition.*
'Stories happily conceived and finely executed. There is strength and genius in Mr. Parker's style.'—*Daily Telegraph.*

MRS. FALCHION. *Fourth Edition.*
'A splendid study of character.'—*Athenæum.*
'But little behind anything that has been done by any writer of our time.'—*Pall Mall Gazette.*   'A very striking and admirable novel.'—*St. James's Gazette.*

THE TRANSLATION OF A SAVAGE.
'The plot is original and one difficult to work out; but Mr. Parker has done it with great skill and delicacy. The reader who is not interested in this original, fresh, and well-told tale must be a dull person indeed.'—*Daily Chronicle.*

THE TRAIL OF THE SWORD. *Fifth Edition.*
'Everybody with a soul for romance will thoroughly enjoy "The Trail of the Sword."'—*St. James's Gazette.*
'A rousing and dramatic tale. A book like this, in which swords flash, great surprises are undertaken, and daring deeds done, in which men and women live and love in the old straightforward passionate way, is a joy inexpressible to the reviewer.'—*Daily Chronicle.*

WHEN VALMOND CAME TO PONTIAC: The Story of a Lost Napoleon. *Fourth Edition.*
'Here we find romance—real, breathing, living romance, but it runs flush with our own times, level with our own feelings. The character of Valmond is drawn unerringly; his career, brief as it is, is placed before us as convincingly as history itself. The book must be read, we may say re-read, for any one thoroughly to appreciate Mr. Parker's delicate touch and innate sympathy with humanity.'—*Pall Mall Gazette.*
'The one work of genius which 1895 has as yet produced.'—*New Age.*

AN ADVENTURER OF THE NORTH: The Last Adventures of 'Pretty Pierre.' *Second Edition.*
'The present book is full of fine and moving stories of the great North, and it will add to Mr. Parker's already high reputation.'—*Glasgow Herald.*

THE SEATS OF THE MIGHTY. *Illustrated. Eighth Edition.*
'The best thing he has done; one of the best things that any one has done lately.'—*St. James's Gazette.*
'Mr. Parker seems to become stronger and easier with every serious novel that he attempts. . . . In "The Seats of the Mighty" he shows the matured power which his former novels have led us to expect, and has produced a really fine historical novel. . . . Most sincerely is Mr. Parker to be congratulated on the finest novel he has yet written.'—*Athenæum.*
'Mr. Parker's latest book places him in the front rank of living novelists. "The Seats of the Mighty" is a great book.'—*Black and White.*
'One of the strongest stories of historical interest and adventure that we have read for many a day. . . . A notable and successful book.'—*Speaker.*

Conan Doyle. ROUND THE RED LAMP. By A. CONAN DOYLE, Author of 'The White Company,' 'The Adventures of Sherlock Holmes,' etc. *Fifth Edition. Crown 8vo. 6s.*
'The book is, indeed, composed of leaves from life, and is far and away the best view that has been vouchsafed us behind the scenes of the consulting-room. It is very superior to "The Diary of a late Physician."'—*Illustrated London News.*

Stanley Weyman. UNDER THE RED ROBE. By STANLEY WEYMAN, Author of 'A Gentleman of France.' With Twelve Illustrations by R. Caton Woodville. *Twelfth Edition. Crown 8vo. 6s.*
'A book of which we have read every word for the sheer pleasure of reading, and which we put down with a pang that we cannot forget it all and start again.'—*Westminster Gazette.*
'Every one who reads books at all must read this thrilling romance, from the first page of which to the last the breathless reader is haled along. An inspiration of "manliness and courage."'—*Daily Chronicle.*

Lucas Malet. THE WAGES OF SIN. By LUCAS MALET. *Thirteenth Edition. Crown 8vo. 6s.*

Lucas Malet. THE CARISSIMA. By LUCAS MALET, Author of 'The Wages of Sin,' etc. *Third Edition. Crown 8vo. 6s.*

Arthur Morrison. TALES OF MEAN STREETS. By ARTHUR MORRISON. *Fourth Edition. Crown 8vo. 6s.*
'Told with consummate art and extraordinary detail. He tells a plain, unvarnished tale, and the very truth of it makes for beauty. In the true humanity of the book lies its justification, the permanence of its interest, and its indubitable triumph.'—*Athenæum.*
'A great book. The author's method is amazingly effective, and produces a thrilling sense of reality. The writer lays upon us a master hand. The book is simply appalling and irresistible in its interest. It is humorous also; without humour it would not make the mark it is certain to make.'—*World.*

Arthur Morrison. A CHILD OF THE JAGO. By ARTHUR MORRISON. *Third Edition. Crown 8vo. 6s.*
This, the first long story which Mr. Morrison has written, is like his remarkable 'Tales of Mean Streets,' a realistic study of East End life.
'The book is a masterpiece.'—*Pall Mall Gazette.*
'Told with great vigour and powerful simplicity.'—*Athenæum.*

Mrs. Clifford. A FLASH OF SUMMER. By Mrs. W. K. CLIFFORD, Author of 'Aunt Anne,' etc. *Second Edition. Crown 8vo. 6s.*
'The story is a very sad and a very beautiful one, exquisitely told, and enriched with many subtle touches of wise and tender insight. It will, undoubtedly, add to its author's reputation—already high—in the ranks of novelists.'—*Speaker.*

Emily Lawless. HURRISH. By the Honble. EMILY LAW-
LESS, Author of 'Maelcho,' etc. *Fifth Edition. Crown 8vo.* 6s.
A reissue of Miss Lawless' most popular novel, uniform with 'Maelcho.'

Emily Lawless. MAELCHO: a Sixteenth Century Romance.
By the Honble. EMILY LAWLESS. *Second Edition. Crown 8vo.* 6s.
'A really great book.'—*Spectator.*
'There is no keener pleasure in life than the recognition of genius. Good work is
commoner than it used to be, but the best is as rare as ever. All the more
gladly, therefore, do we welcome in "Maelcho" a piece of work of the first order,
which we do not hesitate to describe as one of the most remarkable literary
achievements of this generation. Miss Lawless is possessed of the very essence
of historical genius.'—*Manchester Guardian.*

J. H. Findlater. THE GREEN GRAVES OF BALGOWRIE.
By JANE H. FINDLATER. *Fourth Edition. Crown 8vo.* 6s.
'A powerful and vivid story.'—*Standard.*
'A beautiful story, sad and strange as truth itself.'—*Vanity Fair.*
'A work of remarkable interest and originality.'—*National Observer.*
'A very charming and pathetic tale.'—*Pall Mall Gazette.*
'A singularly original, clever, and beautiful story.'—*Guardian.*
'"The Green Graves of Balgowrie" reveals to us a new Scotch writer of undoubted
faculty and reserve force.'—*Spectator.*
'An exquisite idyll, delicate, affecting, and beautiful.'—*Black and White.*

H. G. Wells. THE STOLEN BACILLUS, and other Stories.
By H. G. WELLS, Author of 'The Time Machine.' *Second Edition.
Crown 8vo.* 6s.
'The ordinary reader of fiction may be glad to know that these stories are eminently
readable from one cover to the other, but they are more than that; they are the
impressions of a very striking imagination, which, it would seem, has a great deal
within its reach.'—*Saturday Review.*

H. G. Wells. THE PLATTNER STORY AND OTHERS. By H.
G. WELLS. *Second Edition. Crown 8vo.* 6s.
'Weird and mysterious, they seem to hold the reader as by a magic spell.'—*Scotsman.*
'Such is the fascination of this writer's skill that you unhesitatingly prophesy that
none of the many readers, however his flesh do creep, will relinquish the volume
ere he has read from first word to last.'—*Black and White.*
'No volume has appeared for a long time so likely to give equal pleasure to the
simplest reader and to the most fastidious critic.'—*Academy.*
'Mr. Wells is a magician skilled in wielding that most potent of all spells—the fear
of the unknown.'—*Daily Telegraph.*

E. F. Benson. DODO: A DETAIL OF THE DAY. By E. F.
BENSON. *Sixteenth Edition. Crown 8vo.* 6s.
'A delightfully witty sketch of society.'—*Spectator.*
'A perpetual feast of epigram and paradox.'—*Speaker.*

E. F. Benson. THE RUBICON. By E. F. BENSON, Author of
'Dodo.' *Fifth Edition. Crown 8vo.* 6s.
'An exceptional achievement; a notable advance on his previous work.'—*National
Observer.*

Mrs. Oliphant. SIR ROBERT'S FORTUNE. By MRS.
OLIPHANT. *Crown 8vo.* 6s.
'Full of her own peculiar charm of style and simple, subtle character-painting comes
her new gift, the delightful story before us. The scene mostly lies in the moors,
and at the touch of the authoress a Scotch moor becomes a living thing, strong,
tender, beautiful, and changeful.'—*Pall Mall Gazette.*

Mrs. Oliphant. THE TWO MARYS. By MRS. OLIPHANT. *Second Edition. Crown 8vo. 6s.*

W. E. Norris. MATTHEW AUSTIN. By W. E. NORRIS, Author of 'Mademoiselle de Mersac,' etc. *Fourth Edition. Crown 8vo. 6s.*

'"Matthew Austin" may safely be pronounced one of the most intellectually satis-factory and morally bracing novels of the current year.'—*Daily Telegraph.*

W. E. Norris. HIS GRACE. By W. E. NORRIS. *Third Edition. Crown 8vo. 6s.*

'Mr. Norris has drawn a really fine character in the Duke of Hurstbourne, at once unconventional and very true to the conventionalities of life.'—*Athenæum.*

W. E. Norris. THE DESPOTIC LADY AND OTHERS. By W. E. NORRIS. *Crown 8vo. 6s.*

'A budget of good fiction of which no one will tire.'—*Scotsman.*

W. E. Norris. CLARISSA FURIOSA. By W. E. NORRIS, Author of 'The Rogue,' etc. *Crown 8vo. 6s.*

'One of Mr. Norris's very best novels. As a story it is admirable, as a *jeu d'esprit* it is capital, as a lay sermon studded with gems of wit and wisdom it is a model which will not, we imagine, find an efficient imitator.'—*The World.*
'The best novel he has written for some time: a story which is full of admirable character-drawing.'—*The Standard.*

Robert Barr. IN THE MIDST OF ALARMS. By ROBERT BARR. *Third Edition. Crown 8vo. 6s.*

'A book which has abundantly satisfied us by its capital humour.'—*Daily Chronicle.*
'Mr. Barr has achieved a triumph whereof he has every reason to be proud.'—*Pall Mall Gazette.*

J. Maclaren Cobban. THE KING OF ANDAMAN: A Saviour of Society. By J. MACLAREN COBBAN. *Crown 8vo. 6s.*

'An unquestionably interesting book. It would not surprise us if it turns out to be the most interesting novel of the season, for it contains one character, at least, who has in him the root of immortality, and the book itself is ever exhaling the sweet savour of the unexpected. . . . Plot is forgotten and incident fades, and only the really human endures, and throughout this book there stands out in bold and beautiful relief its high-souled and chivalric protagonist, James the Master of Hutcheon, the King of Andaman himself.'—*Pall Mall Gazette.*

J. Maclaren Cobban. WILT THOU HAVE THIS WOMAN? By J. M. COBBAN, Author of 'The King of Andaman.' *Crown 8vo. 6s.*

'Mr. Cobban has the true story-teller's art. He arrests attention at the outset, and he retains it to the end.'—*Birmingham Post.*

H. Morrah. A SERIOUS COMEDY. By HERBERT MORRAH. *Crown 8vo. 6s.*

'This volume is well worthy of its title. The theme has seldom been presented with more freshness or more force.'—*Scotsman.*

H. Morrah. THE FAITHFUL CITY. By HERBERT MORRAH, Author of 'A Serious Comedy.' *Crown 8vo.* 6s.

'Conveys a suggestion of weirdness and horror, until finally he convinces and enthrals the reader with his mysterious savages, his gigantic tower, and his uncompromising men and women. This is a haunting, mysterious book, not without an element of stupendous grandeur.'—*Athenæum.*

L. B. Walford. SUCCESSORS TO THE TITLE. By MRS. WALFORD, Author of 'Mr. Smith,' etc. *Second Edition. Crown 8vo.* 6s.

'The story is fresh and healthy from beginning to finish ; and our liking for the two simple people who are the successors to the title mounts steadily, and ends almost in respect.'—*Scotsman.*

T. L. Paton. A HOME IN INVERESK. By T. L. PATON. *Crown 8vo.* 6s.

'A pleasant and well-written story.'—*Daily Chronicle.*

John Davidson. MISS ARMSTRONG'S AND OTHER CIRCUMSTANCES. By JOHN DAVIDSON. *Crown 8vo.* 6s.

'Throughout the volume there is a strong vein of originality, and a knowledge of human nature that are worthy of the highest praise.'—*Scotsman.*

M. M. Dowie. GALLIA. By MÉNIE MURIEL DOWIE, Author of 'A Girl in the Carpathians.' *Third Edition. Crown 8vo.* 6s.

'The style is generally admirable, the dialogue not seldom brilliant, the situations surprising in their freshness and originality, while the subsidiary as well as the principal characters live and move, and the story itself is readable from title-page to colophon.'—*Saturday Review.*

J. A. Barry. IN THE GREAT DEEP : TALES OF THE SEA. By J. A. BARRY. Author of 'Steve Brown's Bunyip.' *Crown 8vo.* 6s.

'A collection of really admirable short stories of the sea, very simply told, and placed before the reader in pithy and telling English.'—*Westminster Gazette.*

J. B. Burton. IN THE DAY OF ADVERSITY. By J. BLOUNDELLE BURTON.' *Second Edition. Crown 8vo.* 6s.

'Unusually interesting and full of highly dramatic situations.'—*Guardian.*

J. B. Burton. DENOUNCED. By J. BLOUNDELLE BURTON. *Second Edition. Crown 8vo.* 6s.

The plot is an original one, and the local colouring is laid on with a delicacy and an accuracy of detail which denote the true artist.'—*Broad Arrow.*

W. C. Scully. THE WHITE HECATOMB. By W. C. SCULLY, Author of 'Kafir Stories.' *Crown 8vo.* 6s.

'The author is so steeped in Kaffir lore and legend, and so thoroughly well acquainted with native sagas and traditional ceremonial that he is able to attract the reader by the easy familiarity with which he handles his characters.'—*South Africa.*

'It reveals a marvellously intimate understanding of the Kaffir mind, allied with literary gifts of no mean order.'—*African Critic.*

H. Johnston. DR. CONGALTON'S LEGACY. By HENRY JOHNSTON. *Crown 8vo.* 6s.

'A worthy and permanent contribution to Scottish literature.'—*Glasgow Herald.*

J. F. Brewer. THE SPECULATORS. By J. F. BREWER. *Second Edition. Crown 8vo. 6s.*
'A pretty bit of comedy. . . . It is undeniably a clever book.'—*Academy.*
'A clever and amusing story. It makes capital out of the comic aspects of culture, and will be read with amusement by every intellectual reader.'—*Scotsman.*
'A remarkably clever study.'—*Vanity Fair.*

Julian Corbett. A BUSINESS IN GREAT WATERS. By JULIAN CORBETT. *Crown 8vo. 6s.*
'Mr. Corbett writes with immense spirit, and the book is a thoroughly enjoyable one in all respects. The salt of the ocean is in it, and the right heroic ring resounds through its gallant adventures.'—*Speaker.*

L. Cope Cornford. CAPTAIN JACOBUS: A ROMANCE OF THE ROAD. By L. COPE CORNFORD. Illustrated. *Crown 8vo. 6s.*
'An exceptionally good story of adventure and character.'—*World.*

C. P. Wolley. THE QUEENSBERRY CUP. A Tale of Adventure. By CLIVE PHILLIPS WOLLEY. *Illustrated. Crown 8vo. 6s.*
'A book which will delight boys: a book which upholds the healthy schoolboy code of morality.'—*Scotsman.*

L. Daintrey. THE KING OF ALBERIA. A Romance of the Balkans. By LAURA DAINTREY. *Crown 8vo. 6s.*
'Miss Daintrey seems to have an intimate acquaintance with the people and politics of the Balkan countries in which the scene of her lively and picturesque romance is laid.'—*Glasgow Herald.*

M. A. Owen. THE DAUGHTER OF ALOUETTE. By MARY A. OWEN. *Crown 8vo. 6s.*
A story of life among the American Indians.
'A fascinating story.'—*Literary World.*

Mrs. Pinsent. CHILDREN OF THIS WORLD. By ELLEN F. PINSENT, Author of 'Jenny's Case.' *Crown 8vo. 6s.*
'Mrs. Pinsent's new novel has plenty of vigour, variety, and good writing. There are certainty of purpose, strength of touch, and clearness of vision.'—*Athenæum.*

Clark Russell. MY DANISH SWEETHEART. By W. CLARK RUSSELL, Author of 'The Wreck of the Grosvenor,' etc. *Illustrated. Fourth Edition. Crown 8vo. 6s.*

G. Manville Fenn. AN ELECTRIC SPARK. By G. MANVILLE FENN, Author of 'The Vicar's Wife,' 'A Double Knot,' etc. *Second Edition. Crown 8vo. 6s.*

L. S. McChesney. UNDER SHADOW OF THE MISSION. By L. S. McCHESNEY. *Crown 8vo. 6s.*
'Those whose minds are open to the finer issues of life, who can appreciate graceful thought and refined expression of it, from them this volume will receive a welcome as enthusiastic as it will be based on critical knowledge.'—*Church Times.*

Ronald Ross. THE SPIRIT OF STORM. By RONALD ROSS, Author of 'The Child of Ocean.' *Crown 8vo. 6s.*
A romance of the Sea.   'Weird, powerful, and impressive.'—*Black and White.*

R. Pryce. TIME AND THE WOMAN. By RICHARD PRYCE. *Second Edition. Crown 8vo. 6s.*

Mrs. Watson. THIS MAN'S DOMINION. By the Author of 'A High Little World.' *Second Edition. Crown 8vo. 6s.*

Marriott Watson. DIOGENES OF LONDON. By H. B. MARRIOTT WATSON. *Crown 8vo. Buckram. 6s.*

M. Gilchrist. THE STONE DRAGON. By MURRAY GILCHRIST. *Crown 8vo. Buckram. 6s.*

　'The author's faults are atoned for by certain positive and admirable merits. The romances have not their counterpart in modern literature, and to read them is a unique experience.'—*National Observer.*

E. Dickinson. A VICAR'S WIFE. By EVELYN DICKINSON. *Crown 8vo. 6s.*

E. M. Gray. ELSA. By E. M'QUEEN GRAY. *Crown 8vo. 6s.*

THREE-AND-SIXPENNY NOVELS　3/6
Crown 8vo.

DERRICK VAUGHAN, NOVELIST. By EDNA LYALL.

MARGERY OF QUETHER. By S. BARING GOULD.

JACQUETTA. By S. BARING GOULD.

SUBJECT TO VANITY. By MARGARET BENSON.

THE SIGN OF THE SPIDER. By BERTRAM MITFORD.

THE MOVING FINGER. By MARY GAUNT.

JACO TRELOAR. By J. H. PEARCE.

THE DANCE OF THE HOURS. By 'VERA.'

A WOMAN OF FORTY. By ESMÉ STUART.

A CUMBERER OF THE GROUND. By CONSTANCE SMITH.

THE SIN OF ANGELS. By EVELYN DICKINSON.

AUT DIABOLUS AUT NIHIL. By X. L.

THE COMING OF CUCULAIN. By STANDISH O'GRADY.

THE GODS GIVE MY DONKEY WINGS. By ANGUS EVAN ABBOTT.

THE STAR GAZERS. By G. MANVILLE FENN.

THE POISON OF ASPS. By R. ORTON PROWSE.

THE QUIET MRS. FLEMING. By R. PRYCE.

DISENCHANTMENT. By F. MABEL ROBINSON.

THE SQUIRE OF WANDALES. By A. SHIELD.

A REVEREND GENTLEMAN. By J. M. COBBAN.

A DEPLORABLE AFFAIR. By W. E. NORRIS.
A CAVALIER'S LADYE. By Mrs. DICKER.
THE PRODIGALS. By Mrs. OLIPHANT.
THE SUPPLANTER. By P. NEUMANN.
A MAN WITH BLACK EYELASHES. By H. A. KENNEDY.
A HANDFUL OF EXOTICS. By S. GORDON.
AN ODD EXPERIMENT. By HANNAH LYNCH.

HALF-CROWN NOVELS   2/6
A Series of Novels by popular Authors.

1. HOVENDEN, V.C. By F. MABEL ROBINSON.
2. ELI'S CHILDREN. By G. MANVILLE FENN.
3. A DOUBLE KNOT. By G. MANVILLE FENN.
4. DISARMED. By M. BETHAM EDWARDS.
5. A MARRIAGE AT SEA. By W. CLARK RUSSELL.
6. IN TENT AND BUNGALOW. By the Author of 'Indian Idylls.'
7. MY STEWARDSHIP. By E. M'QUEEN GRAY.
8. JACK'S FATHER. By W. E. NORRIS.
9. JIM B.
10. THE PLAN OF CAMPAIGN. By F. MABEL ROBINSON.
11. MR. BUTLER'S WARD. By F. MABEL ROBINSON.
12. A LOST ILLUSION. By LESLIE KEITH.

Lynn Linton. THE TRUE HISTORY OF JOSHUA DAVIDSON, Christian and Communist. By E. LYNN LINTON. *Eleventh Edition. Post 8vo. 1s.*

Books for Boys and Girls   3/6
A Series of Books by well-known Authors, well illustrated.

1. THE ICELANDER'S SWORD. By S. BARING GOULD.
2. TWO LITTLE CHILDREN AND CHING. By EDITH E. CUTHELL.
3. TODDLEBEN'S HERO. By M. M. BLAKE.
4. ONLY A GUARD-ROOM DOG. By EDITH E. CUTHELL.
5. THE DOCTOR OF THE JULIET. By HARRY COLLINGWOOD.
6. MASTER ROCKAFELLAR'S VOYAGE. By W. CLARK RUSSELL.
7. SYD BELTON : Or, The Boy who would not go to Sea. By G. MANVILLE FENN.

The Peacock Library

A Series of Books for Girls by well-known Authors, handsomely bound in blue and silver, and well illustrated. **3/6**

1. A PINCH OF EXPERIENCE. By L. B. WALFORD.
2. THE RED GRANGE. By Mrs. MOLESWORTH.
3. THE SECRET OF MADAME DE MONLUC. By the Author of 'Mdle Mori.'
4. DUMPS. By Mrs. PARR, Author of 'Adam and Eve.'
5. OUT OF THE FASHION. By L. T. MEADE.
6. A GIRL OF THE PEOPLE. By L. T. MEADE.
7. HEPSY GIPSY. By L. T. MEADE. 2s. 6d.
8. THE HONOURABLE MISS. By L. T. MEADE.
9. MY LAND OF BEULAH. By Mrs. LEITH ADAMS.

University Extension Series

A series of books on historical, literary, and scientific subjects, suitable for extension students and home-reading circles. Each volume is complete in itself, and the subjects are treated by competent writers in a broad and philosophic spirit.

Edited by J. E. SYMES, M.A.,
Principal of University College, Nottingham.

Crown 8vo. Price (with some exceptions) 2s. 6d.

The following volumes are ready:—

THE INDUSTRIAL HISTORY OF ENGLAND. By H. DE B. GIBBINS, D.Litt., M.A., late Scholar of Wadham College, Oxon., Cobden Prizeman. *Fifth Edition, Revised. With Maps and Plans.* 3s.
'A compact and clear story of our industrial development. A study of this concise but luminous book cannot fail to give the reader a clear insight into the principal phenomena of our industrial history. The editor and publishers are to be congratulated on this first volume of their venture, and we shall look with expectant interest for the succeeding volumes of the series.'—*University Extension Journal.*

A HISTORY OF ENGLISH POLITICAL ECONOMY. By L. L. PRICE, M.A., Fellow of Oriel College, Oxon. *Second Edition.*

PROBLEMS OF POVERTY: An Inquiry into the Industrial Conditions of the Poor. By J. A. HOBSON, M.A. *Third Edition.*

VICTORIAN POETS. By A. SHARP.

THE FRENCH REVOLUTION. By J. E. SYMES, M.A.

PSYCHOLOGY. By F. S. GRANGER, M.A.

THE EVOLUTION OF PLANT LIFE: Lower Forms. By G. MASSEE. *With Illustrations.*

AIR AND WATER. Professor V. B. LEWES, M.A. *Illustrated.*

THE CHEMISTRY OF LIFE AND HEALTH. By C. W. KIMMINS, M.A. *Illustrated.*

THE MECHANICS OF DAILY LIFE. By V. P. SELLS, M.A. *Illustrated.*

ENGLISH SOCIAL REFORMERS. H. DE B. GIBBINS, D.Litt., M.A.

ENGLISH TRADE AND FINANCE IN THE SEVENTEENTH CENTURY. By W. A. S. HEWINS, B.A.

THE CHEMISTRY OF FIRE. The Elementary Principles of Chemistry. By M. M. PATTISON MUIR, M.A. *Illustrated.*

A TEXT-BOOK OF AGRICULTURAL BOTANY. By M. C. POTTER, M.A.. F.L.S. *Illustrated.* 3s. 6d.

THE VAULT OF HEAVEN. A Popular Introduction to Astronomy. By R. A. GREGORY. *With numerous Illustrations.*

METEOROLOGY. The Elements of Weather and Climate. By H. N. DICKSON, F.R.S.E., F.R. Met. Soc. *Illustrated.*

A MANUAL OF ELECTRICAL SCIENCE. By GEORGE J. BURCH, M.A. *With numerous Illustrations.* 3s.

THE EARTH. An Introduction to Physiography. By EVAN SMALL, M.A. *Illustrated.*

INSECT LIFE. By F. W. THEOBALD, M.A. *Illustrated.*

ENGLISH POETRY FROM BLAKE TO BROWNING. By W. M. DIXON, M.A.

ENGLISH LOCAL GOVERNMENT. By E. JENKS, M.A., Professor of Law at University College, Liverpool.

THE GREEK VIEW OF LIFE. By G. L. DICKINSON, Fellow of King's College, Cambridge. *Second Edition.*

Social Questions of To-day

Edited by H. DE B. GIBBINS, D.Litt., M.A.
Crown 8vo. 2s. 6d.

2|6

A series of volumes upon those topics of social, economic, and industrial interest that are at the present moment foremost in the public mind. Each volume of the series is written by an author who is an acknowledged authority upon the subject with which he deals.

The following Volumes of the Series are ready :—

TRADE UNIONISM—NEW AND OLD. By G. HOWELL, Author of ' The Conflicts of Capital and Labour.' *Second Edition.*

THE CO-OPERATIVE MOVEMENT TO-DAY. By G. J. HOLYOAKE, Author of ' The History of Co-Operation.' *Second Edition.*

MUTUAL THRIFT. By Rev. J. FROME WILKINSON, M.A., Author of ' The Friendly Society Movement.'

PROBLEMS OF POVERTY : An Inquiry into the Industrial Conditions of the Poor. By J. A. HOBSON, M.A. *Third Edition.*

THE COMMERCE OF NATIONS. By C. F. BASTAPLE, M.A., Professor of Economics at Trinity College, Dublin.

THE ALIEN INVASION. By W. H. WILKINS, B.A., Secretary to the Society for Preventing the Immigration of Destitute Aliens.

THE RURAL EXODUS. By P. ANDERSON GRAHAM.

LAND NATIONALIZATION. By HAROLD COX, B.A.

A SHORTER WORKING DAY. By H. DE B. GIBBINS, D.Litt., M.A., and R. A. HADFIELD, of the Hecla Works, Sheffield.

BACK TO THE LAND: An Inquiry into the Cure for Rural Depopulation. By H. E. MOORE.

TRUSTS, POOLS AND CORNERS: As affecting Commerce and Industry. By J. STEPHEN JEANS, M.R.I., F.S.S.

THE FACTORY SYSTEM. By R. COOKE TAYLOR.

THE STATE AND ITS CHILDREN. By GERTRUDE TUCKWELL.

WOMEN'S WORK. By LADY DILKE, Miss BULLEY, and Miss WHITLEY.

MUNICIPALITIES AT WORK. The Municipal Policy of Six Great Towns, and its Influence on their Social Welfare. By FREDERICK DOLMAN.

SOCIALISM AND MODERN THOUGHT. By M. KAUFMANN.

THE HOUSING OF THE WORKING CLASSES. By R. F. BOWMAKER.

MODERN CIVILIZATION IN SOME OF ITS ECONOMIC ASPECTS. By W. CUNNINGHAM, D.D., Fellow of Trinity College, Cambridge.

THE PROBLEM OF THE UNEMPLOYED. By J. A. HOBSON, B.A., Author of ' The Problems of Poverty.'

LIFE IN WEST LONDON. By ARTHUR SHERWELL, M.A. *Second Edition.*

Classical Translations

Edited by H. F. FOX, M.A., Fellow and Tutor of Brasenose College, Oxford.

Messrs. Methuen are issuing a New Series of Translations from the Greek and Latin Classics. They have enlisted the services of some of the best Oxford and Cambridge Scholars, and it is their intention that the Series shall be distinguished by literary excellence as well as by scholarly accuracy.

ÆSCHYLUS—Agamemnon, Chöephoroe, Eumenides. Translated by LEWIS CAMPBELL, LL.D., late Professor of Greek at St. Andrews, 5*s.*

CICERO—De Oratore I. Translated by E. N. P. MOOR, M.A. 3*s.* 6*d.*

CICERO — Select Orations (Pro Milone, Pro Murena, Philippic II., In Catilinam). Translated by H. E. D. BLAKISTON, M.A., Fellow and Tutor of Trinity College, Oxford. 5*s.*

CICERO—De Natura Deorum. Translated by F. BROOKS, M.A., late Scholar of Balliol College, Oxford. 3s. 6d.

LUCIAN—Six Dialogues (Nigrinus, Icaro-Menippus, The Cock, The Ship, The Parasite, The Lover of Falsehood). Translated by S. T. IRWIN, M.A., Assistant Master at Clifton; late Scholar of Exeter College, Oxford. 3s. 6d.

SOPHOCLES—Electra and Ajax. Translated by E. D. A. MORSHEAD, M.A., Assistant Master at Winchester. 2s. 6d.

TACITUS—Agricola and Germania. Translated by R. B. TOWNSHEND, late Scholar of Trinity College, Cambridge. 2s. 6d.

Educational Books
CLASSICAL

PLAUTI BACCHIDES. Edited with Introduction, Commentary, and Critical Notes by J. M'COSH, M.A. *Fcap. 4to.* 12s. 6d.
'The notes are copious, and contain a great deal of information that is good and useful.'—*Classical Review.*

TACITI AGRICOLL With Introduction, Notes, Map, etc. By R. F. DAVIS, M.A., Assistant Master at Weymouth College. *Crown 8vo.* 2s.

TACITI GERMANIA. By the same Editor. *Crown 8vo.* 2s.

HERODOTUS: EASY SELECTIONS. With Vocabulary. By A. C. LIDDELL, M.A., Assistant Master at Nottingham High School. *Fcap. 8vo.* 1s. 6d.

SELECTIONS FROM THE ODYSSEY. By E. D. STONE, M.A., late Assistant Master at Eton. *Fcap. 8vo.* 1s. 6d.

PLAUTUS: THE CAPTIVI. Adapted for Lower Forms by J. H. FRESSE, M.A., late Fellow of St. John's, Cambridge. 1s. 6d.

DEMOSTHENES AGAINST CONON AND CALLICLES. Edited with Notes and Vocabulary, by F. DARWIN SWIFT, M.A., formerly Scholar of Queen's College, Oxford; Assistant Master at Denstone College. *Fcap. 8vo.* 2s.

GERMAN

A COMPANION GERMAN GRAMMAR. By H. DE B. GIBBINS, D.Litt., M.A., Assistant Master at Nottingham High School. *Crown 8vo.* 1s. 6d.

GERMAN PASSAGES FOR UNSEEN TRANSLATION. By E. M'QUEEN GRAY. *Crown 8vo.* 2s. 6d.

SCIENCE

THE WORLD OF SCIENCE. Including Chemistry, Heat, Light, Sound, Magnetism, Electricity, Botany, Zoology, Physiology, Astronomy, and Geology. By R. ELLIOTT STEEL, M.A., F.C.S. 147 Illustrations. *Second Edition. Crown 8vo.* 2s. 6d.
'If Mr. Steel is to be placed second to any for this quality of lucidity, it is only to Huxley himself; and to be named in the same breath with this master of the craft of teaching is to be accredited with the clearness of style and simplicity of arrangement that belong to thorough mastery of a subject.'—*Parents' Review.*

ELEMENTARY LIGHT. By R. E. STEEL. With numerous Illustrations. *Crown 8vo.* 4s. 6d.

ENGLISH

ENGLISH RECORDS. A Companion to the History of England. By H. E. MALDEN, M.A. *Crown 8vo.* 3*s.* 6*d.*
A book which aims at concentrating information upon dates, genealogy, officials, constitutional documents, etc., which is usually found scattered in different volumes.

THE ENGLISH CITIZEN: HIS RIGHTS AND DUTIES. By H. E. MALDEN, M.A. 1*s.* 6*d.*
'The book goes over the same ground as is traversed in the school books on this subject written to satisfy the requirements of the Education Code. It would serve admirably the purposes of a text-book, as it is well based in historical facts, and keeps quite clear of party matters.'—*Scotsman.*

METHUEN'S COMMERCIAL SERIES
Edited by H. DE B. GIBBINS, D.Litt., M.A.

BRITISH COMMERCE AND COLONIES FROM ELIZABETH TO VICTORIA. By H. DE B. GIBBINS, D.Litt., M.A., Author of 'The Industrial History of England,' etc., etc., 2*s.*

COMMERCIAL EXAMINATION PAPERS. By H. DE B. GIBBINS, D.Litt., M.A., 1*s.* 6*d.*

THE ECONOMICS OF COMMERCE. By H. DE B. GIBBINS, D.Litt., M.A. 1*s.* 6*d.*

A MANUAL OF FRENCH COMMERCIAL CORRESPONDENCE. By S. E. BALLY, Modern Language Master at the Manchester Grammar School. 2*s.*

GERMAN COMMERCIAL CORRESPONDENCE. By S. E. BALLY, Assistant Master at the Manchester Grammar School. *Crown 8vo.* 2*s.* 6*d.*

A FRENCH COMMERCIAL READER. By S. E. BALLY. 2*s.*

COMMERCIAL GEOGRAPHY, with special reference to Trade Routes, New Markets, and Manufacturing Districts. By L. W. LYDE, M.A., of the Academy, Glasgow. 2*s.*

A PRIMER OF BUSINESS. By S. JACKSON, M.A. 1*s.* 6*d.*

COMMERCIAL ARITHMETIC. By F. G. TAYLOR, M.A. 1*s.* 6*d.*

PRÉCIS WRITING AND OFFICE CORRESPONDENCE. By E. E. WHITFIELD, M.A.

WORKS BY A. M. M. STEDMAN, M.A.

INITIA LATINA: Easy Lessons on Elementary Accidence. *Second Edition. Fcap. 8vo.* 1*s.*

FIRST LATIN LESSONS. *Fourth Edition. Crown 8vo.* 2*s.*

FIRST LATIN READER. With Notes adapted to the Shorter Latin Primer and Vocabulary. *Third Edition.* 18*mo.* 1*s.* 6*d.*

EASY SELECTIONS FROM CAESAR. Part I. The Helvetian War. 18*mo.* 1*s.*

EASY SELECTIONS FROM LIVY. Part I. The Kings of Rome. 18*mo.* 1*s.* 6*d.*

EASY LATIN PASSAGES FOR UNSEEN TRANSLATION. *Fifth Edition. Fcap. 8vo.* 1*s.* 6*d.*

EXEMPLA LATINA. First Lessons in Latin Accidence. With Vocabulary. *Crown 8vo.* 1*s.*

EASY LATIN EXERCISES ON THE SYNTAX OF THE SHORTER AND REVISED LATIN PRIMER. With Vocabulary. *Sixth Edition. Crown 8vo.* 2*s.* 6*d.* Issued with the consent of Dr. Kennedy.

THE LATIN COMPOUND SENTENCE : Rules and Exercises. *Crown 8vo. 1s. 6d.* With Vocabulary. *2s.*

NOTANDA QUAEDAM : Miscellaneous Latin Exercises on Common Rules and Idioms. *Third Edition.* *Fcap. 8vo. 1s. 6d.* With Vocabulary. *2s.*

LATIN VOCABULARIES FOR REPETITION : Arranged according to Subjects. *Sixth Edition. Fcap. 8vo. 1s. 6d.*

A VOCABULARY OF LATIN IDIOMS AND PHRASES. *18mo. 1s.*

STEPS TO GREEK. *18mo. 1s.*

EASY GREEK PASSAGES FOR UNSEEN TRANSLATION. *Second Edition. Fcap. 8vo. 1s. 6d.*

GREEK VOCABULARIES FOR REPETITION. Arranged according to Subjects. *Second Edition. Fcap. 8vo. 1s. 6d.*

GREEK TESTAMENT SELECTIONS. For the use of Schools. *Third Edition.* With Introduction, Notes, and Vocabulary. *Fcap. 8vo. 2s. 6d.*

STEPS TO FRENCH. *Second Edition. 18mo. 8d.*

FIRST FRENCH LESSONS. *Second Edition. Crown 8vo. 1s.*

EASY FRENCH PASSAGES FOR UNSEEN TRANSLATION. *Second Edition. Fcap. 8vo. 1s. 6d.*

EASY FRENCH EXERCISES ON ELEMENTARY SYNTAX. With Vocabulary. *Crown 8vo. 2s. 6d.*

FRENCH VOCABULARIES FOR REPETITION : Arranged according to Subjects. *Fifth Edition. Fcap. 8vo. 1s.*

SCHOOL EXAMINATION SERIES

EDITED BY A. M. M. STEDMAN, M.A. *Crown 8vo. 2s. 6d.*

FRENCH EXAMINATION PAPERS IN MISCELLANEOUS GRAMMAR AND IDIOMS. By A. M. M. STEDMAN, M.A. *Ninth Edition.* A KEY, issued to Tutors and Private Students only, to be had on application to the Publishers. *Fourth Edition. Crown 8vo. 6s. net.*

LATIN EXAMINATION PAPERS IN MISCELLANEOUS GRAMMAR AND IDIOMS. By A. M. M. STEDMAN, M.A. *Seventh Edition.* KEY issued as above. *6s. net.*

GREEK EXAMINATION PAPERS IN MISCELLANEOUS GRAMMAR AND IDIOMS. By A. M. M. STEDMAN, M.A. *Fifth Edition.* KEY issued as above. *6s. net.*

GERMAN EXAMINATION PAPERS IN MISCELLANEOUS GRAMMAR AND IDIOMS. By R. J. MORICH, Manchester. *Fifth Edition.* KEY issued as above. *6s. net.*

HISTORY AND GEOGRAPHY EXAMINATION PAPERS. By C. H. SPENCE, M.A., Clifton College.

SCIENCE EXAMINATION PAPERS. By R. E. STEEL, M.A., F.C.S., Chief Natural Science Master, Bradford Grammar School. *In two vols.* Part I. Chemistry ; Part II. Physics.

GENERAL KNOWLEDGE EXAMINATION PAPERS. By A. M. M. STEDMAN, M.A. *Third Edition.* KEY issued as above. *7s. net.*

Printed by T. and A. CONSTABLE, Printers to Her Majesty at the Edinburgh University Press

Lightning Source UK Ltd.
Milton Keynes UK
UKHW022113080223
416681UK00011B/2640